CRUISING THE PANAMA CANAL

Richard Detrich

Photos, unless otherwise noted, are by the author, are historical images believed to be in the public domain or are US government photos and illustrations

Copyright 2012 Richard Detrich

Boquete 0413, Chiriqui, Republic of Panama
RichardDetrich.com

"While lecturing on ships transiting the Canal I realized that there was a need for a simpler, more readable book written for cruise passengers that included information about the Canal as well as information about Panama. I wanted to write a book that would be helpful to folks planning a Panama Canal trip as well as serve as a guide during the voyage."

Richard Detrich

* * * *

Guaranteed to help you get the most out of your Canal Cruise!

Which itinerary to pick
The best time of the year
Which side of the ship
What to look for
What to expect
How to pick shore excursions
What you need to know
A guide for your passage through the Canal

* * * *

"This is **the best Panama Canal book for cruise ship passengers.**"

"Richard's commentary, history and background **made our Canal trip come alive!**"

"Unlike some of the standard Canal books, Richard's book is **concise and readable.**"

"**Everything I ever wanted to know about the Panama Canal.**"

"The ultimate authority on cruising the Canal . . . **Easy-going writing style makes this a cinch for anyone to read.**"

"This is the book you will want to buy for planning your cruise and to **use as a guide during the Canal cruise itself.**"

* * * *

Contents

Foreword - 7

MV JUST CRUISING – 8

1 - It's 4:30 am on the MV JUST CRUISING - 9

2 - South Bound Transit - Atlantic to Pacific - 25
A - The Approach - Colon - 25
B - Atlantic Locks - 33
C - Gatun Lake - 46
D - Gamboa & Gaillard Cut - 61
E - Pacific Locks - 71
F - Balboa & Amador - 83

3 - North Bound Transit - Pacific to Atlantic - 91
A - The Approach - Amador & Balboa - 91
B - Pacific Locks - 100
C - Gaillard Cut - 118
D - Gamboa & Gatun Lake - 137
E - Atlantic Locks - 152
F - Colon & Limon Bay - 154

4 - Cruising Panama - 158

5 - Panama 101 - 181

6 - The Big Ditch - 193

7 - A Complicated Marriage of Sorts - 216

8 - Moving Forward - 232

9 - Questions & Answers - 242

The Bill for MV JUST CRUISING Transit – 257
Key Dates in Panama History - 258
For Further Reading - 264
Panama Canal by The Numbers - 266

Foreword

When we owned travel agencies I always gave clients who booked Panama Canal cruises a copy of David McCullough's definitive Panama Canal book, THE PATH BETWEEN THE SEAS. It took me a while to realize that although it is the definitive story of the Canal, it is also a long and heavily footnoted historical tome, so few people actually read it.

While lecturing on ships transiting the Canal I realized that there was a need for a simpler, more readable book written for cruise passengers that included information about the Canal as well as information about Panama. I wanted to write a book that would be helpful to folks planning a Panama Canal trip as well as serve as a guide during the voyage.

The most challenging thing about giving lectures on board ship is to take a mass of information and distill it all down into a 45-minute talk that keeps people awake, interested, and at times laughing. This is particularly challenging with a topic like the Panama Canal. I'm not a historian. My challenge is to take this enormous story and distill it down to an interesting tale which for you will be a "page turner" that will make your day in the Canal more meaningful and memorable.

If you look at the map you will see that Panama runs east west, so the Panama Canal actually runs north-south. When you are going from the Atlantic to the Pacific, although your ship may be heading west, it is a "Southbound" Canal transit. Pacific to Atlantic is a "Northbound" transit.

Since the sequence is different I've provided commentary in Chapter 2 for a "Southbound" transit and in Chapter 3 for a "Northbound" transit. You can read the Chapter that applies to your cruise, or both, if you'd like. A lot of folks ask which direction is "best" and as you can see, they're the same just in different sequence.

The only thing that might make a Southbound trip better is that many ships make a time change the night before the Canal, giving you an extra hour of sleep, which makes getting up at 5 am a little easier!

A good trip has three memorable parts: anticipating and planning, taking the trip, and reliving the experience when you get home. Reading this book will help you understand the history and know what to expect, which will make your day in the Canal even more special!

MV JUST CRUISING

We need a hypothetical ship for our journey since Canal tolls and procedures vary according to the size of the ship, so meet   . . .

MV JUST CRUISING - Operating by Dripping-In-Royalty Cruise Line or DIR Cruises

Built 1999 at Fincantieri, Monfalcone, Italy

Cost $350 million US

Gross Registered Tonnage 77,441 tons

Net Registered Tonnage 44,193 tons

Panama Net Registered Tonnage 63,441 tons

Length 856 feet (260.9 meters)

Breadth 105 feet (32 meters)

Draft 26 feet (7.9 meters)

Total Berths 3,070

Propulsion 4 Diesel Electric Engines

Thrusters 2 Bow, 2 Stern

Cruising Speed 21 knots

1 - It's 4:30 am on the MV JUST CRUISING

Since 4 am people have been out on deck to capture the "best" spot for viewing the Panama Canal almost as if lining up for tickets to a hot concert or the day-after-Thanksgiving sale at Wal-Mart. The reality: there is no one "best" spot on the ship for Canal Day, but folks will figure that out eventually.

The MV JUST CRUISING arrived "on station" just outside the breakwater at Colon this morning at about 3 am just to be certain to be on time for the arrival of the Panama Canal authorities and pilot, scheduled to arrive at 5 am. At 4:18 am MV JUST CRUISING contacted the pilot station to confirm an ETA of 5 am.

Dripping-In-Royalty cruise line has reserved this slot to go through the Panama Canal three years ago when it developed this year's itineraries. To reserve this slot Dripping-In-Royalty cruise line, hereinafter "DIR Cruises", and as per terms of the 36-page "Passenger Contract" written in legalese and printed in unreadable 8-point type, has paid a preferential booking fee of $25,000.

If MV JUST CRUISING doesn't show up on the designated day, the Panama Canal Authority [*Autoridad de Canal de Panama* or "ACP"] just like the Shore Excursion office onboard, doesn't give any refunds, so we loose our money, and pay all over again and there goes the captain's bonus. If we show up late we pay a 50 - 100% penalty. So we are on time.

Excitement is running high on MV JUST CRUISING.

Folks turned in early last night, leaving the nightclub almost deserted. Everyone set early morning wake up calls, determined not miss a single moment of our passage between the oceans. Even on the bridge excitement is high. No matter how many times you have been through the Canal, it's hard to sleep the night before. Generally I sense when the ship's engines shift and wake up almost automatically about 4:00 am.

It's 4:45 am and after a quick shower I head to the bridge

The bridge, like the engine room and communications center, is a secure area of the ship. There are reinforced doors, security protocols, and . . . panic buttons with which to notify authorities in case of attack. Although cruising is all about fun and relaxation, behind the scenes it is all work in order to protect the fun and relaxation. In today's world a high level of security is essential.

Like many cruise lines, on DIR Cruises, the bridge has two "zones": "Green" and "Red". When the bridge is in "Green" non-essential people and crew are allowed to phone and visit the bridge. Sometimes special VIP or Royal Suite guests are invited to the bridge, or crew members and sometimes their family members are allowed to visit. But when the bridge is in "Red" only essential people and emergency phone calls are allowed.

As one, somewhat over-the-top, captain explained to me, "When the bridge is in 'Red' it is like landing a fighter plane on an aircraft carrier: everyone needs to be totally focused." And, yes, his bridge felt very focused : . . also quite uptight and super tense. It may have just been military training, seamanship, or potty training . . . who knows. But on most ships being on the bridge is like being in a hospital operating theater where a group of skilled professionals are focused on doing what they do best. Folks are cool, and confident, doing the job they do well without any drama. I've been through the Canal on ships where the captain was doing what everyone else on the ship was doing . . . taking pictures. And I've also been on ships where the captain had ordered rock salt . . . just like you use for winter ice on the driveway . . . thrown all around the bridge to insure good luck for our Canal crossing.

So I push the security button for access, hear the click and step into an anteroom bathed in red light. Bridges are dark and the red-light anteroom keeps a bright swath of light from messing up the night vision of the guys driving the ship. I walk into the darkness of the bridge where all I can make out are shadows of people, lots of people. It seems like the entire deck team are on the bridge this morning. This is one day everyone wants to experience, especially junior officers and deck cadets for whom this might be their first Canal transit.

"Morning Captain!"

Today will be an interesting day for the captain since he won't be the one giving the orders.

Usually pilots give the captains suggestions, but not in the Panama Canal. The Panama Canal is the only place in the world where, if you want to use the Canal, the ship must be signed over the ACP and the Canal pilot is calling the shots. It's not easy for a captain to turn over control of a $350 million dollar ship, when, even although he's not calling the shots, if something goes wrong it's his reputation on the line.

"Morning guys . . . and gals!" At this point, my eyes only just adjusting to the darkness, they are all just shadowy figures.

I scrounge around in the darkness for a flashlight and some spare batteries for the wireless microphone. It will be a long day. I feel around for a chair without accidentally feeling up a deck officer and pull the chair up to the bridge window. Already I see the shadowy shapes of guests lining the foredecks.

My eyes now accustomed to the darkness, I walk out onto the open wing bridge to get a feel for the weather . . . and to inhale the muggy morning air of home. It already feels and smells like Panama. Although my home, up in the Chiriqui mountains near to the Costa Rican Border, is over six hours away, it is still good to be home in my adopted land.

* * * *

Early morning on Canal Day is a magical time. On Southbound ships the clock is usually turned back the night before the Canal, so you end up with an extra hour of sleep to make up for the early morning wake up. A plus I guess for going south! Because Panama is about nine degrees north of the Equator, there is very little variance not only in temperature but also in the time of sunrise and sunset. Generally in Panama the sun comes up around 6:30 am. Some ships make a big deal out of Panama Canal morning . . . setting out coffee and tea and even, on Holland America, serving a special treat called "Panama Canal Rolls". I've tried, without success, to find the claimed historical association of these treats, but they are Dam good! To be out on the forward deck in the darkness, watching the ships from the nighttime convoy sail by and experiencing all the activity as the sun comes up . . . is just plain magical!

The last of the nighttime convoy ships

It's 5:00 am and Canal Day on MV JUST CRUISING!

Good morning MV JUST CRUISING! *"Bienvenidos a Panamá"* and welcome to the Panama Canal! And it's going to be a beautiful day as we make our way across what has been called "the path between the seas."

Since I now live in Panama, for me to be able to guide you through the Canal is a great pleasure. I still get excited every time I do this, which I why I didn't sleep very well last night.

* * * *

You'll notice all of the ships anchored out here. Generally there are twenty to thirty ships waiting to get through the Canal. The number of ships waiting is a good indication of the state of the world's economy. A few years ago some ships were sitting out here waiting for up to five weeks to get through the Canal. With the world's financial crises Canal traffic is off a bit, although the profits are up due to increased tolls.

If you want to go through the Canal you don't just show up! The Canal works on a slotting system. The Canal can handle forty ships a day, and there are usually more ships wanting to pass through the Canal than the Canal can accommodate.

In good economic times there are usually about sixty ships waiting, thirty ships on each side. If there is maintenance going on in one of the lock chambers the line can be longer.

Consider that a ship sailing from New York to San Francisco via the Canal travels 6,000 miles (9,656 kilometers), well under half the distance of the previous 14,000 mile (22,531 kilometer) route around Cape Horn.

Now assume you're a toy manufacturer in China and have a container of toys going to Wal-Mart, toys you need to get to Houston or New York, and have on the shelves by some upcoming holiday. Losing a few days waiting to get through the Canal is a long time! But the alternatives are traveling around the tip of South America, or trying to get them into Los Angeles harbor, where there is an enormous bottleneck of containers, and then trucked or rail freighted across the US. So it's worth a little wait to get through the Canal.

Over a million ships have transited the Canal since it was opened in 1914.

One hundred years ago, when the Canal was built, the demands were far different than they are today. There are only three of locks, each with two "lanes" . . . and the process takes as long as it takes. Although there has been continuing improvement and widening of the Canal there are now many ships that are just too large to fit through the Canal. So all of this has led to "amplification" or expansion of the Canal, in order to widen the choke-point areas and install a "third lane" of new locks. As you make your way through the Canal you will see a lot of work going on for the Canal expansion which was originally scheduled to be completed in 2014 for the 100th Anniversary of the Panama Canal.

With all these ships waiting, how is it that MV JUST CRUISING goes to the front of the line?

First, we reserved our spot, paying $25,000 for the privilege. This works well for cruise ships since we know exactly when we are going to be at the entrance to the Canal. But it doesn't work as well for many ships who might be delayed along the way or have to pick up or drop off additional cargo, so for them it's often not only cheaper but also more efficient to just wait around a few days to get a slot to pass through the Canal. And during that wait . . . you just sit there and wait. No shore leave for the crew.

Second, the Canal gives preference to passenger ships with 50 or more passengers. Every ship entering the Canal is given an identification code "N" for Northbound or "S" for Southbound. Following the directional letter is a schedule number, odd numbers for Northbound transits and even numbers for Southbound transits. Passenger ships are given the "Zulu" preferential identification.

So if our ship, MV JUST CRUISING, is making a Southbound transit, our identification would be Zulu 8 meaning that we are a preferential vessel, the eighth ship of the day making the Southbound transit. Were we making a Northbound transit, we would have an odd number like Zulu 7.

If you look at the flags flying on your ship you will see the cruise line's house flag, the flag of the country where your ship is registered, the flag of Panama, and a red and white flag called "Hotel" which is the maritime signal for "I have a pilot on board." If it is a Southbound transit below the Hotel flag will be flags giving the identification number for your ship, or, if it is a Northbound transit the numbers will be above the Hotel flag. In our case we will fly the "Zulu" flag and our transit number.

If you see a ship next to you in the locks flying a red pendant or "Bravo" flag it means the vessel is carrying flammable or explosive material. In the Canal a ship flying the "Tango" flag with vertical red, white and blue strips means it carries toxic or radioactive material.

* * * *

The Panama Canal takes cash only. No credit. No credit cards. And the check must have cleared with the cash in the ACP account before you get in the line . . . so no toll both. The ship's agent will handle the transaction and wire the cash into the Panama Canal's account.

Tolls for the Canal are decided by the Panama Canal Authority and are based on vessel type, size, and the cargo carried. Large passenger vessels like MV JUST CRUISING are charged per passenger berth. The current rate is $134 per berth, so with a 3,070 berths, our toll is $411,380. So that's our toll. If you think of an airline ticket, that toll is like the cost of the ticket. But then you have . . . the fees. In addition to the toll, somewhat like going into an a la carte restaurant, you pay extra for each tug boat, each mule, each inspection, etc.

Tug boats, $11,445, line handlers $4,745, a fee for this, fee for that . . . so it adds up quickly.

My estimate for the MV JUST CRUISING . . .

Toll $411,380
Fees around $47,398

Total: somewhere around $458,778 . . . give or take a few thousand. But what's money among friends? So, with fees, we're paying around $149 per berth.

So . . . cha-ching! The Canal makes a direct contribution to Panama, not an just economic contribution but a direct check to the government each year, of over $400 million per year. In a country of 3.3 million people that's significant. So thank you for your business!

MV JUST CRUISING is a Panamax ship or one of the largest ships that can transit the Canal. Ships that are too large to pass through the current Canal are called Post-Panamax ships.

A Panamax vessel, such as MV JUST CRUISING, usually requires up to 22 line handlers, six to eight locomotives (half at the bow and half at the stern), and two tugs to assist the vessel. One pilot will remain on the bridge at all times, moving between the wheel room and to either wing bridge to call out instructions, "full ahead," "ahead one-third," "amidships," etc. The other pilot will move about the vessel from bow to stern, port to starboard, keeping watch on the ship's progress.

The lowest toll ever paid was 36 cents, paid by Richard Halliburton for swimming the Canal in 1928. Richard Halliburton was an adventurer and author who in the '30s made headlines with his adventures.

* * * *

The bridge has ordered one of the shell doors opened on the hull to prepare for arrival of a number of small boats approaching the ship. These boats carry Panama Canal pilots and officials, Panamanian immigration officials and the ship's agent.

Generally a ship like MV JUST CRUISING will use two pilots.
A pilot who takes a Panamax ship through the Canal is a senior pilot who generally has been at it about ten years. A Panama Canal pilot has one of the highest paying jobs in Panama. In the Panama Canal the pilot is in charge.

My neighbor in Panama is a woman by the name of Sarah Terry, who was the first woman in the US to get her master's license and the first woman Panama Canal pilot. Sarah says that at the beginning, when a pilot who was a woman often was a surprise, that the most important thing was to establish your "command presence." Not every captain is eager to relinquish control . . . and in those early days, certainly not to a woman.

Canal Day on the bridge

The pilot is a licensed captain, with a master's license, and during our voyage through the Canal, although our captain must be on the bridge, the Canal pilot will be in charge: "The pilot assigned to a vessel shall have control of the navigation and movement of such a vessel." But if something goes wrong . . . it's the captain who has to explain to the home office.

So how it works is the pilot gives the instruction to the captain and the captain relays the pilot's instructions to his crew members, who perform the proper maneuver. To make sure everyone understands the instruction, as is typical on the bridge, the instruction is repeated . . . so throughout the day so there is a lot of background "chatter" as orders are given and repeated for confirmation.

If the captain doesn't like taking orders from the pilot . . . there is always the long way around the southern tip of South America.

Control Central – Marine Traffic Control

The pilot climbs aboard carrying what is known as the "orange box", a computer hookup to Marine Traffic Control. Marine Traffic Control is a heavily secured small building far from the shores of the Canal that controls the movement of all ships in Canal waters. Our passage through the Canal was slotted, and the pilots were assigned to our ship by Marine Traffic Control. Additionally in Marine Traffic Control are television screens that show movement in the Canal and in the locks. And, interestingly, especially once you've made this passage, you can go online to the Panama Canal Authority Web site and see these live Web cams at PanCanal.com.

Sarah Terry retired about the time of the Canal Turnover. She first was captain of one of the tugs, became a Canal pilot, a senior pilot and finally was one of the port captains. There are two port captains on duty at any given moment that ultimately control all movement in the Canal, one in Panama City and the other in Colon.

A senior Panama Canal pilot can make over $300,000 a year – in a country where the minimum wage is about $1.15 an hour, and an experienced construction worker makes about $35,000 a year – so the Canal pilot is at the top of the food chain.

It's 5:04 am The first set of pilots were boarded

"Pilot on board."

"Pilot on board."

A ship cadet continues writing in the logbook, "At 4:18 the ACP was contacted to confirm ETA. At 5:04 am the first set of pilots were boarded."

The pilot is escorted to the bridge by ship security along with the Canal inspection officers and a Canal computer technician.

"Morning Captain!" There are introductions and offers of coffee. The ACP computers are set up and connections with Marine Traffic Control are established. A Canal inspection officer is quickly running through a checklist.

Since this is a regular run at this time of year for MV JUST CRUISING the Canal folks already know the ship. If it was our first time in the Panama Canal, or if the ship had any modifications since the last time it was in the Canal, the inspection officer may have some questions or may even want to see the plans. He gets an update on the status of the engines and bow thrusters: all is in order. He may want to flash some lights, or toot the horn as a perfunctory check, but we are good to go.

* * * *

Down in the Purser's Office the "PRACTICA" or port paper officer ["PPO"] is with the ship's agent, Panama immigration and inspection officers along with other officials who are sitting around drinking coffee, munching breakfast pastries and reviewing, stamping and signing a three-inch high stack of papers, declarations and documents. There are lists of passengers and crew, all of which has been previously conveyed to Panamanian authorities in advance via computer. And, this being Panama, there is a lot of rubber stamping to be done.

The authorities want to know if anyone is in quarantine or if there are any medical emergencies to be offloaded. This morning on MV JUST CRUISING there are two crew members quarantined to their cabins for 36 hours for suspected Noro-virus and four guests quarantined for the same reason, below 1% and well below any cause for concern.

First officer, pilot, captain, Canal official on the Bridge

One guest is scheduled to be disembarked with the Ship Agent because of concerns about an arrhythmia that the Senior Doctor feels needs to be evaluated ashore and because, frankly, the cruise line's policy is to get people with any questionable medical conditions off the ship ASAP.

Also, yours truly, having completed my pre-Canal lectures and after giving my Canal transit commentary, is all packed and ready to climb down the ladder and leave with the pilot on the other end of the Canal. I go back home to my wife, dogs and coffee farm high in the Chiriqui mountains of Panama, just outside the little town of Boquete. The Canal pilots always find this interesting since Boquete is a favorite vacation destination of folks living in Panama City.

The Isthmus of Panama, home to the Republic of Panama, is a little squiggle that joins the continents of North and South America. At 28,702 square miles (74,340 square kilometers), the Republic of Panama is little smaller than South Carolina. Panama has 1,547 miles (2,490 kilometers) of coastline on both the Atlantic Ocean (Caribbean Sea) and Pacific Ocean. The highest point is Volcan Baru, 11,398 feet (3,474 meters), the mountain on which I live.

Panama runs east to west with the western border being with Costa Rica, and the eastern border with Colombia. Because the Isthmus joins North and South America many people wrongly assume the country runs north – south.

The Panama Canal, although facilitating transits between east and west, actually runs north and south.

Since the introduction of lighting in 1963 the Canal operates 24 hours a day, 365 days a year and is bi-directional, that is with ships moving in both directions a maximum of 14,600 ships a year. The Canal has carefully worked out scenarios to get the maximum traffic through the Canal, and so during the night they usually run a north and south convoy of ships, entering opposite ends at roughly the same time, passing one another in the middle, and exiting in the early morning. So the ships we see slowly passing are part of the convoy that went through the Canal during the night. Once they have cleared the locks MV JUST CRUISING will start the transit.

The "orange box" amongst other things gives the distance to the lock

From beginning to end the Canal is 50 miles (80.5 kilometers).

* * * *

When the first European explorers came to this region they were looking for a path between east and west. Your journey through the Canal, "the path between the seas", is the realization of the dream of those early explorers.

Christopher Columbus, on his fourth voyage in 1502, embittered and sickly, sailed in these very same waters, searching for the illusive "hidden straight" that would get him to the Far East. In 1502 Columbus anchored in the very spot in the Caribbean where ships now wait to enter the Canal. Columbus died believing that he had encountered the outer islands of India and so they were named the West Indies.

Due east of the Atlantic entrance to the Canal is a cove in the Darien first reached by Europeans in 1501 and seen by Columbus on his last voyage. In 1510 the first successful European settlement on the mainland of the Americas was established on the western side of the Gulf of Urabá and named Santa María de la Antigua del Darien. The settlement was short lived and abandoned in 1524 after being attacked and burned by the Indigenous people.

Balboa claiming and naming the "South Sea"

But it was from Santa María de la Antigua del Darien that Balboa made his famous march to the Pacific. Hearing the Indigenous people talk of a "great ocean" across the mountains to the south, Balboa led an expedition in 1513 to follow the Indian trail. Accompanied by 190 Spaniards, all wearing unbelievably hot helmets, breastplates of polished steel, thick leather breaches, woolen stockings and high boots, Balboa trekked through the jungle across the Isthmus to discover what he called the "South Sea." It was not until much later that Magellan would later rename this vast body of water the Pacific Ocean.

So . . . the dream began! Unable to find a natural path across the Isthmus, people began dreaming of a canal.

* * * *

In 1534 King Charles V of Spain ordered that the Chagres River be mapped and cleared all the way to what by then was already Panama City. He ordered land studies with a view toward excavating a canal. At the same time he was also looking at the San Juan River that runs from Lake Nicaragua to the Caribbean, creating what would eventually become a rivalry between Nicaragua and Panama.

The discovery of the Pacific and the further conquests of the Spanish Conquistadors produced a flood of gold and silver from the New World which dwarfed any treasure the Spanish might have gotten from the Indies had Columbus been successful in finding a path to the East by going west. Panama became the crossroads of Spain's empire in the New World. Gold and silver were brought by ship from across the Americas to Panama City.

Without the canal Charles V had dreamed about, King Phillip II devised a system of convoys in the 1560s that would not only get the riches of Spain's vast empire back home, but also ward off attacks of privateers and pirates.

The "*Flota de Indias*" fleet left Spain in two convoys bound for the treasure cities of Veracruz, Portobelo, Nombre de Dios and Cartagena where treasure was being stored in warehouses awaiting the fleet's arrival. All of these ships would rendezvous in Havana before sailing for Spain as one mighty naval force. Additional treasures were brought from the Philippines to Acapulco, then across Mexico to Veracruz where they were loaded onto the Caribbean treasure fleet.

To get the gold and silver from Panama City back to Spain it had to first be transported across the Isthmus of Panama by mule train. A single mule train could include hundreds of mules all loaded down with gold and silver!

The route across the Isthmus became known as the Camino Real, or the Royal Road, although it was more commonly called the *"Camino de Cruces"* ("Road of the Crosses") because of the abundance of gravesites along the way. Don't let the name fool you: it was really nothing more than a jungle trail, often knee deep with mud and frequently washed out by landslides. After the trek across the jungle of Panama the gold and silver ended up in the custom house in Portobelo to await the arrival of the treasure fleet. Sometimes mules laden with silver fell off the path and tumbled down ravines and, being Panama even back then, sometimes a mule and with its load of treasure would just disappear with the loot hidden in the jungle to be recovered later. It is believed there still may be lodes of lost silver and gold still buried in the mud and jungle overgrowth along the Royal Road even to this day.

Portobelo is about a half hour east of Limon. You can go there and still see the old Spanish Forts which guarded the town and the restored Custom House where the treasure was stored to await the Spanish Fleet and shipment to Spain. Today the Spanish fortifications from Portobelo to San Lorenzo - just west of the Atlantic entrance to the Canal - are UNESCO World Heritage sites.

The restored Custom House in Portobelo

Of course Portobelo was too good for pirates and privateers to pass up!

In 1572 Sir Francis Drake carried an enormous pile of silver back to England, silver he had looted in Panama from the Spanish. Working as a privateer for the Queen of England, Drake seized Spanish ships off the coast of Panama, captured and looted Number de Dios, and ambushed a mule train carrying Peruvian silver across the Isthmus.

Drake returned twenty years later in an attempt to capture the entire Isthmus for England only to die of dysentery . . . and to be buried in a lead coffin just east of the Bay of Limon.

Another English privateer Henry Morgan sacked Panama . . . first sacking Portobelo in 1671 and then marching across the Isthmus to sack Panama City, then the richest city in the world.

Captain Morgan Interrogating Panamanians

2 - Southbound Transit - Atlantic to Pacific

> This part is for those of you crossing from the Atlantic to the Pacific. If you are making a Northbound trip, Pacific to Atlantic, you can just skip to Chapter 3. Both chapters are designed to give you a narrative of what you will experience during your Canal passage, a guidebook if you will. *So although the content is pretty much the same, it is presented in a different order.*

2A- The Approach - Colon

The Bay of Limon is the huge natural bay, 4.5 miles (7 kilometers) long and 2.5 miles (4 kilometers) wide, that provides anchorage for ships awaiting transit.

In the darkness you can generally just make out the breakwaters that extend from the west and east sides of the entrance to the approach to the Canal. The breakwaters are themselves a great engineering achievement - 6 miles (9.6 kilometers) long, and 425 feet (130 meters) wide at the base.

The breakwaters were originally built to protect the Canal from torpedoes. As the ship passes through the breakwater it is headed due south, and if it is clear at certain times of the year you can see the Southern Cross just above the horizon dead ahead. Once we are inside the breakwater the ship turns southeast to the entrance of Gatun Locks. Torpedoes went straight ahead, so if one was fired from outside the breakwater it would miss the Canal entrance.

Today the breakwaters serve a useful function of protecting the inner harbor against storms and protecting the Canal channel from silting and surf.

The mast lights marking the entrance to the breakwater are among the tallest in the world.

From the outer breakwater to the entrance of Gatun Locks is 5.4 miles (7.2 kilometers).

Way off on the starboard side, in the distance there is a navigation light that marks where the former US Fort Sherman was located. And off to the port side, around the end of the breakwater, was another US installation called Coco Solo. During the US Canal period there were 12-16 military forts and operations in the Canal Zone, including a jungle survival school where Indigenous Embera Indians were used to train troops, including the first US astronauts.

During the US days the Canal Zone was pretty much off limits to Panamanians, unless they worked for the Canal or the US Army. Today there are many Panamanians who are dual citizens of both Panama and the US because they had a parent who worked either for the Canal or the US Army. So judging by the number of folks in Panama who are both Panamanian and US, the fence along the Canal Zone was pretty porous!

The lights off the port side in the distance are lights of the city of Colon. Colon was a very important area during the US Canal occupation and home to several major US military operations that provided a lot of local revenue and employment. Today Colon is the second largest city in Panama and home to the Colon Free Zone, the second largest free port in the world, second only to Hong Kong. It's not "duty free shopping" in the cruise port sense, but a port where goods can be assembled, purchased wholesale and distributed by container loads around the world. Location at the "crossroads of the Americas" is one of the main keys to the enormous success of the Colon Free Zone.

Other than the Free Zone, and a few new hotel and shopping complexes, the center of Colon is a pretty depressed area. It was actually used in the James Bond film "Quantum of Solace" to represent Haiti . . . it's that bad. Although much of the city was burned during a Colombian civil war in 1885, and again in a massive fire in 1915, many of the surviving buildings still reflect the French style architecture of the Canal construction days. With some government investment and employment projects for locals, downtown Colon could be developed into a real tourist center.

There are two places cruise ships dock in Colon. Colon 2000 is a terminal used by a lot of Carnival Corporation companies. Home Port is used mostly by Royal Caribbean companies. Royal Caribbean homeports in a ship Panama during the North American winter cruise season.

For many years there was an old pier built in 1919 as a coaling station that was known as Pier 6 or Cristobal. In 2010 the old historic pier was demolished to allow more space for containerized port operations.

The huge port here is operated by the Panama Ports Company, part of Hutchinson Port Holdings, which operates 355 berths in 44 ports around the world. Hutchinson in turn is owned by Cheung Kong Group, one of Hong Kong's leading multi-national conglomerates. This company also operates a port on the other end of the Canal at Balboa. This has led to one of those crazy rumors, rampant in some places, including the US, that the People's Republic of China is running the Canal.

Not so! Panama, not China, owns and runs the Canal. With few exceptions, if you work in Panama you have to be Panamanian. But the People's Republic recognizes what hopefully are good investments, things like investing in US Treasury Bonds . . . and investing in Panama's port infrastructure.

Royal Caribbean has done very well home porting ships in Panama. Guests from Asia, Europe and Central and South America and even Canada can avoid the hassles of US immigration that they would encounter sailing from Florida. Guests from the US can begin their cruise right in the heart of the Caribbean and enjoy more of the southern Caribbean area. I predict in coming years you will see more cruise lines home porting vessels in Panama using Colon on the Atlantic side and Amador on the Pacific.

* * * *

From King Charles V of Spain (1534) onward many people have looked longingly at the idea of a canal across Central America. Benjamin Franklin was entranced by the idea of a canal. When Thomas Jefferson became US ambassador to France, he was interested in seeing a canal in Panama. Simon Bolivar chose Panama City as the site for his Latin American Congress claiming that if the world would have a capital, it would be Panama. Bolivar was passionately in favor of a canal.

Panama was captivated by the "Great Liberator" Simon Bolivar and his vision of a coalition of former Spanish colonies to be called Gran Colombia. Panama along with Colombia, Venezuela and Ecuador joined Gran Colombia which lasted from 1819 to 1831. Plagued by internal squabbling Gran Colombia dissolved and Panama ended up part of Colombia with whom it had little in common. Panama became a largely neglected region of Colombia except when Colombia needed to conscript troops.

But Panama wasn't the only canal option. The Dutch were looking at Nicaragua as a potential site for a canal. Britain was also in the game. The French had managed to wrest a concession from Colombia for a railway across Panama, but the French syndicate failed to raise sufficient funds for the railway so the concession was taken over by a New York businessman by the name of William Aspinwall. Aspinwall was already running a steamship service between Panama and San Francisco and thought a canal across Panama would greatly enhance his operation.

When gold was discovered in California there was a rush for people to get to California to make their fortune in gold. There were three ways to get to California: the plains across, the Cape around, or across the Isthmus of Panama. The Panama route was the quickest, but also the most expensive. Boats would come from New Orleans to Panama and men would get off at the little village of Chagres, up the Chagres River and fight their way across the Isthmus to Panama City where they would board a steamship for California. There was nothing more than a 21-mile muddy trail across the Isthmus. Chagres quickly became known as "American Chagres" loaded down with bars and brothels. It was the American Wild West in Panama. There was no law enforcement so everyone packed their own gun. More than a hundred prostitutes worked the tent town and drinks in the saloon in Chagres cost more than they did in New York City.

Old Colon, Panama

It was an ideal opportunity for Aspinwall to build his railroad. After looking at several options for the western terminus, he settled on a swampy island just off Limon Bay called Manzanillo. As work began on the railroad Manzanillo began to sprout a small town, which the company named Aspinwall after the company president. Fortunately the locals would have none of this, so a law was passed calling the town Colon, after Christopher Columbus.

During the days of the US Canal Zone the area of the city within the Zone was named Cristobal (Christopher) and the old Panamanian area was called Colon (Columbus).

* * * *

As the ship makes its way to the entrance of Gatun Locks there are two interesting passages branching off the main channel, one on either side of the ship.

On the starboard or right side is a little passage known as the French passage. This tiny inlet is all that is left from the original French attempt to dig the Panama Canal, an attempt that cost over 20,000 lives.

At the entrance to the French Passage is a good place to look for the crocs that hang out in this area, but more about those suckers later!

On the port side of the ship you will see another channel and a lot of construction. This is called the US Channel. The Canal opened in 1914 but rather quickly folks began to realize that it wasn't large enough to handle all the demand, and with larger and larger military ships the Canal needed to be enlarged. So in 1939 the US began an ambitious program to expand the Canal, enlarging it and building a "third lane" of larger locks . . . very similar in concept to the huge expansion project now being undertaken by Panama. The US project began in 1939 but the effort was abandoned when the US entered World War II. The idea was revisited periodically but with price tags in the billions of dollars nothing happened. The US Channel is what remains of that attempt.

But the work isn't going to go to waste since the original US Channel is actually being used as the entrance channel to the new set of Gatun Locks being built by Panama as a part of the current "third lane" or Canal expansion or "amplification" project, which is why you see all the dredging and construction going on.

* * * *

The image and expectation that many people have is that they will see wildlife and birds along the shoreline as they transit the Canal. Although Panama is one of the most bio-diverse areas in the world, and the rainforests you will see along the sides of the Canal have an amazing diversity of birds and animals, don't expect to see much. Unless you have really good eyes and a great pair of binoculars the Canal channels are too far from shore to see much more than spectacular foliage. And we are transiting during the middle of the day when most respectable animals are napping. But they are there! Anteaters, jaguars, cougars, monkeys, deer, agouti, parrots, toucans, sloths, snakes, hundreds of butterflies including the iridescent Blue Morpho . . . they're all there. All of this giving you a great reason to come back and visit Panama and stay a while!

What you can look for are crocs! The Canal has American crocodile as well as caiman. Although often locally called "alligators", they are in fact crocodiles. How I remember: "canal" and "crocodile" both start with "C". Crocodiles like to hang out near the entrance to Gatun Locks. Some of these guys have been here since before the Canal was built and some are huge! These big suckers can be very aggressive so Canal workers have to be very cautious when doing maintenance work in this area. Look on the banks . . . or watch in the water. The tip off is what looks like a log . . . moving in the wrong direction or against the current. And yes, both the crocodiles and caiman have attacked and killed people. Caiman grow as large as 12 to 15 feet (3.7 to 4.6 meters), and crocodiles can get as large as 18 feet (5.5 meters) and weigh as much as a ton. People have been killed in this area, in Gatun Lake and in Miraflores Lake and since it is common for the animal to take its victim and hide the body underwater, the bodies of those attacked are usually never found. So keep your hands and feet inside the ship!

People always ask about the large birds with the forked tails. These are frigates, and you see lots of them around the Canal. Panama has 940 bird species, but unfortunately you aren't going to see a lot from the middle of the Canal. You may hear first, then see, some flocks of the little green parrots we have . . . noisy buggers. You'll probably see them in the tops of the trees along the Canal.

Up close and personal with the Canal on the Promenade Deck

There is no one "best" vantage point on the ship. If you want to get the most out of your day in the Canal, move around the ship. Coming into the locks the forward part of the ship is the best place to be. When the ship is in the locks move around! The view from the aft end is totally different.

Sometime when you are in the locks go down to the promenade deck and you will really appreciate just how little room there is to spare! It is so close that you feel as if you can almost reach out and touch the sides of the Canal. If you have a balcony the best time to enjoy that vantage point is when you sailing through Gatun Lake.

If you have an outside cabin without a balcony, but with a window, while you are in the locks you should run down to your cabin and look out the window. Outside you will see the massive wall of the lock, just inches away!

* * * *

A lot of times when planning their cruise people will ask, "Which is the best side of the ship to book our stateroom? We want the best view." Again, there is no one best vantage point. There is no way of know in advance which lock chamber will be assigned. If your stateroom is on the port side and you happen to be assigned the right or starboard chamber, you will have the "best" view of the action and of any other vessel that may be in the chamber next to you. But if you happened to be assigned the port or starboard lock chamber, the "best" view will be on the other side! There is no way to know in advance! So, again, my advice is . . . move around!

Once you are in Lake Gatun there is no advantage to being on one side or the other.

* * * *

Once the ship clears Gatun Locks is a good time to have breakfast. If your ship offers the option of having a champagne breakfast served on your stateroom balcony, a good time to schedule it is once you are through Gatun Locks, just entering Gatun Lake. If things are running on schedule, around 8:30 am or 9 am is a good time for your champagne breakfast. It will make a memorable day even more special!

It will be a long day so stay hydrated, wear a hat and sunscreen, and pace yourself. By the end of the day the rails won't be nearly as crowded. People will be playing cards, working out in the gym, lying about on deck.

To prove the point, I actually took a picture of a couple for whom the trip through the Canal was a bucket-list trip of a lifetime. We were actually in the locks and these folks were on the promenade deck sound asleep!

To each his own, but I hope you don't miss a thing.

Can you believe it? Asleep IN the locks on the trip of a lifetime!

2B - The Atlantic Locks

It's 6:00 am approaching Gatun Locks

There are two "lanes" through the lock complexes and in the case of Gatun each lane has three lock chambers. They are bi-directional and you can go in either direction. All this is done to maximize the number of ships passing through the Canal.

Prior to entering the locks a small boat will bring the Panama Canal line handlers on board to assist MV JUST CRUISING in connecting to the engines or "mules" that will help guide us through the locks.

The Canal has thirty two tug boats and two will be standing by to assist us as necessary and if necessary nudge the ship into the correct position to enter the locks. At some times of the year the wind blows from the north, sometimes quite strongly, so a Panamax ship can act like a huge sail, and the tugs are sometimes essential.

The Arrow is an additional communication tool

The big arrow is a visual communication from the lock to the pilot. The position of the arrow indicates the readiness of the lock for the ship to enter and which side of the chamber will be used.

So you can read the arrow signals and tell all your fellow passengers what is going on . . .

Signal	Meaning	Signal	Meaning
↑	Not ready; lockage cannot take place for some time	↘	Moor to approach wall near jaws on right-hand side
↑	Not ready; stand off well clear of lock, prepared to approach on signal	↙	Moor to approach wall near jaws on left-hand side
↖	Locks making preparation, probably be ready for lockage in 10 minutes or less; you may approach with caution, prepared to tie up or enter on right hand side on signal	→	Enter right-hand side
↗	Locks making preparation, probably be ready for lockage in 10 minutes or less; you may approach with caution, prepared to tie up or enter on left hand side on signal	←	Enter left-hand side

Now you'll be the only one "in the know" thanks to me! Impress your friends, make a bet and get them to buy you a drink!

* * * *

The ship is getting ready to enter the Gatun Lock complex, a three-stage flight of locks that will lift the MV JUST CRUISING up 85 feet (26 meters) above sea level to the level of Gatun Lake. Then we will sail across Panama 85 feet (26 meters) above sea level to the Pedro Miguel and Miraflores Locks on the Pacific side. There we will drop back down to sea level and sail off into the sunset.

There is no way to know in advance of the signal which of the lock chambers will be assigned to MV JUST CRUISING. So you are wasting your time trying to psych out which is "the best side of the ship" to book your cabin.

* * * *

Each lock chamber is 1,000 feet (304.8 meters) long and 110 feet (33.5 meters) wide. Our hypothetical MV JUST CRUISING is 856 feet (260.9 meters) long and 105 feet (32 meters) wide so, unless guests have been eating too many desserts, we should fit with about 2.5 feet (about .8 meters) to spare on either side.

The lock chambers are seven stories high! The maximum draft is 39.5 feet (12.04 meters) in tropical fresh water (which is a slightly different than in salt water or cold fresh water).

Panamax vessels navigate under-draft-depth restrictions that do not allow them their full cargo capacity. Part of the expansion program is to increase the depth of the locks to make it possible for vessels to carry a full load..

The pilot maneuvers the ship to the approach wall where the line handlers attach the cables of the locomotives to the vessel. As the pilot calls out maneuvers to the captain, the vessel continues forward with assistance from the tug at the stern. When the ship reaches the first chamber of the lock, line handlers will attach the cables of the remaining locomotives to the vessel and draw them tight to stabilize the ship for entry into the chamber.

Together with the locomotives and tugs and under its own power, the ship moves into the first chamber, where gates close behind the vessel's stern to lock it into the chamber.

6:20 am connecting to the mules

In order to tie the ship up to the "mules" or locomotives lines have to be passed from the shore to the ship. This job is handled by the Panama Canal line handlers. Over the years they have tried many ways to get the lines from the vessel to the shore. They've tried everything including shooting the lines on board, which ended up putting out a few people's eyes. So it turns out that the very best way is to send a little rowboat to bring the lines from the ship to the engines.

Line handlers preparing to bring lines out to the ship

Here's this high-tech cruise ship with our sophisticated, computerized bridge . . . and the little row boat is still the best way!

* * * *

As we enter the locks you will notice some round things that look like giant tires on the Canal walls. These are the "bumpers" . . . just like in a pinball machine . . . designed to roll and keep the Canal walls from putting a hole in the ship hull should the ship accidentally drift or make too sharp a turn. Nobody wants to bring the "family" ship back with a giant gash in the hull . . . or paint off the fender . . . but the fact is the cosmetic paint on the hull of many ships passing through the Canal takes a beating.

* * * *

There are three places along the Canal where locals and visitors can get a good view of the action. The first is going to be on the port side of the first lock chamber, the Gatun Locks Observation Center. If you look down on the port side of the first chamber, just before the observation center, you will see one of the huge old gears that were used to open the lock gates.

One of the old gears used to open and close lock gates

Originally 50 horsepower motor operated gears to open and close lock leaves. Now a 15 horsepower motor operates hydraulic arms that open and close the leaves.

* * * *

Just below the steps that lead up to the observation platform you can see one of the early locomotives or "mules" used on the Canal that was built by General Electric.

One of the early General Electric "mules"

The number of locomotives or "mules" that are used depends on the size of the ship. MV JUST CRUISING will use six. The Canal is kind of like an a la carte restaurant. There is a basic toll that's based on the size and amount of cargo plus all the extra fees. Although on a cruise people come on as guests, but after eating all that spectacular food, end up being classed as "cargo", the reality is that cruise ships are charged according to the number of berths regardless of the weight of the "cargo."

In addition to the basic toll you pay extra for each tug, each locomotive, each line handler . . . cha ching, cha ching. So on behalf of the people of Panama, thank you very much! All over Panama you will see big blue signs designating projects that are a direct result of Canal revenues: basketball courts in tiny little towns, new roads, new bridges, school renovations . . . even the new road in front of my house in the little hamlet of Palmira.

The locomotives have been called "mules" through the years, but not because animals were ever used in Panama to assist ships through the Canal. In the early history of canals in the US and Europe mules were used to pull barges along. So it is because of that history, that the engines used in Panama came to be called "mules."

There have been three generations of locomotives, the first built by General Electric, the second built by Mitsubishi, and the current generation built by Mitsubishi. The newest were assembled in Panama, and each cost $1.9 million. The Canal has 100 of these electric engines, powered by a third rail, geared to run on tracks. Each locomotive weighs 50 tons and operates with two 290 HP traction units with a towing capacity of 178 to 311.8 kilo new tons depending on their speed. Their maximum return speed is 16 kilometers per hour which is important when a lockage is completed and the engines have relay down the center track back to the beginning.

Each locomotive has two powerful winches controlled by the driver to take cable in or pay it out as ordered by the pilot. Ships travel through the Canal on their own power. The locomotives have several important functions:

Keeping the vessel centered;
Assisting in towing if needed;
Stopping the forward motion if needed as a safety feature.

* * * *

The folks back home can follow your journey through the Canal online by accessing the three Web cams that are located on the official site of the Panama Canal Authority [PanCanal.com]. There are Web cams at Gatun Locks, Centennial Bridge, and Miraflores Locks. The Web cams are located on the red and white communication towers.

* * * *

6:46 am inside the first chamber and gate closed

The function of the locks is to act as a "water elevator" that lifts the ship up from sea level to the level of Gatun Lake, 85 feet (26 meters) above sea level. There the ship sails across the Isthmus of Panama and when it gets to the other side, another series of locks acts as a "water elevator" to lower the ship back to sea level.

The Gatun Lock complex has three lock chambers. Water from the second chamber flows into the first chamber and lifts the vessel to the water level of the second chamber. When the ship has been raised to the proper level the gates in front open and the vessel moves ahead into the second chamber under its own power. The process repeats for the second chamber. In the third chamber the ship is lifted up to the level of Gatun Lake.

Once the ship is inside the chamber and the lock gates are closed, it takes only about thirty minutes for the ship to be raised. Assuming everything flows smoothly the ship will be in the Gatun lock complex for about an hour. This depends not only on the lockage of your ship, but also the ship ahead of you. Sometimes the process gets delayed and everything does not move on schedule. With some of the larger, boxy ships, like bulk carriers and tankers, it takes longer for the water to flow around the hull.

Entering Gatun Locks

The lockmaster at each lock has the responsibility for handling ships in the locks. The control house is the center of operations. The pilot, lockmaster and control house operator are in constant radio communication.

For the efficient operation of the locks some ships may be assigned to tie along the lock walls to wait while other vessels are inside the locks. To maximize traffic and efficiency a relay system of locomotives is often used where locomotive teams change mid-lockage.

As we make our way through the locks the pilot is continually giving commands to the locomotive operators by radio. The bells and lights on the locomotives are additional ways of communicating and confirming commands. The green light means the locomotive is "up to speed". The red light "confirms pilot order" and the yellow light means the locomotive is "standing by".

The locomotive bells are an additional means of communication between the pilot and the locomotive operator. Two "distinct taps" on the locomotive bell means the order has been received, understood and will be executed as directed. Three taps on the bell means the locomotive operator does not understand or cannot execute the order or wants to attract the attention of the pilot. Continual ringing of the bell is a general alarm signal.

* * * *

The Canal uses only fresh water. Neither the Canal nor Gatun Lake is salt water. Not only would salt water have a corrosive effect on the cement and the metal, but the challenge of the Canal historically has been what to do with all the water that flows into Gatun Lake from the Chagres River during the rainy season. It is not unheard of in Panama to have rain falling at times at 3 to 4 inches (76 to 102 millimeters) an hour.

So the Canal uses fresh water and it uses a lot of water. Each time a ship transits the Canal 53.4 million US gallons (202,000 cubic meters) of water is passed from the lake into the sea. With some 14,600 vessel transits per year, this represents a huge demand for fresh water. Since rainfall is seasonal in Panama, Gatun Lake acts as a water store, allowing the Canal to continue operation through the dry season.

One of the most fascinating things about the Canal is the way in which water from Gatun Lake flows through the locks. Deep within the walls are huge culverts 18 feet (5.5 meters) in diameter. When the Canal was built the tunnels were the same size as the tunnels under the Hudson River in New York that were built to bring the railroad into New York City.

From the main culvert there are 14 lateral culverts running underneath the lock floor. In the floor of the lock there are 70 holes, each about 4 feet (1.2 meters) wide. These many holes allow the lock chamber to either fill or empty with minimal turbulence. It all happens so smoothly that you don't even know the ship is being lifted until you happen to look at a ship in the next chamber or a point on shore.

The water from the highest lock, makes its way to the next lock, then on to the lowest lock, and finally it is emptied out flushing into the approach and out to sea.

Since all the equipment of the locks is operated electrically, the whole process of locking a ship up or down is controlled from a central control room located on the center wall of the upper flight of locks. The controls are designed to minimize the chances of operator error so there is an actual model of the locks with moving components that mirror the actual state of the locks. An operator can see at a glance exactly the position of all locks and valves. Interlocks are built into the controls so that no component can be moved if another is not in the right position.

Cross-section of Lock Chamber and Walls, Panama Canal

A section across the width of the locks, showing the culverts for filling and draining the chambers. One side is shown; the other is the same.

There are walkways across the lock gates that allow Canal workers to pass from one side of the lock chamber to the other. When the gates are closed and about to open a bell warns workers before the rails collapse into the gate.

Sometimes you will see the red lights flashing on the center wall and hear a siren. This is a warning that hazardous cargo is on the ships and no open flames, smoking or electrical tools are permitted.

7:25 am Medical evacuation complete - passing to the second chamber

It was actually Leonardo da Vinci who first came up with the design used by the Canal's current miter gates: double-leaf doors hinged on chamber walls and sealed by water pressure.

---

[1] GNU Free Documentation License, Version 1.2

Each steel lock leaf is 65 feet (19.8 meters) wide, 7 feet (2.1 meters) thick, and from 47 to 82 feet (14.3 to 25 meters) high and weighs from 390 to 730 tons. The largest gates are at Miraflores Locks and were so designed because of the vast tidal variances on the Pacific side. Tides on the Atlantic are only 1 or 2 feet (.3 or .6 meters) whereas on the Pacific they can run as high as 23 feet (7 meters).

The lock leaves are hollow, so for repairs and maintenance they can be lifted out by one of the Canal's giant cranes and floated off to be repaired. Of course that requires shutting down a traffic lane and causing delays, so the new lock complexes now under construction for the expansion of the Canal will use the rolling-type gates which are more efficient and easier to maintain.

* * * *

The Canal runs 24 hours a day, 365 days a year. It only ran during daylight hours until 1963 when new lighting was introduced and the Canal began round the clock operations.

The Canal has only been closed three times in its history, once in 1986 when a landslide in Gaillard Cut blocked the Canal for twelve hours, and again for an entire day starting at midnight December 20, 1989 when the US invaded Panama. Following the invasion, from December 21 to December 27, the Canal only operated during daylight hours. December 8, 2010 the Canal was closed for 17 hours when extreme rains forced the opening of spillways. The combination of entire small islands washing down from the Chagres River into the Canal channel and extreme currents created by opening the spillways made navigation unsafe.

The Canal follows somewhat the route of the original Panama Railroad. To create the Canal and particularly when Lake Gatun was created and flooded there were little towns that disappeared under the surface. The three lock complexes – Gatun, Pedro Miguel and Miraflores were named after towns that were flooded creating the Canal.

8:00 am Moving into the third chamber - line handlers and first pilot disembark, second pilot on board

People are always curious about the bulls-eye targets on the center wall of the third chamber. These are used by the line handlers to practice throwing hawser lines, the object being to put the "monkey fist" at the end of the line through the center hole. Line handlers have competition events to determine who wins the prize for accuracy and height.

Another competitive event that has been around the Canal since 1954 is the annual Cayuco Race. A *cayuco* is the traditional Indigenous canoe made by hollowing out a giant log. The race started when a Panama Canal worker had the great idea to take a group of Boy Scouts to meet a native Embera Indian community on the Chagres. The boys learned how to paddle the traditional Indian *cayuco* which eventuated in an annual race through the Panama Canal, from one side to the other covering a 41 mile (66 kilometer) long route over three days. Over 75 boats make the trek each year.

* * * *

In the third chamber you will notice that there are two sets of gates. The second is a security gate. In the event a vessel would not be able to slow its forward motion and damage the integrity of the first gate, the second gate would prevent Gatun Lake from draining.

Double lock gates protect Gatun Lake water supply in the event of an accident in the locks

* * * *

While in the third chamber, if you look to the right or starboard side of the ship, in the distance, you will see Gatun Dam and the hydroelectric plant that generates electricity.

Gatun Dam is an earthen dam built across the Chagres River, constructed between 1907 and 1913. The dam creates the large artificial Gatun Lake that allows ships, once they are lifted by the Gatun Locks up 85 feet (26 meters) above sea level, to sail across the Isthmus of Panama. The dam, lake and locks are all named the honor the town of Gatun which was flooded in order to create the Canal.

Construction of the dam was itself a stunning engineering achievement, eclipsed only by the simultaneous excavation of the Gaillard Cut.

Originally there was a gap in the hills around the Chagres Valley of about 1.2 miles (2 kilometers). This gap was filled with material excavated from Culebra Cut and the Gatun lock site to create a dam 2,100 feet (640 meters) thick at the bottom, 7,500 feet (2,300 meters) long along the top and 98 feet (30 meters) thick at the top. At the normal level of Gatun Lake the top of the dam is 30 feet (9 meters) above the lake level.

To create the dam two parallel walls of stone were built and then clay dredged out of the river base of the Chagres River was pumped into the center of the walls to create, in effect, a solid core of natural material within the dam.

As you look to the starboard or right side what you see primarily is the spillway which regulates the flow of water from Gatun Lake down a concrete channel. The crest of the spillway dam is 16 feet (4.9 meters) below the normal lake level. The spillway dam has 14 electrically operated gates, each 46 feet (14 meters) wide by 20 feet (6 meters) high. These gates are used to control the flow of water and the height of water in Gatun Lake. The capacity of the spillway is 140,000 cubic feet (4,100 cubic meters) of water per second which is more than the maximum flow of the Chagres River.

Sometimes during the rainy season so much water is pouring into Gatun Lake that the lake needs to be lowered and the spillway gates are opened, which is a spectacular sight that always draws locals to watch. Should this not be sufficient to lower the lake, the culverts in the locks theoretically could release an additional 49,000 cubic feet (1,400 cubic meters) of excess water per second probably flooding part of Colon.

The dam contains some 22 million cubic yards (17 million cubic meters) of material, and weighs some 30 million short tons (27 million long tons). It covers 290 acres (1.17 square kilometers) of ground. There is enough earth and rock in Gatun Dam to build a wall almost five feet (1.5 meters) high and a foot (.3 meters) thick all around the earth at the Equator!

A hydroelectric power plant at the dam produces power that in the US Canal days was just used for the operation of the Canal Zone. Today the plant provides enough electricity for the Canal as well as additional power which is sold onto the Panama grid. Under Panamanian operation, the Canal generates significant revenue from the sale of surplus electricity.

It is more fun if there is another ship in the next chamber

2C - Gatun Lake

8:55 am Exiting the third chamber and cruising into Gatun Lake

Once we make our way through into Gatun Lake, if you look back on the port side you will see some of the construction that is going on to create the new Atlantic lock complex.

At the time it was built, Gatun Lake was the largest man-made lake in the world. Today, Gatun Lake doesn't even make the top-thirty list of man-made bodies of water. Gatun Lake has an area of 164 square miles (425 square kilometers) at its normal level. The lake stores 4,200,000 acre feet of water (5.2 cubic kilometers) which is about as much water as comes down the Chagres River during an average year. Which means if you emptied Gatun Lake, it would only take an average year's rainfall to refill the lake, which gives you some idea of the enormous amount of rain that falls in this area of Panama, something like 200 inches (5 meters) a year! So my usual weather forecast for the Panama Canal is that sometime it's going to rain, even if just a few sprinkles. But when it really decides to rain in Panama it rains! Sometimes when it really decides to rain in Panama it's like someone in the heavens is dumping out oil barrels full of water.

We'll talk later about the history of the Canal, and about the initial French attempt under de Lesseps but one of the reasons why de Lesseps' plan for a sea level canal would not have worked was the tremendous amount of water that comes down through the Chagres River. Look at all this water! And you're only going to see a tiny part of Gatun Lake: remember the lake moves off into lots of little coves behind the islands. What de Lesseps' sea level canal plan never anticipated was how to handle this enormous flow of water, rushing through his canal into the sea. Creating Gatun Lake not only solved the problem of not having to dig all the way through the Continental Divide, but it created a positive solution to the Chagres River water problem!

* * * *

This morning we will be cruising about 23 miles (37 kilometers) miles across Gatun Lake to the entrance of Gaillard Cut

From the bridge entering Gatun Lake

Gatun Lake has a 1,100 mile (1,770 kilometer) shoreline. The lake is about 85 feet (25.9 meters) deep, but, as part of the Canal Expansion program with the new locks, the Canal will require more water, so Gatun Lake needs to be increased. One way, raise the dam, but . . . oops . . . the existing locks are then eight feet (2.4 meters) under water . . . so they are increasing the water in Gatun Lake by deepening the lake. And you will see as we go through the Canal work in progress as they are dynamiting the bottom of the lake and dredging to increase the depth. That will increase the volume of water as well as enable ships with deeper draft to get through the Canal.

What you see as islands in Gatun Lake today are actually the tops of mountains that used to be here before the lake was flooded.

One of the tours offered on cruises that stop in Panama is Peacock Bass fishing on Gatun Lake. Peacock Bass are not native to Panama but originate in the Rio Negro river basin in the Amazon. A renowned Panamanian aquarist and doctor was raising the fish in a pond for sale as an aquarium fish. In 1958 a flood wiped out his pond and the Peacock Bass accidentally got into Gatun Lake. The Peacock Bass have flourished and have become the dominant game fish in the Panama Canal. I've done the fishing tour and I've caught fish. Nothing like the 32 pound record, but it was fun.

Another tour offered on cruises that stop in Panama is a tour where you take a small motor boat and explore some of the little islands and many coves along the shoreline of Gatun Lake. In some of these coves the monkeys come down and jump on the boat for grapes. The guy who conducts one of these tours lives on a houseboat on Gatun Lake, so you go to his houseboat for a Panamanian lunch!

Many of these islands have been pretty much undisturbed for almost 100 years because of the Canal's policy, both during the US Canal days and today with Panama running the show, that all of the area around the Canal needs to be preserved as a protected area to protect the rain forest and watershed that provide the fresh water necessary to operate the Canal.

One of the most interesting islands, Barro Colorado, is home to a research center of the Smithsonian Tropical Research Institute, locally called "STRI". STRI provides a unique opportunity for long-term ecological studies in the tropics, and every year is used by visiting scientists from academic and research institutions in the US and around the world. Thirty eight staff scientists reside at STRI and are encouraged to pursue their own research priorities without geographic limitations.

* * * *

The French viewed themselves as the "great engineers" and were building fantastic bridges and buildings across Europe. Although Ferdinand de Lesseps is often called "the great engineer" he was not an engineer but a promoter. De Lesseps was riding high after his incredible achievement in building the Suez Canal, which only added to French confidence that, "We are the French: we can do anything."

The creation of the Suez Canal was a phenomenal achievement, in its day the equivalent of landing a man on the moon. But Suez was a sea level canal. It involved excavating a channel for water across the desert. Panama would prove quite different.

As we mentioned the idea of a canal in Panama had been around since the earliest Spanish explorers. Riding on the success of Suez, and sensing the time was right for a canal across Panama, in 1876 the French sent over a preliminary exploration team. Their report recommended a canal design that would include locks and a series tunnels through the mountains. De Lesseps, already committed to a sea level canal, didn't like this idea and so sent over a second team in 1877. This team basically mapped out the route along the original Panama Railroad, which is somewhat the route the Canal follows today. They called for just one tunnel through the Continental Divide at Culebra.

Ferdinand de Lesseps 1805 – 1894

Meanwhile, a concession to build a canal was negotiated by the French with Colombia, since Panama was then part of Colombia. The concession gave the French a 99-year lease without paying any compensation to Colombia and at the end of the lease the canal would revert to Colombia.

Sometimes people say, "I thought the US had a 99-year lease", confusing the French agreement with Colombia with the agreement the US would make with the newly minted Republic of Panama.

* * * *

An International Congress was held in Paris to consider fourteen plans that had been offered for consideration. Only one of the engineers had any construction experience in the tropics, and he urged a canal that using locks. But de Lesseps, at the time called "the greatest Frenchman who ever lived", had organized the conference with only one purpose and that was to have his plan rubber-stamped. Before the final vote half of the Committee walked out in disgust, but de Lesseps' popularity managed to carry the day.

The resolution for a sea level canal passed with only eight of the remaining delegates opposed.

* * * *

The French were big on ceremony and festivities, and so with great celebration the canal construction in Panama was begun. As de Lesseps was a trained diplomat and not an engineer, his son Charles took on the task of supervising the daily work. De Lesseps himself handled the important work of promoting and raising money for the project from private subscription. His boundless confidence and enthusiasm for the project and his consummate faith in the miracles of technology attracted stockholders.

The French had no concept of what they faced in the tropics. Disease such as malaria and yellow fever was rampant and nobody understood the disease or the cause. When the French arrived in Panama they loved all the palm trees and indoor foliage that was the decorating rage in Europe. They decorated their homes with palm trees sitting in saucers of standing water, without knowing that mosquitoes were the cause of their illnesses. If you went into hospital you had a 75% chance of being carried out in a coffin. In hospitals to keep ants from invading patients' beds, the posts of the beds were placed in bowls of water, again, creating the ideal breeding ground for mosquitoes.

French Hospital Ancon 1900

Machinery came from many quarters -- France, the US and Belgium. Equipment was constantly being modified and used in experimental combinations. A growing accumulation of discarded, inoperative equipment along the canal route testified to earlier mistakes. But most importantly, the technology to perform the Herculean task simply didn't exist. Each of five excavators working on the Atlantic side could remove 392 cubic yards (300 cubic meters) each day, but lack of spoil trains defeated their work. The equipment wasn't the right type, and was too small and too light. French bucket-chain excavators got caught and halted by stones and rock.

The Chagres could rise and flood in an hour, sweeping away men and materials. Isthmus is one of the wettest places on earth where rain can fall at what would be an hourly rate of 4 inches (10.2 centimeters) per hour. The French had no idea what to do with all the water flowing from the Chagres River. The US would come along and wisely utilize all of this water . . . and even to this day, it is the water generated by the Chagres River that allows the Canal to function.

It was becoming clear to nearly everyone except Ferdinand de Lesseps that a sea level canal would not work. Eventually, and reluctantly, he agreed to change, but . . . suddenly, there was no more money. The company was broke . . . 20,000 men had died . . . and there was no canal.

The French failed because they were ahead of their time. The medical understanding and technology needed to conquer the Isthmus just did not exist.

A "new" Panama Canal Company was organized, but with insufficient working capital, and a public that had soured on the idea of a canal, the idea was abandoned and the rights to build a canal were eventually sold to the Americans.

* * * *

California and Oregon had achieved statehood and there still wasn't a transcontinental railroad, so the US had an economic need for a canal. Additionally, President Teddy Roosevelt was trying to establish a US naval supremacy that would support an expansionist policy. A naval base had been established in Cuba in the Spanish-American War. When the battleship MAINE was blown up in Cuba, the nearest battleship was the OREGON up in San Francisco. It took the OREGON sixty seven days to steam from San Francisco to Cuba, just about the time the war was over. The experience clearly showed the military significance of an Isthmian canal.

Philippe Bunau-Varilla, chief engineer for de Lesseps, had managed to get his hands on shares of the new company and became the major salesman for a Panama canal. Congress was arguing between canal routes through Nicaragua or Panama, Just before the vote to decide a route, Bunau-Varilla mailed a letter to every Congressman enclosing a one-centavo Nicaraguan stamp showing Nicaragua's famous Momotombo volcano in full eruption. The stamp clearly pointed out a difference between the countries and Bunau-Varilla argued the volcanoes made Nicaragua inherently unsafe for a canal. On June 19, 1902, the Senate vote favored a Panama canal route by just eight votes.

US Secretary of State John Hay in his office

Now that the route was decided, the US needed to get a concession from Colombia. US Secretary of state John Hay negotiated a treaty with the Colombian chargé d'affaires, but this was turned down by the Colombian legislature.

Impatient to build the canal, Roosevelt supported Panama's independence movement, dispatching warships to both sides of the Isthmus blocking sea approaches, just in time for Panama to declare independence from Colombia on November 3, 1903.

Philippe Bunau-Varilla, the guy representing the French concession, now claiming to be the official ambassador of this newly minted country, negotiated a treaty giving the US full rights and sovereignty over a 10 mile (16 kilometer) wide Canal Zone that split Panama in two. The new country of Panama had the choice to accept the treaty or have all US support for their new country withdrawn.

* * * *

If the Americans were to be successful, they had to control disease and death. Chief Sanitary Officer of the US Army Corps of Engineers, Dr. William Crawford Gorgas and his staff set up operations. Dr. Walter Reed, Gorgas' commanding officer, had identified the mosquito as the disease-carrying culprit. Gorgas, who himself had survived yellow fever and was now immune, knew that he needed to eradicate mosquitoes on the Isthmus before new workers arrived, became infected, and died.

Previously unscreened offices and houses got window screens and screen doors. Mosquito nets were distributed. Fumigation brigades went house to house spraying against mosquitoes in homes, cisterns and cesspools. Clean running water was introduced to do away with the need for standing water containers that could breed mosquitoes. Thanks to Gorgas yellow fever was completely wiped out in Panama with the last reported case in 1905.

Often when people are planning a cruise through the Canal they visit their local public health office or seek out a tropical medicine specialist. Then they come on the ship laden down with malaria pills and having received yellow fever shots . . . and gotten stuck with a $500 medical bill.

Pay your money and take your choice, but yellow fever is not a problem in Panama and hasn't been since 1905. Malaria? Unless you are planning to visit a remote part of the Darien jungle, and I have no idea why you would want to do this unless you are going to break bread with Colombian FARC rebels or visit the jungle lab of a Colombian drug lord, you don't have to worry about malaria. If you get malaria, in most cases it is readily cured by the same pills you take to prevent it. Hear out your doctor and make your own decision. But $500 is $500, and might be better spent on Panama tours or Embera Indian basketry.

The greater problem today in Panama and in South and Central America and the islands of the Caribbean is dengue fever for which there is no preventative pill or cure. So Panama is very concerned about controlling mosquitoes. But on the ship . . . in the Canal . . . you're not going to need any bug spray. The wind alone will keep you bug-free.

Do as you wish, and of course listen to your physician, but as for me, I wouldn't even think about taking malaria pills . . . and I live in Panama!

Malaria, unlike yellow fever, does not confer immunity and you can get it again, so malaria was the cause of more deaths during the French and US construction periods than yellow fever. During the first year of the American effort, 1905, nearly everyone, including Gorgas, had contracted malaria.

Gorgas said, "If we cannot control malaria, I feel very little anxiety about other diseases. If we do not control malaria our mortality is going to be heavy."

Gorgas said that getting rid of the mosquito that carried yellow fever carrier was like "making war on the family cat," while a campaign against the malaria-carrying mosquito was "like fighting all the beasts of the jungle."

The task to eradicate disease-carrying mosquitoes from the Isthmus was almost as big as the task of building the Canal itself. Vegetation around houses and buildings was removed. More than 100 square miles of swamp was drained. Ditches were installed so water would not pool. Thousands of minnows were hatched and released and spiders, ants and lizards were bred and released to feed on adult insects. A mixture of carbolic acid, resin and oil was sprayed monthly in areas where standing water might collect. It was said by tourists who came to Panama to observe the Canal construction that the entire Isthmus smelled like an oil refinery.

* * * *

John Wallace was the first man in charge of the US construction effort. Wallace tried picking up where the French had left off, but without support from Washington ended up frustrated and resigned.

Teddy Roosevelt's famous remark regarding the Canal effort, after the US-supported, convenient creation of the Republic of Panama, was, "Let the dirt fly!" And the man who finally made the "dirt fly" was John F. Stevens, the second man in charge of the American effort.

Steven's background was as a railroad engineer and his ability to design a railroad was critical. Virtually none of the equipment the French had left was useable. Everything that was needed for Canal construction had to be brought to the Isthmus and distributed efficiently along the construction line. Stevens completely overhauled the Panama Railroad, which would not only carry workers, materials and supplies, but also move the dirt and rock.

Later Stevens would comment, "This is no reflection on the French, but I cannot conceive how they did the work they did with the plant they had." Stevens built an efficient railroad operation to support the construction effort, in essence building a new railroad from scratch with everything needing to be imported, including experienced railroaders.

The size of the work force tripled in six months. To support this rapidly growing workforce Stevens built entire communities including housing, mess halls, YMCAs, hospitals, hotels, schools, churches, laundries and cafeterias. Communities were designed from scratch. Complex schedules were devised so that the work never stopped and trains carrying the spoil of rock and dirt were at the right place at the right time.

In comparison to the Americans, the French had used a primitive rail system. Stevens developed a complex system of railroad tracks at different levels within the Culebra Cut that would enable the spoil to be removed. The tracks could be moved as necessary so that the spoil trains kept pace with the excavation, thus enabling the giant Bucyrus steam shovels to keep working continuously.

It was Stevens who pushed for a lock canal rather than a sea level canal. Congress voted approval by a narrow margin, the margin being the difference between US success and a repeat of the French failure.

With all systems "go" and work proceeding efficiently and on schedule, in 1907 Stevens suddenly retired without giving any explanation other than that it was "personal."

Frustrated by the loss of Stevens, Roosevelt decided to go to Panama himself to survey the situation on the ground.

* * * *

In 1907 Roosevelt went to Panama, the first president in history to leave the US while in office. He chose November, the worst time of year to visit, at the height of the rainy season, because he wanted to see Panama at its worst and understand the challenges faced. He visited the construction sites, talked to the workers and even had an early presidential "photo op" sitting at the controls of a steam shovel in Culebra Cut.

Roosevelt came to view the building of the Canal as a mighty battle, pitting the US against the unbelievable challenge of building a path between the seas.

Even back then, the famous presidential photo-op

* * * *

Determined not to lose another capable leader, Roosevelt appointed someone who could not resign, then Lieutenant Colonel George Washington Goethals of the US Army Corps of Engineers, an Army man used to taking orders. Determined that Goethals get the job done, the President gave Goethals absolute authority, answerable only to the Secretary of War and the President himself.

Accepting the challenge, Goethals said, "I am no longer a commander in the US Army. I now consider that I am commanding the Army of Panama, and that the enemy we are going to combat is the Culebra Cut and the locks and dams at both ends of the Canal, and any man here on the work who does his duty will never have any cause to complain of militarism."

Goethals would never wear a military uniform in Panama, but in the end would become *General* George Washington Goethals. He was a West Point graduate who had previous experience not only with organization and command but with the "nuts and bolts" of locks and dams.

Workers from Barbados arriving on the SS ANCON

The Isthmus of Panama lacked a population large enough to provide laborers for such a vast project, so Goethals assigned recruiting agents to scour the world for people to work on the Canal. The US may have thought it was building the Canal, but generally there were no more than 5,000 Americans employed. Almost all of the down and dirty workers came from the rest of the world. Like the French, the Americans looked to the nearest source of cheap labor, the Caribbean. Almost 20,000 laborers came from Barbados, representing about 30 to 40 percent of the adult men of Barbados.

Canal workers were paid in either gold or silver. US, mostly white, workers were paid in gold, and everyone else was paid in silver. (Of course any US citizen today would love to be paid in either gold or silver!) The pay car had separate windows for people being paid in gold and in silver. Thus began the distinction that ruled life in the Canal Zone and became a euphemism for racism, a highly stratified system of "Gold" and "Silver."

Signs on toilets, drinking fountains, shops, and railway cars noted "Gold" or "Silver" which effectively was a nice way of saying "White" or "Colored." Those paid in gold were all white Americans, and those paid in silver were all persons of color, including local Panamanians. A stated goal of life within the Canal Zone was to prevent "intermingling of the races". Most Panamanians working within the Zone were people of color who had menial jobs and quite naturally came to resent not only the system, but the US and the Canal Zone occupation.

Long after the signs were pulled down the attitudes within the Canal Zone remained. We have friends, neighbors, who have been in Panama for years. He is Panamanian, went to the US for college and fell in love with a beautiful gal from Iowa. They married and came back to Panama where both worked for the US Army. Both are US citizens, but she is a white, blond-haired, blue-eyed, Dutch girl from Iowa and he is a Panamanian. Up until the 1977 treaty, if they went to shop in the "PX" or military store in the Canal Zone, she was allowed in, but he was not, even although they were married and both worked for the US Army. Problem was that he was a person of color, number one, and a Panamanian, number two.

That gives you some idea of the feelings of resentment that Panamanians felt about the Canal Zone. And it helps you understand what was behind US President Jimmy Carter's statement, at the turnover of the Canal at the turn of the Century,

"We didn't understand clearly enough the feeling of many Panamanians that the arrangement implied an element of colonialism and subjugation and not an equal representation . . ."

* * * *

The Panama Canal cost Americans around $375 million, including the $10 million paid to Panama and the $40 million paid to the French company. It was the single most expensive construction project in US history to that time. Amazingly, unlike any other such project on record, the American canal had cost less than estimated, with the final figure some $23 million below the 1907 estimate, in spite of landslides and a design change to a wider canal.

Plans for a grand celebration of the opening of the Panama Canal were abruptly put on hold by World War I. A tug boat festooned with flags made its way through the Canal, and then on August 15, 1914 the Canal opened with the ANCON making the first official transit.

Unlike any other government project, the Canal finished under budget, ahead of schedule, and without scandal.

By July 1, 1914, a total of 238.8 million cubic yards (about 36.5 million cubic meters) had been excavated during the American construction era. Together with 30 million cubic yards (about 4.6 million cubic meters) excavated by the French, gives a total of around 268.8 cubic yards (about 41.1. million cubic meters) or more than four times the volume originally estimated for de Lesseps' sea level canal. It is said that if de Lesseps had pursued his original idea of a sea level canal, he would still be digging!

The greater cost was in the cost of human lives. Hospital records during the US construction era record 5,609 lives were lost from disease and accident. The estimate for the French era is 20,000, although because people were dying so rapidly during the French era, accurate hospital records were not kept. It is likely that the number of people who died during the 10 years of the French effort far exceeds the estimate of 20,000. Adding the deaths during the French era would likely bring the total deaths to some 25,000 based on an estimate by Gorgas. However, the true number will never be known, since the French only recorded the deaths that occurred in hospital.

SS ANCON making the first official transit of the Canal 1914

As you make your way through the Canal a sober fact to ponder is that almost 500 people died for every mile of the Panama Canal.

Engraved in the rotunda of the Panama Canal Administration building are these words of Theodore Roosevelt:

"It is not the critic who counts, not the man who points out how the strong man stumbled, or where the doer of deeds could have done them better. The credit belongs to the man who is actually in the arena; whose face is marred by dust and sweat and blood; who strives valiantly, who errs and comes short again and again; who knows the great enthusiasms, the great devotions, and spends himself in a worthy cause; who, at the best, knows in the end the triumph of high achievement; and who, at the worst, if he fails, at least fails while daring greatly, so that his place shall never be with those cold and timid souls who know neither victory nor defeat."

David McCullough in his book THE PATH BETWEEN THE SEAS writes:

"The creation of a water passage across Panama was one of the supreme human achievements of all time, the culmination of a heroic dream of over four hundred years and of more than twenty years of phenomenal effort and sacrifice . . . Primarily the canal is an expression of that old and noble desire to bridge the divide, to bring people together. It is a work of civilization."[2]

---

[2] David McCullough, THE PATH BETWEEN THE SEAS.

2D - Gamboa & Gaillard

Many cruise passengers opting for a shore excursion riding the rails of the Panama Canal Railway assume that they are following the route of the original Panama Railroad and that they will wind their way along the Panama Canal. One cruise line even hyped this excursion on their Internet site by saying that as you rode along you could "watch for monkeys and toucans."

First, the original Panama Railroad had a different route than today's Panama Canal Railway.

Second, the current Panama Canal Railway exists primarily to move shipping containers across the Isthmus and the route, although it occasionally provides glimpses of the Canal, runs mostly through jungle and not next to the Canal.

Third, about that rain forest and those "monkeys and toucans" . . . Yes, the animals are there, but being self-respectable animals they are not hanging around next to the railroad tracks and, even if they were, the train is whizzing along at 40 mph. You can "watch for monkeys and toucans" all you want, but don't expect to see any from the train.

The Panama Canal Railway runs over a little bridge that spans the Chagres River so often you will see a train on the port side of the ship as you pass where the Chagres flows into Gatun Lake.

William Aspinwall's initial plan was to combine his existing wooden paddle-wheel steamships with the Panama Railroad as a way to get mail across the US from one side to the other, by way of Panama, before the existence of a transcontinental railroad. But all that changed when gold was discovered in California. Suddenly the money wasn't in moving the mail, but in moving those wishing to strike it rich in California. With a concession from Colombia to build a railroad, Aspinwall seized this golden opportunity and began work on the project.

The Panama Railroad would become one of the most expensive railroads ever built. With only 7 miles (11.3 kilometers) of track laid, the railroad was already doing a brisk business with prospectors climbing aboard the partially completed railroad. The stock soared on Wall Street providing an additional $4 million to push construction ahead through the jungle.

The completed railroad was only a single railroad track running 47 miles (75.6 kilometers) following the Chagres River across the Isthmus of Panama, but when it opened in January 1855 the transoceanic railroad was even enthusiastically dubbed the first transcontinental railroad.

Although the railroad had cost $6.5 million, over $137,000 per mile, it turned almost an instant profit carrying prospectors and gold across the Isthmus. Over $700 million in gold was carried on the railroad between 1855 and 1867. When the Gold Rush petered out and the first transcontinental railroad opened in the US, the bottom fell out for the Panama Railroad. Share price plummeted from $369 to $52.

When de Lesseps arrived he snapped up the failing railroad at inflated prices of up to $250 per share. The French paid $25 million for the railroad. When the US bought the French rights to build a canal they got the railroad rights as well. Since the canal followed the route of the railroad along the Chagres, it cost the US $9 million to relocate the railroad.

When the Carter-Torrijos Treaty turned what remained of the Panama Railroad over to Panama, the railroad was in poor repair and losing $4 million a year. Panama's aggressive process of privatizing many of the assets it acquired with the Canal turnover included the railroad.

Today the Panama Canal Railway is a very profitable operation moving containers across the Isthmus. Panama is the only place in the world where it is possible to transship containers in-bond from the Atlantic to the Pacific in under four hours. Often container ships have containers stacked too high to meet Canal restrictions, and so they can offload extra containers at one end of the Canal and by the time they reach the other end the containers are waiting to be reloaded. Because containers can be transshipped in bond, they can be sent from the Pacific port to the gigantic Colon Free Zone on the other side of the Isthmus.

Today's Panama Canal Railway is used primarily to move containers

A tiny part of the railroad operation is the one passenger train that runs in the morning from Panama City to Colon and in the evening from Colon to Panama City, mainly to transport business men who are doing business at the Colon Free Zone. When cruise ships are in port, the passenger train operates during the day as a shore excursion for cruise ship visitors. All of the rolling stock of the present railroad is refurbished old engines and cars brought in from the US.

* * * *

As you make your way through the Canal you will see a number of navigational lights, as well as nineteen different lighthouses in the Canal designed originally as navigational lights.

* * * *

Dredging is a continuing operation in the Canal with routine dredging maintenance before the expansion program running about $150 million annually. Now, with the expansion, there is major additional dredging going on as part of the Canal expansion. As you pass by the little old Canal Zone town of Gamboa, on the left or port side of the ship, you will see the Panama Canal Dredging Division.

Just before the Dredging Division is a small dock used by the Smithsonian Tropical Research Institute. A boat leaves here each morning to take day workers on the forty minute ride out to Barro Colorado, and then returns each afternoon.

* * * *

The lock leaves or gates for the Canal are made of steel and each weighs from 390 to 730 tons. The gates are hollow so that they can be floated out for repair. Nice, but . . . how do you pick up a 390-730 ton steel gate to be able to float it out?

Enter the cranes. The Panama Canal has had two giant floating cranes; the largest is named "Titan", and the smaller one, "Hercules". Titan was originally built by Hitler's Germany and claimed by the US as war booty. Titan spent 50 years in Long Beach, California before being moved to Panama in 1999. The crane can be floated into the locks of the Panama Canal and is used for the heavy lifting required to maintain the doors of the locks of the canal. It can lift 350 metric tons and is one of the strongest cranes in the world. If the cranes are not in use elsewhere in the Canal they are docked at the Dredging Division.

* * * *

On the port or left side of the ship is a small bridge crossing the Chagres River. The bridge carries the Panama Canal Railway and one lane of traffic at a time.

The Chagres River with all its many tributaries upstream is the source of the water in Gatun Lake and provides the fresh water necessary to run the Panama Canal.

Bridge where the Chagres River flows into Gatun Lake

Upstream is another dam called Madden Dam that created Alajuela Lake. The lake is an important part of the Canal water system and is 250 feet (76.2 meters) above sea level. It can store one third of the Canal's annual water need. Madden Dam controls the possible torrential flow of the Chagres river into the navigational route of Lake Gatun. The water is also used to generate hydroelectric power, and to supply Panama City's freshwater. Its upper basin is covered by dense tropical forests and to protect it, Panama created Chagres National Park in 1985.

* * * *

One of the fantastic opportunities when you visit Panama is the chance to actually go up into Chagres National Park and visit the Indigenous group of Embera Indians who live in the Chagres. To visit my Embera Indian friends who live in a tiny village on Rio San Juan de Pequini that feeds into Alajuela Lake, you first go to Alajuela Lake where the Embera will meet you with a dug out canoe. You travel across the lake, then up the river through dense jungle for another 45 minutes to visit their village. It's a fantastic, once-in-a-lifetime experience.

* * * *

Embera wood carvers at Embera Puru, San Juan de Pequini

Just before the tiny bridge across the mouth of the Chagres River is the entrance to Gamboa Rainforest Resort, a luxury destination resort located on the Panama Canal, in the heart of the Panamanian rainforest. The Gamboa Rainforest Resort is designed to provide a variety of educational and adventure experiences in addition to a luxury resort vacation.

* * * *.

When you drive from Panama City to Chagres you drive through Soberania National Park, just 15 miles (24 kilometers) from Downtown Panama City. The park was established in 1980 and is a strip bordering much of the eastern side of the Canal. In the protected area there are 105 species of mammals, 525 species of birds, 79 reptiles, 55 amphibious and 36 species of fresh water fish, so the park is an important wildlife refuge.

Among the mammals you can find jaguar, the white-tailed deer, neques, raccoons, ant eaters, sloths, herds of wild pigs and various species of monkeys.

* * * *

Along that road you come to a hillside cemetery beside the road called the Mount Hope Cemetery or the French Cemetery. This is the resting place of some of the workers of the Panama Canal from the French period, many of whom came from Martinique, Jamaica and St. Lucia. It is estimated that 20,000 workers died during the French era, but nobody knows for sure. The French recorded only people who died in hospitals, but people were dying so fast that many never made it to hospital.

A West Indian worker named Alfred Dottin recalled,

"Death was our constant companion. I shall never forget the trainloads of dead men being carted away, daily, as if they were just so much lumber. Malaria with all its horrible meaning those days was just a household word. I saw mosquitoes, I say this, without fear of exaggerating, by the thousands attack one man. There were days when we could only work a few hours because of the high fever racking our bodies – it was a living hell."[3]

Workers wrote their wills before leaving for Panama: a few had the foresight to bring their coffins with them from France.

* * * *

Culebra Cut passes through what was once nine miles of solid rock including what was known as Culebra Mountain. The mountain was cut in half to allow the Canal to pass through. The two remaining parts of Culebra Mountain are now called, on the left or port side, Gold Hill, and on the right or starboard side, Contractor's Hill.

---

[3] Matthew Parker, PANAMA FEVER, p. xxi.

You will see what is left of Gold Hill rising 662 feet (201.8 meters) above sea level atop a sheer cliff, its side blasted away for the Canal. Gradually over the years to control erosion and slides the hill has been whittled away.

Why "gold" hill? Turns out the overeager and over optimistic writer of a prospectus for the French Canal Company lured investors by saying "this mountain is full of gold and it is believed that the ore from this place alone will be worth more than will be the total cost of the canal construction." Well the prospectus was full of something . . . because there never was any gold. Not an ounce of gold was ever found but the name stuck.

* * * *

The biggest challenge of building a Canal was getting ships through the continental divide in the middle of the Isthmus of Panama. The lowest point was a "saddle" between what is now called Gold Hill on the east and Contractors Hill on the west. To complete the Canal it was necessary to somehow get over, under or through this mountain. The Canal builders decided to cut an 8.75 mile (14.1 kilometer) stretch through the Continental Divide from Gamboa to the little town of Pedro Miguel on the South. Ships would be lifted up to the level of a newly created lake and then sail across the Isthmus 85 feet (26 meters) above sea level. To get the ships through the Continental Divide the cut through the mountain would have to take it from 210 feet (64 meters) to 40 feet (12.2 meters) above sea level.

Holes were drilled and filled with explosives to loosen the dirt and rock. Gigantic steam shovels would pile the spoil on railroad cars that would haul it away to fill or dump sites. This is where the railroad system designed by John L. Stevens would prove essential. Wooden flatcars, each carrying 19 cubic yards (69.6 cubic meters) of spoil, would be pulled by long trains to the designated dump sites. Stevens had designed a unique rail car where both sides could be dropped and a huge scoop dragged along the line of cars that efficiently pushed the spoil off the sides as it was winched along.

More than 100 million cubic yards (about 76.5 million cubic meters) of spoil had to be hauled away from the excavation site and dumped. Part of the spoil was used to link four small islands on the Pacific side to create a breakwater which is today known as the Amador Peninsula running over three miles (4.8 kilometers) out into the Pacific. Spoil was also used as fill to create the town of Balboa and what became the Fort Amador military reservation.

Cutting through Culebra Mountain

The unstable nature of the geology of Culebra and the frequency of heavy rains in Panama made earth slides a constant threat to Canal builders. During the French era land slides would sweep away both machinery and people burying both under tons of earth. On October 4, 1907 after several days of heavy rain 500,000 cubic yards (382,277 cubic meters) of material slid into the cut and the slide continued for ten days moving an average of 14 feet (4.3 meters) every 24 hours.

The worst slide happened on the east side of Gold Hill when the mountain slid covering a 75 acre (30.4 hectare) area, destroying buildings in Culebra village and requiring the removal of some 10 million cubic yards (7,645,540 cubic meters) of material. Another Gold Hill slide required removal of some 7 million cubic yards (5,351,884 cubic meters) of material.

The genius behind the massive Culebra excavation was a young engineer, David Gaillard, a graduate of the United States Military Academy at West Point. Goethals brought Gaillard with him and put the young engineer in charge of the Culebra Cut excavation.

David Gaillard 1859-1913

The cut was the most difficult part of the construction taking nine years to excavate, during which 100 million tons of rock were removed and the mountain was cut down from 210 feet (64 meters) to 40 feet (12.2 meters).

Gaillard was evacuated from Panama in 1913 with what was thought to be nervous exhaustion. In fact it was a brain tumor and Gaillard died at the age of 54 only nine months before the opening of the Panama Canal. In recognition of his achievement Culebra Cut was renamed in his honor.

Outside the Miraflores Visitor Center is a memorial plaque to David Gaillard and the men who did the "impossible".

Culebra Cut, later to be known as Gaillard Cut, is one of the special wonders of the Canal. Here is where you should stand with you mouth gaping in awe of what men and machines were able to accomplish almost 100 years ago.

At the entrance to the Miraflores Visitor's Center stands one of the trains that was used by the French found buried in the mud while the Canal was being dredged.

* * * *

Centennial Bridge, built to celebrate the 100th anniversary of the Republic of Panama, was dedicated in 2004. It is the second bridge across the Panama Canal joining the continents. The bridge crosses Gaillard Cut just before the Pedro Miguel locks. The Bridge didn't actually open to traffic until 2005 while the US and Panama argued about who was responsible to clean up the cache of poisonous gas canisters and other weapons that the US had left buried near the bridge site.

Centennial Bridge

Centennial is a cable-stayed bridge with a total span of 3,451 feet (1,052 meters). The main span is 1,051 feet (320 meters). The supporting towers are 604 feet (184 meters) high. The bridge clears the Canal by 262 feet (80 meters), allowing large vessels and even "Titan", Hitler's giant floating crane, to pass under the bridge.

The west tower of the bridge is set back about 164 feet (50 meters) to allow for future widening of the Canal.

2E - The Pacific Locks

12:10 pm Another team of linesmen and another pilot is boarded

What astounds me every time I go through the Canal is that here is something that was built almost 100 years ago, and it still works exactly the same way it was designed to work. We live in a throw-away society. How long does a toaster last? One or two years if you're lucky. Every few years you dump your old computer and monitor. Your printer is broken: it's cheaper to throw it away and buy a new one than try to fix it. But here is this engineering marvel, still working after almost 100 years . . . working 24 hours a day, 365 days a year.

Captain and pilot on wing bridge

* * * *

The average depth of the Canal channel is 43 feet (13 meters) and the minimum depth is 41 feet (12.5 meters), although these numbers are changing as the Canal is deepened as part of the Canal Expansion program.

* * * *

The width varies from 500 to 1,000 feet (150 to 300 meters), and again this is increasing as the Canal is enlarged with the expansion.

* * * *

The average time to pass from ocean to ocean is about 10 hours, down from the 12.5 hours just a few years ago. Panamax ships, like ours, generally take 10 to 12 hours. Often cargo ships have to tie up for periods at several spots along the Canal or anchor for a while in Gatun Lake in order to maximize traffic flow. Passenger ships generally are given a priority transit.

* * * *

Approximately 35-40 ships a day pass through the canal.

* * * *

The top five customers of the Canal are the US, People's Republic of China, Chile, Japan and Korea.

* * * *

The first lock on the Pacific side is Pedro Miguel, again named after one of the little towns that were flooded during the construction of the Canal. Pedro Miguel has only one chamber which will lower the vessel 29 feet (8.9 meters) into a small transit area known as Miraflores Lake. We travel about 1.3 miles (2 kilometers) through this small lake to Miraflores Locks, where two additional chambers lower the vessel to sea level.

On the port side just before Pedro Miguel you will see a parking area where folks who live in Panama City like to bring visitors to see ships in the Canal. There aren't always ships actually in the locks, so sometimes you have to try a couple of spots if you want your friends to see more than an empty lock.

12:32 pm Vessel enters Pedro Miguel

Since the turnover of the Canal Panama has been on an economic roll, on track to become what is already being called "The Singapore of the Americas". When the US started closing down bases and pulling out of Panama after the 1977 Treaty times were tough for Panama. All those US jobs suddenly disappeared. In the 86 years the US operated the Canal in Panama it had paid the original $10 million, plus $250,000 per year after the first nine years, or a total of $29.25 million. In the *first year* of Panama's ownership and stewardship of the Canal, the Canal made a direct transfer to the national treasury of $252 million!

During the *first four years* of Panamanian operation the Canal made direct contributions to the national treasury of $1.1 billion plus all the additional indirect contributions to the national economy such as salaries, taxes, procurement and local business.

Today the Canal writes an annual direct check to the government of Panama for about $400 million. It's estimated that by the time the Canal expansion is finished in 2015 that amount will be $1.25 billion a year and remember, this is in a country of 3.3 million people.

There were a lot of doomsayers who predicted Panama couldn't manage the Canal, and that it would fall apart once the Turnover took place. The reality is that the Canal is doing better than ever!

So how has Panama done?

There has been a 35% decrease in waiting time, granted assisted slightly by lower demand.

Transit time has been decreased by 25%.

There has been a 30% reduction in accidents.

There has been continuing upgrading and maintenance of items the US delayed prior to the Turnover. The Canal has spent $1.5 billion in improvements since the Turnover.

The Americans ran the Canal as a federally operated service with tolls just covering operating costs: the Panamanians run it as a very profitable business.

The Canal now generates $2 billion a year.

The Canal is being expanded to accommodate larger vessels at a cost of $5.2 billion originally scheduled to be completed by 2014.

Of the $5.25 billion expansion program, $3 billion will come from retained earnings, and the rest from bilateral and multilateral lenders, led by the Japan Bank for International Cooperation, European Investment Bank and the Inter-American Development Bank.

* * * *

1:10 pm Gates are opened, mules disconnected and vessel moves into Miraflores Lake

One safety concern always has been the failure of the lock gates, perhaps caused by a runaway ship hitting a gate. This could not only unleash a flood, but drain the entire lock system and even Gatun Lake.

Originally the locks had chain barriers stretched across the lock to prevent a ship from ramming a gate. These were lowered into the lock floor when it was time for the ship to pass. These "fender chains" were designed to stop ships up to 10,000 tons, but with ships getting much larger and the expense of maintaining the chains they were removed in 1980.

Extra safety against flooding the system and draining Gatun Lake is provided by an extra set of gates at both ends of the upper chambers on both sides. All four gates would all have to fail to create a disaster. The additional gates are 70 feet (21 meters) from the operating gates.

Extra set of gates and raised walkway for workers

* * * *

Miraflores Lake is a small, man-made lake that serves only as a connection between the single lock at Pedro Miguel and the double locks at Miraflores, and is 54 feet (16.5 meters) above sea level.

* * * *

In our post 9/11 world Canal Security is a major concern. Whereas in the past the Canal's neutrality and usefulness avoided conventional threats, since 9/11 the "rules of engagement" are different. Now you have fanatical groups who aren't afraid to hurt themselves or to die in the process and are looking for spectacular targets of particular interest and concern to the US.

There are several avenues of protection for the Panama Canal.

First, Panama is neutral country and the Panama Canal is open to everyone.

Part of Panama's defense is the famous "Swiss strategy", a take-off of the phrase, "If you have them by the balls, their hearts and minds will follow." In this case, "If you have them by their money, their hearts and minds will follow." It worked for Switzerland and it is working for Panama.

Panama's second line of defense is the US. Many people do not realize that there were actually two treaties signed in 1977. The first treaty turned the Canal over to Panama. In the second treaty the US agreed to protect the neutrality of the Canal in perpetuity. Panama abolished the army after the dictatorship. It doesn't need an army.

The Canal uses an Electronic Data Collection System that requires all pre-arrival information to be submitted to the Canal in advance so that a risk assessment can be made and to insure that all international security regulations are followed. Cargo manifests, crew and passenger lists are carefully monitored and checked against US security databases.

Each year the US sponsors and finances "Operation Panamax", a security exercise that simulates an attack on the Canal. The exercise involves as many as fifteen countries in addition to Panama. Additionally it provides the US an opportunity to showcase military hardware for sale to friendly countries.

* * * *

Looking over to the left or port side of the ship as we enter Miraflores locks you will see a large complex of buildings that was Fort Clayton during the US occupation of the Canal Zone. Today it is known as the "City of Knowledge" and is home to a number of large high tech and computer operations, call centers, and university buildings. There are hotels and housing developments and the gigantic, sprawling US Embassy.

2:02 pm Gates to Miraflores opened and mules connected

Since MV JUST CRUISING is 105 feet (32 meters) wide and the locks are 110 feet (33.5 meters) wide we have only a 2.5 foot (about .8 meter) clearance on either side of the ship.

Miraflores is the last of the Canal lock complexes. By now you are an expert and know to watch for the row boat, the "bumpers", and understand the role of the locomotives and how water flows through the lock system and eventually out to sea.

Because of the extreme tides on the Pacific it was decided to split the lock complexes on the Pacific side with one chamber at Pedro Miguel and two chambers at Miraflores. The drop from Miraflores Lake to the Pacific approach varies due to the tidal differences on the Pacific, between 43 feet (13.1 meters) at extreme high tide and 64.5 feet (19.7 meters) at extreme low tide.

Panama Canal linesmen at work connecting to mules

* * * *

When it was built the concrete construction of the Panama Canal was the largest ever undertaken and the record remained until the construction of the Hoover Dam in the 1930s. Pedro Miguel was the first lock complex, completed in 1911, and Miraflores was finished in 1913.

Since much of the concrete in the Canal is now almost 100 years old, the Canal Authority spends a great deal of money to repair and replace deteriorating concrete. It is believed that within the Canal walls there still are pockets of concrete which have not completely dried.

Passing through the locks it is hard to imagine the immense size of the culverts deep within the walls that carry the water necessary for the lock chambers to work. You get a better idea when you look at one of the old photos taken at the time of construction. If you look carefully you can make out several figures in the lower left hand corner.

The main culverts are 18 feet (5.5 meters) in diameter, the same size of the tunnels that carried the railroad lines under the Hudson River into New York City.

2:39 pm entering Miraflores locks

As ships have gotten bigger the Panama Canal Authority has realized the necessity of enlarging the Canal. And as we said, this is nothing new. The US began a program to enlarge the Canal and in effect build a "third lane" back in 1939. They started and actually dug channels which have become a part of the new expansion program, but World War II came along and the project had to be abandoned. The current Expansion or Amplification of the Canal is once again a "third lane" concept. The program consists in the construction of two new sets of locks - one on the Pacific and one on the Atlantic side of the Canal. Each lock will have three chambers and each chamber will have three water reutilization basins.

The program also entails the widening and deepening of existing navigational channels in Gatun Lake and Gaillard Cut.

If you look to the starboard side you will see one of the major construction sites of new lock construction. The new locks will be large enough to accommodate most ships now on the drawing boards, and even larger ships.

The Canal Authority is not building a new Canal that will parallel the existing Canal, but another lane with the necessary approach channels. The present locks will continue to be used, but the new lock complexes will allow for larger vessels. All traffic will feed into the existing Canal route which is being enlarged and deepened as part of the expansion project.

I know, it's an old photo, but if you look very carefully at the lower left corner you can see a man walking along the wall and another guy getting ready to climb up

2:50 pm Inside first lock chamber

The new locks will be different not only in size but also in operation. Instead of the existing swing or miter gates, the locks will have rolling gates which are easier to maintain. And the new locks will feature water saving basins that will recycle 60% of the fresh water.

For generations electric locomotives have been used to assist ships through the locks, but the size of the new locks would have required twelve to sixteen mules. So . . . the mules will disappear in the new lock chambers. The size of the new locks makes it possible to use two of the existing tug boats, one at each end of the ship, allowing for a more efficient transit.

The existing chambers will continue to be used for smaller vessels increasing not only the size of ships that can use the Canal but the number of ships that can transit on a given day.

The cost of the expansion program is budget at $5.25 billion and was originally scheduled to be completed by 2014 at the beginning of the Canal's second century.

The large building with the observation decks on the port or left side is the Miraflores Visitor Center. The center provides observation decks, restaurant, areas for meetings and events, and a museum honoring the thousands of men and women who made this achievement possible. The better of the Canal museums is the Interoceanic Canal Museum in the old Casco Viejo area of Panama City. The Interoceanic Canal Museum is located in what was a fancy hotel during the French era.

* * * *

Looking ahead in the distance you will see Ancon Hill, a 654 foot (199.2 meter) hill overlooking Panama City on the other side of the hill. On top of the hill are a giant Panamanian flag and an overlook where you get a fantastic view of the city. I've sometimes stayed at a little bed and breakfast up on Ancon Hill. Because the hill was never developed in the US Canal Zone days, monkeys still come to eat bananas off your balcony, and you see brightly colored toucans. When I've stayed there I've gotten up early to hike to the top of Ancon Hill and watch the sun rise over the Pacific. Yes, sunrise over the Pacific! Remember Panama runs east to west, so it is possible to watch the sun rise over the Pacific. The view of Panama City and the Bay of Panama is breathtaking.

Entering Miraflores from the bridge

3:29 pm inside the second lock chamber

Just down the hill is a series of tunnels built by the US during the war. The tunnels have wooden floors designed to prevent an enemy from listening. There are dorm rooms, a hospital, chapel, cafeteria and even a machine to shred tons of documents. Interestingly the present government in Panama has announced plans to remodel these tunnels as an emergency hide out for the President of Panama should Panama or the Canal ever be attacked.

During the US days the lower slopes of Ancon Hill contained residences for officers and Gorgas Hospital. Higher up was the residence of the Governor of the Canal Zone. Originally the Governor's residence was the mansion de Lesseps had built for himself on the Continental Divide. It was later moved to Ancon Hill and has expanded over the years. Today it is the home of the Administrator of the Panama Canal Authority. On up was the headquarters of the US Southern Army Command. Under US jurisdiction it always irked the Panamanians that the US flag flew over Ancon Hill, so when Panama regained control of the hill, following the 1977 Panama Canal Treaty, one of the first things the country did was fly a large oversized Panamanian flag from the top of Ancon hill. Today the flag flies day and night, lit up at night by spotlights.

* * * *

Van Ingen mural in rotunda of Panama Canal Headquarters

The most pretentious old public building in Panama is the Panama Canal Headquarters Building on Ancon Hill. If you look over to Ancon Hill while you are still in the locks you can see the Panama Canal Headquarters about halfway up the hill. The building opened in 1914.

Inside are remarkable murals depicting the history and construction of the Canal that were created by William B. Van Ingen of New York. Van Ingen, who had achieved considerable fame for his murals in the Library of Congress, agreed to produce the murals at $25 a square foot. The artist visited Panama twice during the Canal construction and made charcoal sketches. The murals were painted in his New York studio and eventually moved to Panama.

* * * *

The Panama Canal Authority, or ACP, which operates the Canal is an autonomous government legal entity with exclusive charge of the operation, administration, management, preservation, maintenance, and modernization of the Canal so that the Canal may operate in a safe, continuous, efficient, and profitable manner. Because of its importance and uniqueness, the ACP is financially autonomous and has its own, non-political hiring and operational authority. An Administrator is appointed for a seven-year term, and may be re-elected for an additional term. There is an eleven-member board of directors, nine appointed by the president and one by the legislature. An advisory board is composed representatives from the world's largest shipping firms and representatives from the biggest customers.

* * * *

The Panama Canal Authority has three Web cams and the last one is midway up the red and white communications tower next to the Miraflores Visitors Center. On one ship they convinced guests to prepare signs for the folks back home and to wave flags as we passed by the final Canal Web cam.

People had a lot of fun getting ready for the grand event, and the ship's photographers and videographers had a field day, but the folks back home . . . Well, if they looked very closely they might have seen a few pixels that were their friends with their carefully crafted signs. But it did look good on the videos and pictures the ship photographers shot.

* * * *

From the start of the Canal effort there was recognition that the Canal would split Panama in two. This was a challenge even during the US construction the split created challenges. Barges were used to ferry construction workers back and forth.

The old swing bridge at Miraflores, no longer used, was built in 1942, but could be used only when ships weren't passing. In 1942 ferry service was added as well, known as the Thatcher Ferry after a former member of the Canal Commission who introduced the legislation that created the ferry. Until the Bridge of the Americas was built in 1962 there was no other way to cross.

Until the Bridge of The Americas this old swing bridge was only way to cross the Canal

2F - Balboa & Amador

4:00 pm gates opened and we left Miraflores

On the port side is the area of Panama City known as Balboa. The Balboa area is mostly reclaimed land created with spoils from Culebra Cut. During the days of the US Canal Zone Balboa was the central downtown for the US Canal Zone with civic buildings, hospitals, movie theaters, a huge YMCA, and the major church in the Canal Zone.

Another US installation, Albrook Air Force Station, was located just to the east of Balboa. Today it is Albrook or Gelabert Airport which is the national airport for flights within Panama. There is also a huge bus terminal with buses departing to all parts of Panama and Costa Rica as well as the gigantic Albrook Mall.

* * * *

The Balboa port on the port or left side is another massive port owned by the same Chinese company that owns the port on the Atlantic side.

The Chinese have been here since before there was a country named Panama. In 1852, "The Chinamen, one thousand in number, had been brought to the Isthmus by the [Panama Railroad] Company, and every possible care taken which could conduce to their heath and comfort. Their hill-rice, their tea, and opium, in sufficient quantity to last for several months, had been imported with them - they were carefully housed and attended to - and it was expected that they would prove efficient and valuable men. But they had been engaged upon the work scarcely a month before almost the entire body became affected with a melancholic, suicidal tendency, and scores of them ended their unhappy existence by their own hands."[4]

---

[4] F. N. Otis, ILLUSTRATED HISTORY OF THE PANAMA RAILROAD, PP. 35-36

The Chinese were involved in both the French and American efforts to build the Panama Canal. When we go under the Bridge of the Americas, which you see up ahead, on the west side of the Bridge, which we can't see, is a Chinese pagoda and a monument to the Chinese presence in and contributions to Panama for the past 100 years. Outside of Panama City most of the little "corner" stores are run by Chinese. We have tons of Chinese restaurants. Unfortunately for me, since I'm used to Chinese food in San Francisco, Chinese food in Panama has been somewhat corrupted by 100 years in Panama. (No Chinese restaurant in San Francisco considers *patacones* or fried green plantain slices a staple of Chinese cuisine!)

Panama is one of the few countries in the world to recognize Taiwan. And since you can't recognize both, Panama doesn't officially recognize the People's Republic of China. To help preserve that relationship Taiwan has given Panama enormous amounts of aid. Of course the People's Republic of China, second largest customer of the Panama Canal, would dearly like to be the ones with official recognition, so it also gives enormous amounts of aid to Panama. Panama sits in the catbird seat, collecting cash from both sides.

It's not only the Chinese. Japan is also big contributor. For years every time it rains hard Panama City's storm water system overflows and gets mixed in with raw sewage, and so, pretty as it is, nobody can swim in the Bay of Panama. When Donald Trump agreed to build the new Trump Ocean Club in Panama, which looks a lot like the sail-shaped Al Arab hotel in Dubai, he insisted that Panama agree to deal with traffic congestion and the sewage flowing into the Bay of Panama. The result was a beautiful landscaped park and freeway called "*Cinta Balboa*" and a project to build new sewer lines in Panama City. An initial $25 million for the sewer project came from Japan. The Dutch and other European countries contribute to Panama to buy carbon emission credits.

* * * *

The Bridge of the Americas was built by the US in 1962 at a cost of $20 million and became the first permanent, non-swinging bridge to link together not just the country of Panama but also the continents of North and South America. Originally the bridge was called the Thatcher Ferry Bridge after the ferry service it replaced, but quickly became known as the Bridge of the Americas. When it was built it was the only permanent connection between the continents. Today there is also the Centennial Bridge, the new one we sailed under earlier. A new road and bridge is proposed on the Atlantic side that will link Colon to the rest of the country and really open up development along the beautiful Caribbean coast of Panama and there are tentative plans for an additional bridge on the Pacific side to connect to new development around the old Howard Air Force Base.

Captain and pilot on bridge – On most ships the captain spends very little actual time on the bridge leaving driving the ship to his bridge team, except in the Canal where he is required to be on the bridge

The Bridge of The Americas has a total length of 5,425 feet (1,654 meters) in 14 spans, abutment to abutment. The main span measures 1,128 feet (344 meters) and the tied arch (the center part of the main span) is 850 feet (259 meters). The highest point of the bridge is 385 feet (117 meters) above mean sea level; the clearance under the main span is 210 feet (61.3 meters) at high tide. MV JUST CRUISING should clear the bridge with 36 feet (11 meters) to spare.

On May 18, 2010, the bulk cargo ship ATLANTIC HERO struck one of the protective bases of the bridge after losing engine power partially blocking this section of the Canal to shipping traffic.

The Bridge of the Americas as seen from the top of Ancon Hill

The Bridge carries the Pan-American Highway, a road network running from Prudhoe Bay, Alaska to the southern tip of Chile and Argentina. Except for a 54 mile (87 kilometer) break in the Darien jungle of Panama, the road links together the Americas for 29,800 miles (47,958 kilometers). Although the road is quite good and safe through Panama, in some countries it is passable only in the dry season and in many places unsafe, particularly at night.

Colombia would like to complete the section through the Darien jungle and connect with Panama, but that is unlikely. The Darien is a dense, impenetrable jungle that separates Colombia and Panama. Panama has enough problems with FARC Rebels from Colombia in that area, drug runners and clandestine drug laboratories set up by the Colombians. Panama has begun working with the US military to help with the problems along the border with Colombia in the Darien.

Sometimes when listening to Panamanians, it sounds like all of the problems in Panama are caused by the Colombians. Drugs, en route to the US, are an enormous problem. Panama has this huge coastline, much of it lined with jungle, and it is right next door to Colombia. The drug problem will continue to worsen until the US decriminalizes drug use, regulates and taxes distribution, and removes the enormous illegal profit incentive.

Once I have fought my way through Panama City traffic and I am up on the Bridge of The Americas, it is a seven hour drive to my house in Boquete, not very far from the Costa Rican border.

* * * *

On the port or left side, just beyond the fuel tanks is the Country Inn hotel, complete with a TGIF Friday's restaurant. It costs about $155 a night for a room facing the Panama Canal. Frequently when I'm getting off a ship either with the pilot in the Canal or if the ship docks in Amador, I like to use this hotel. If I'm flying home, only about fifteen minutes from Albrook Airport, or if I'm driving its easy to get on the Pan American Highway.

* * * *

The area on the left or port side is called Amador because it was part of Fort Amador during the US Canal Zone days. During the construction of the Canal, spoil from the Culebra Cut was used to create the breakwater. Later the breakwater was expanded to create the Amador Peninsula linking together the mainland with the nearest offshore island of Naos.

Three forts protected the Canal. On the left or port side was Fort Amador is named for Manuel Amador Guerrero, the first president of Panama. Fort Grant consisted of the islands just offshore, some connected to Amador by the causeway. Fort Grant was named after the future US president, then Captain Ulysses S. Grant, who marched across Panama in 1852. On the starboard or right side was Fort Sherman.

The islands were favorites of the English pirates and privateers who raided the Spanish ships visiting Panama City. Sir Francis Drake, Captain Henry Morgan, and Captain James Cook all hid out in these islands.

During the US Canal Zone years the area was closed to all but military personnel. After it was turned over to Panama, Amador was opened up and became a favorite place to stroll, bike, skate, walk, or just enjoy the fantastic view of Panama City. There is a major Convention Center which, among other things, has hosted the Miss Universe Contest. There are shops, hotels, condos, marinas, restaurants and clubs. The Smithsonian Tropical Research Institute (STRI) has a marine research station and a small museum area on one of the islands.

* * * *

On the port side is the new Bridge of Life Museum of Biodiversity, designed by Frank Gehry who designed the Walt Disney Concert Hall in Los Angeles and the Experience Music project in Seattle. Panama's secret to getting this world-renowned architect to design this museum: his wife is Panamanian. The brightly colored jagged roofs are intended to represent the forces of nature that shape our world and created the Isthmus of Panama, the "bridge of life" connecting the continents.

* * * *

On the port side on the Amador Peninsula is the Pacific pilot Station where we bid farewell to our pilot. As the pilot leaves us we officially leave the Panama Canal. As we do so we should remember that the conservative death toll to construct the Canal, including both the French and American efforts, is 25,000 . . . that's five hundred lives for every mile of the Canal that you travelled today. They were ordinary people, struggling to make a living and striving to do the impossible.

5:15 pm pilot disembarked and ship headed out to sea

If you look back over Amador you will catch a glimpse of modern day Panama City. Panama's population is around 3.3 million, and about 2 million of those folks live in and around Panama City. Panama has one of the strongest economies in the region and is rapidly developing. The modern Panama City is crowded with high rise towers.

One of the iconic towers of Panama City is the Trump Ocean Club, a sail shaped building similar to the Al Arab hotel in Dubai. If you have good eyes, or binoculars, you may be able to catch a glimpse of the Trump Ocean Club on the port or left side, off in the distance over Amador peninsula.

* * * *

To the right or starboard side of the ship is what used to be Howard Air Force Base. Since the US pulled out of Panama, turning over all US facilities to the Panamanians, Howard has sat virtually untouched. Panama wisely chose to wait on developing many of the former US facilities. Recently the giant former USAF airstrip has been opened to charter flights. Copa Airlines, Panama's private flag carrier, has its maintenance center at Howard, and also maintains the aircraft of Singapore Airlines. Copa flies out of Panama's Tocumen International Airport, operating 148 daily scheduled flights to 45 destinations in 24 countries in North, South, and Central America and the Caribbean. The airline has 50 planes and 25 new Boeing aircraft currently on order. Tocumen is growing so rapidly that Copa and the airport facilities can hardly keep up with the demand. Much of the demand is from folks who don't want to put up with the intrusive hassle of connecting through the US, so they choose Panama instead.

I predict you're going to see the same thing with the cruise industry. Two years ago Royal Caribbean began home porting a ship in Colon with the idea of attracting European passengers who didn't want to endure the hassle of US immigration in Miami. The ship sold out every sailing, so Royal Caribbean is moving another ship from Europe to Colon. My prediction is that Amador will become a major cruise port once a proposed pier is built at Amador.

There are ambitious plans to develop Howard into a brand new city and free zone to be called Panama Pacifico, which will be one of the largest planned master developments in the hemisphere. The first stage of the project is a 58 acre (23.5 hectare) International Business Park that will offer industrial and commercial office space. Panama is working on a new underground subway system which may eventually go under the Canal to this new city.

* * * *

On the port side you will see was the cruise lines call *"Fuerte Amador"*, really a fancy name for this area of Panama City, and three islands Naos Island, Perico Island, and Flamenco Island.

At one time these islands were home to Fort Grant and provided major protection to the US Panama Canal Zone. There were gun emplacements, defensive tunnels, and even a Hawk missile installation. Today the island hosts very expensive yachts of the rich and famous, has little boutiques and restaurants and those caves . . . at night are discos where folks can crank up the music as loud as they wish.

Last look back at Panama City

Sometime tomorrow morning as the sun comes up, if the ship turns northward, and just before you get off the coast of Costa Rica, you will cross the Bay of Chiriqui which I can see from my back porch up on the huge mountain you'll see off in the distance. If there isn't fog, and the light is right, I can see cruise ships off in the distance as they sail across. So wave as you go by!

3 - Northbound - Pacific to Atlantic

This part is for those of you doing a Northbound crossing from the Pacific to Atlantic.

Not all ships provide guided commentary from the bridge, and, if they do, the quality and amount of information varies. I wanted CRUISING THE PANAMA CANAL to be a tool you could use in preparation and anticipation of your trip, but also something you could use during your transit. *And yes, it is the same information given in the opposite direction.*

3A - Amador & Balboa

If you are looking to the starboard or right side of the ship, you will be looking east. The sun usually rises in Panama around 6:30 am so this morning, if you are looking off the right or starboard side of the ship, you may actually get to see the sun rising over the Pacific Ocean.

To the west, going up the Panama coast toward Costa Rica, is where a lot of the beachfront development is taking place. Farther up the coast there are a lot of resort communities and there is a lot of development going on the Azuero Peninsula that juts out into the Pacific. Folks like Arnold Schwarzenegger, Brad Pitt and Angelina Jolie have spreads on the Azuero, and Mick Jagger has a private island.

If it is a clear morning you will catch glimpses of Panama City glittering in the distance. Panama's population is around 3.3 million, and about 2 million of those folks live in and around Panama City. Panama has one of the strongest economies in the region and is rapidly developing. The modern Panama City is crowded with high rise towers and I like to think of it as "Miami on steroids".

One of the iconic towers of Panama City is the Trump Ocean Club a sail-shaped building similar to the Al Arab hotel in Dubai. If you have good eyes, or binoculars, you may be able to catch a brief glimpse of the Trump Ocean Club on the starboard or right side, off in the distance as we start our voyage this morning.

* * * *

Panama City skyline as seen from Amador

To the left or port side of the ship is what used to be Howard Air Force Base. Since the US pulled out of Panama turning over all US facilities to the Panamanians, Howard has sat virtually untouched. Panama wisely chose to wait on developing many of the former US facilities. Recently the giant former USAF airstrip has been opened to charter flights. Copa Airlines, Panama's private flag carrier, has its maintenance center at Howard, and also maintains the aircraft of Singapore Airlines. Copa flies out of Panama's Tocumen International Airport, operating 148 daily scheduled flights to 45 destinations in 24 countries in North, South, and Central America and the Caribbean. The airline has 50 planes and 25 new Boeing aircraft currently on order. Tocumen is growing so rapidly that Copa and the airport facilities can hardly keep up with the demand. Much of the demand is from folks who don't want to put up with the intrusive hassle of connecting through the US, so they choose Panama instead.

I predict you're going to see the same thing with the cruise industry. Two years ago Royal Caribbean began home porting a ship in Colon with the idea of attracting European passengers who didn't want to endure the hassle of US immigration in Miami. The ship sold out every sailing, so Royal Caribbean is moving another ship from Europe to Colon. My prediction is that Amador will become a major cruise port over the next several years.

There are ambitious plans to develop Howard into a brand new city and free zone to be called Panama Pacifico, which will be one of the largest planned master developments in the hemisphere. The first stage of the project is a 58 acre (23.5 hectare) International Business Park that will offer industrial and commercial office space. Panama is working on a new underground subway system which, among other things, may eventually go under the Canal to this new city.

* * * *

The area on the right or starboard side is called Amador because it was part of Fort Amador during the US Canal Zone days. During the construction of the Canal, waste material from the Culebra Cut was used to create the breakwater. Later the breakwater was expanded to create the Amador Peninsula linking together the mainland with the nearest offshore island of Naos.

During the US days three forts protected the Canal. On the starboard side was Fort Amador is named for Manuel Amador Guerrero, the first president of Panama. Fort Grant consisted of the islands just offshore, some connected to Amador by the causeway. Fort Grant was named after the future US president, then Captain Ulysses S. Grant, who marched across Panama in 1852. On the port side was Fort Sherman.

The islands were favorites of the English pirates and privateers who raided the Spanish ships visiting Panama City. Sir Francis Drake, Captain Henry Morgan, and Captain James Cook all hid out in these islands.

During the US Canal Zone years Amador was closed to all but military personnel. After it was turned over to Panama, Amador was opened up and became a favorite place to stroll, bike, skate, walk, or just enjoy the fantastic view of Panama City. There is a major Convention Center which, among other things, has hosted the Miss Universe Contest. There are shops, hotels, condos, marinas, restaurants and clubs. The Smithsonian Tropical Research Institute (STRI) has a marine research station and a small museum area on one of the islands.

* * * *

On the starboard side is the new Bridge of Life Museum of Biodiversity, designed by Frank Gehry who designed the Walt Disney Concert Hall in Los Angeles and the Experience Music project in Seattle. Panama's secret to getting this world-renowned architect to design this museum: his wife is Panamanian. The brightly colored jagged roofs are intended to represent the forces of nature that shape our world and created the Isthmus of Panama, the "bridge of life" connecting the continents.

* * * *

On the starboard or right side, is the Country Inn hotel, complete with a TGIF Friday's restaurant. It costs about $155 a night for a room facing the Panama Canal. Frequently when I'm getting off a ship either with the pilot in the Canal or if the ship docks in Amador, I like to use this hotel. If I'm flying home, only about fifteen minutes from Albrook Airport, or if I'm driving its easy to get on the Pan Amcrican Highway.

* * * *

The Bridge of the Americas was built by the US in 1962 at a cost of $20 million and became the first permanent, non-swinging bridge to link together not just the country of Panama but also the continents of North and South America. Originally the bridge was called the Thatcher Ferry Bridge after the ferry service it replaced, but quickly became known as the Bridge of the Americas. When it was built it was the only permanent connection between the continents. Today there is also the Centennial Bridge, which we will sail under later this morning. A new road and bridge is proposed on the Atlantic side that will link Colon to the rest of the country and really open up development along the beautiful Caribbean coast of Panama and there are tentative plans for an additional bridge on the Pacific side to connect to new development around the old Howard Air Force Base.

The Bridge of the Americas has a total length of 5,425 feet (1,654 meters) in 14 spans, abutment to abutment. The main span measures 1,128 feet (344 meters) and the tied arch (the center part of the main span) is 850 feet (259 meters). The highest point of the bridge is 385 feet (117 meters) above mean sea level; the clearance under the main span is 210 feet (61.3 meters) at high tide. MV JUST CRUISING should clear the bridge with 36 feet (11 meters) to spare. Today the bridge carries about 35,000 vehicles per day.

The Bridge of the Americas as seen from the top of Ancon Hill

On May 18, 2010, the bulk cargo ship ATLANTIC HERO struck one of the protective bases of the bridge after losing engine power partially blocking this section of the Canal to shipping traffic.

The bridge carries the Pan-American Highway, a road network running from Prudhoe Bay, Alaska to the southern tip of Chile and Argentina. Except for a 54 mile (87 kilometer) break in the Darien jungle of Panama, the road links together the Americas for 29,800 miles (47,958 kilometers). Although the road is quite good and safe through Panama, in some countries it is passable on in the dry season and in many places unsafe, particularly at night.

Colombia would like to complete the section through the Darien jungle and connect with Panama, but that is unlikely. The Darien is a dense, impenetrable jungle that separates Colombia and Panama. Panama has enough problems with FARC Rebels, drug runners and clandestine drug laboratories set up by the Colombians along the border. Panama has begun working with the US military to help with on the problems along the Colombia border in the Darien.

Sometimes when listening to Panamanians, it sounds like all of the problems in Panama are caused by the Colombians. Drugs, en route to the US, are an enormous problem. Panama has this huge coastline, much of it lined with jungle, and it's right next door to Colombia. The drug problem will continue to worsen until the US decriminalizes drug use, regulates and taxes distribution, and removes the profit incentive.

Once I have fought my way through Panama City traffic and I am up on the Bridge of The Americas, it is a seven hour drive to my house in Boquete, not very far from the Costa Rican border.

* * * *

As we pass under the Bridge of The Americas, on the starboard side of the ship is the area of Panama City known as Balboa. The Balboa area is mostly reclaimed land created with spoils from Culebra Cut. During the days of the US Canal Zone Balboa was the central downtown for the US Canal Zone with civic buildings, hospitals, movie theaters, a huge YMCA, and the major church in the Canal Zone.

Another US installation, Albrook Air Force Station, was located just to the east of Balboa. Today it is Albrook or Gelabert Airport which is the national airport for flights within Panama. There is also a huge bus terminal with buses departing to all parts of Panama and Costa Rica as well as the gigantic Albrook Mall.

* * * *

The Balboa port on the right side is a massive port owned by the same Chinese company that owns the port on the Atlantic side. The Chinese have been here since before there was a country named Panama. In 1852, "The Chinamen, one thousand in number, had been brought to the Isthmus by the [Panama Railroad] Company, and every possible care taken which could conduce to their heath and comfort. Their hill-rice, their tea, and opium, in sufficient quantity to last for several months, had been imported with them - they were carefully housed and attended to - and it was expected that they would prove efficient and valuable men. But they had been engaged upon the work scarcely a month before almost the entire body became affected with a melancholic, suicidal tendency, and scores of them ended their unhappy existence by their own hands." [5]

The Chinese were involved in both the French and American efforts to build the Panama Canal. When we go under the Bridge of the Americas, which you see up ahead, on the west side of the Bridge, which we can't see, is a Chinese pagoda and a monument to the Chinese presence in and contributions to Panama for the past 100 years.

---

[5] Ibid

Outside of Panama City most of the little "corner" stores are run by Chinese. We have tons of Chinese restaurants. Unfortunately for me, since I'm used to Chinese food in San Francisco, Chinese food in Panama has been somewhat corrupted by 100 years in Panama. (No Chinese restaurant in San Francisco considers *patacones* or fried green plantain slices a staple of Chinese cuisine!)

Panama is one of the few countries in the world to recognize Taiwan. And since you can't recognize both, Panama doesn't officially recognize the People's Republic of China. To help preserve that relationship Taiwan has given Panama enormous amounts of aid. Of course the People's Republic of China, second largest customer of the Panama Canal, would dearly like to be the ones with official recognition, so it also gives enormous amounts of aid to Panama. Panama sits in the catbird seat, collecting cash from both sides.

Entering the locks you want to be up front if possible

It's not only the Chinese. Japan is also big contributor. For years every time it rains hard Panama City's storm water system overflows, gets mixed in with raw sewage, and so, pretty as it is, nobody can swim in the Bay of Panama. When Donald Trump agreed to build the new Trump Ocean Club in Panama, which looks a lot like the sail-shaped Al Arab hotel in Dubai, he insisted that Panama agree to deal with traffic congestion and the sewage flowing into the Bay of Panama. The result was a beautiful landscaped park and freeway called "*Cinta Balboa*" and a project to build new sewer lines in Panama City. An initial $25 million for the sewer project came from Japan. The Dutch and other European countries contribute to Panama to buy carbon emission credits.

* * * *

There is no one "best" vantage point on the ship. If you want to get the most out of your day in the Canal, move around the ship. Coming into the locks the forward part of the ship is the best place to be. When the ship is in the locks move around! The view from the aft end is totally different. If you have an outside cabin without a balcony, but with a window, some time when you are in the locks you should run down to your cabin. Outside you will see the massive wall of the lock, just inches away!

This picture, taken from the Canal ferry shore excursion, is the same view as you get from an outside stateroom on the lower deck

Sometime when you are in the locks go down to the promenade deck and you will really appreciate just how little room there is to spare! It is so close that you feel as if you can almost reach out and touch the sides of the Canal. If you have a balcony the best time to enjoy that vantage point is when you sailing through Gatun Lake.

Once the ship clears Pedro Miguel Lock is a good time to order breakfast. If your ship offers the option of having a champagne breakfast served on your stateroom balcony, a good time to schedule it is once you are through Pedro Miguel, usually around 8:30 to 9:30 am.

It will be a long day so stay hydrated, wear a hat and sunscreen, and pace your self. By the end of the day the rails won't be nearly as crowded. People will be playing cards, working out in the gym, lying about on deck.

To prove the point, I actually took a picture of a couple for whom the trip through the Canal was a bucket-list trip of a lifetime. We were actually in the locks and these folks were on the promenade deck sound asleep! To each his own, but I hope you don't miss a thing.

I kid you not! Thousands of dollars for a Canal trip and these folks are sound asleep in the middle of the locks

3B - The Pacific Locks

It's 6:15 am approaching Miraflores Locks

There are two "lanes" through the lock complexes and in the case of Miraflores each lane has two lock chambers. They are bi-directional and you can go in either direction. All this is done to maximize the number of ships passing through the Canal.

Prior to entering the locks a small boat will bring the Panama Canal line handlers on board to assist MV JUST CRUISING in connecting to the engines or "mules" that will help guide us through the locks.

Many of the Canal tugs are named after provinces in Panama

The Canal has thirty two tug boats and two will be standing by to assist us as necessary to nudge the ship into the correct position to enter the locks. At some times of the year the wind blows from the north, sometimes quite strongly, so a Panamax ship can act like a huge sail, and the tugs are essential.

* * * *

The ship is getting ready to enter the Miraflores Lock complex, a two-stage flight of locks that will lift the MV JUST CRUISING up 54 feet (16.5 meters) above sea level to the level of Miraflores Lake. From there we will sail the short distance across Miraflores Lake to Pedro Miguel, a single chamber lock, which will lift us up another 31 feet (9.5 meters) to the level of Gatun Lake. We will then sail across Panama, 85 feet (26 meters) above sea level to the Gatun Locks on the Atlantic side. There we will drop back down to sea level and sail off into the sunset.

There is no way to know in advance which of the lock chambers will be assigned to MV JUST CRUISING.

Arrows at the entrance to the lock provide an additional means of communication

The big arrow is a visual communication from the lock to the pilot. The position of the arrow indicates the readiness of the lock for the ship to enter and which side of the chamber will be used.

If you can read the arrow signals you can impress your fellow passengers with your knowledge of what's happening. If you play this right you should be able to make a "bet" with your friends and get them to buy you a drink!

	Not ready; lockage cannot take place for some time		Moor to approach wall near jaws on right-hand side
	Not ready; stand off well clear of lock, prepared to approach on signal		Moor to approach wall near jaws on left-hand side
	Locks making preparation, probably be ready for lockage in 10 minutes or less; you may approach with caution, prepared to tie up or enter on right hand side on signal		Enter right-hand side
	Locks making preparation, probably be ready for lockage in 10 minutes or less; you may approach with caution, prepared to tie up or enter on left hand side on signal		Enter left-hand side

* * * *

Each lock chamber is 110 feet (33.5 meters) wide and 1,000 feet (304.8 meters) long. Our hypothetical MV JUST CRUISING is 856 feet (260.9 meters) long and 105 feet (32 meters) wide so, unless guests have been eating too many desserts, we should fit with about 2.5 feet (about .8 meters) to spare on either side.

The lock chambers are seven stories high! The maximum draft is 39.5 feet (12.04 meters) in tropical fresh water (which is a slightly different than in salt water or cold fresh water).

Panamax vessels navigate under-draft-depth restrictions that do not allow them their full cargo capacity. Part of the expansion program is to increase the depth of the locks to make it possible for vessels to carry a full load of cargo.

The pilot maneuvers the ship to the approach wall where the line handlers attach the cables of the locomotives to the vessel. As the pilot calls out maneuvers to the captain, the vessel continues forward with assistance from the tug at the stern. When the ship reaches the first chamber of the lock, line handlers will attach the cables of the remaining locomotives to the vessel and draw them tight to stabilize the ship for entry into the chamber.

Together with the locomotives and tugs and under its own power, the ship moves into the first chamber, where gates close behind the vessel's stern to lock it into the chamber.

6:30 am connecting to the mules

In order to tie the ship up to the "mules" or locomotives lines have to be passed from the shore to the ship. This job is handled by the Panama Canal line handlers. Over the years they have tried many ways to get the lines from the vessel to the shore. They've tried everything including shooting the lines on board, which ended up putting out a few people's eyes. So it turns out that the very best way is to send a little rowboat to bring the lines from the ship to the engines.

Here's this high-tech cruise ship with our sophisticated, computerized bridge . . . and the little row boat is still the best way!

* * * *

As we enter the locks you will notice some round things that look like giant tires on the Canal walls. These are the "bumpers" . . . just like in a pinball machine . . . designed to roll and keep the Canal walls from putting a hole in the ship hull should the ship accidentally drift or make too sharp a turn. Nobody wants to bring the "family" ship back with a giant gash in the hull . . . or paint off the fender . . . but the fact is the cosmetic paint on the hull of many ships passing through the Canal takes a beating.

Even with all the modern technology, that tiny little rowboat

* * * *

From the start of the Canal effort there was recognition that the Canal would split Panama in two. This was a challenge even during the US construction when barges had to be used to ferry construction workers back and forth.

The old swing bridge at Miraflores, no longer used, was built in 1942, but could be used only when ships weren't passing. In 1942 ferry service was added as well, known as the Thatcher Ferry after a former member of the Canal Commission who introduced the legislation that created the ferry. Until the Bridge of the Americas was built in 1962 there was no other way to cross.

* * * *

There are three places along the Canal where locals and visitors can get a good view of the action. The first is the Miraflores Visitor Center on the starboard side.

The Visitor Center at Miraflores

Although the Visitor Center is closed this early in the morning, it is very popular with tourists and locals alike. The center provides observation decks, restaurant, areas for meetings and events, and a museum honoring the thousands of men and women who made this achievement possible. The better of the Canal museums is the Interoceanic Canal Museum in the old Casco Viejo area of Panama City. The Interoceanic Canal Museum is located in what was the headquarters building during the French era.

* * * *

The Panama Canal Authority has three Web cams and the first one is midway up the red and white communications tower next to the Miraflores Visitors Center. On one ship they convinced guests to prepare signs for the folks back home and to wave flags as we passed by the final Canal Web cam.

People had a lot of fun getting ready for the grand event, and the ship's photographers and videographers had a field day, but the folks back home . . . Well, if they looked very closely they might have seen a few pixels that were their friends with their carefully crafted signs. But it did look good on the videos and pictures the ship photographers shot.

* * * *

The locomotives have been called "mules" through the years, but not because animals were ever used in Panama to assist ships through the Canal. In the early history of canals in the US and Europe mules were used to pull barges along. So it is because of that history, that the engines used in Panama came to be called "mules."

A center cog track enables the locomotives to climb

There have been three generations of locomotives, the first built by General Electric, the second built by Mitsubishi, and the current generation built by Mitsubishi. The newest were assembled in Panama, and each cost $1.9 million. The Canal has 100 of these electric engines, powered by a third rail, geared to run on tracks. Each locomotive weighs 50 tons and operates with two 290 HP traction units with a towing capacity of 178 to 311.8 kilo new tons depending on their speed. Their maximum return speed is 16 kilometers per hour which is important when a lockage is completed and the engines have relay down the center track back to the beginning. Ships travel through the Canal on their own power. The locomotives have several important functions:

Keeping the vessel centered;
Assisting in towing if needed;
Stopping the forward motion if needed as a safety feature.

The number of locomotives or "mules" that are used depends on the size of the ship. MV JUST CRUISING will use six.

* * * *

Just to the left of the Miraflores Visitor Center, you can see one of the early locomotives or "mules" used on the Canal that was built by General Electric.

At the entrance to the Miraflores Visitor's Center, which unfortunately you can't see from the ship, stands one of the trains that was used by the French found buried in the mud while the Canal was being dredged.

* * * *

6:51 am inside the first chamber and gate closed

The function of the locks at Miraflores and Pedro Miguel is to act as a "water elevator" that lifts the ship up from sea level to the level of Gatun Lake, 85 feet (26 meters) above sea level. There the ship sails across the Isthmus of Panama and when it gets to the other side, another series of locks acts as a "water elevator" to lower the ship back to sea level.

The Miraflores complex has two lock chambers. Water from the second chamber flows into the first chamber and lifts the vessel to the water level of the second chamber. When the ship has been raised to the proper level the gates in front open and the vessel moves ahead into the second chamber under its own power. The process repeats for the second chamber.

Once the ship is inside the chamber and the lock gates are closed, it takes only about thirty minutes for the ship to be raised. Assuming everything flows smoothly the ship will be in the lock complex about an hour. This depends not only on the lockage of your ship, but also the ship ahead of you. Sometimes the process gets delayed and everything does not move on schedule. With some of the larger, boxy ships, like bulk carriers and tankers, it takes longer for the water to flow around the hull.

The lockmaster at each lock has the responsibility for handling ships in the locks. The control house is the center of operations. The pilot, lockmaster and control house operator are in constant radio communication.

For the efficient operation of the locks some ships may be assigned to tie up at the locks. To maximize traffic and efficiency a relay system of locomotives is often used where locomotive teams change mid-lockage.

As we make our way through the locks the pilot is continually giving commands to the locomotive operators by radio. The bells and lights on the locomotives are additional ways of communicating and confirming commands. The green light means the locomotive is "up to speed". The red light "confirms pilot order" and the yellow light means the locomotive is "standing by".

The locomotive bells are an additional means of communication between the pilot and the locomotive operator. Two "distinct taps" on the locomotive bell means the order has been received, understood and will be executed as directed. Three taps on the bell means the locomotive operator does not understand or cannot execute the order or wants to attract the attention of the pilot. Continual ringing of the bell is a general alarm signal.

* * * *

The Canal uses only fresh water. Neither the Canal nor Gatun Lake is salt water. Not only would salt water have a corrosive effect on the cement and the metal, but the challenge of the Canal historically has been what to do with all the water that flows into Gatun Lake during the rainy season from the Chagres River. It is not unheard of in Panama to have rain falling at times at 3 to 4 inches (76 to102 millimeters) an hour.

So the Canal uses fresh water and it uses a lot of water. Each time a ship transits the canal 53.4 million US gallons (202,000 cubic meters) of water is passed from the lake into the sea. With some 14,600 vessel transits per year, this represents a huge demand for fresh water. Since rainfall is seasonal in Panama, the lake acts as a water store, allowing the Canal to continue operation through the dry season.

* * * *

One of the most fascinating things about the Canal is the way in which water from Gatun Lake flows through the locks. Deep within the walls are huge culverts 18 feet (5.5 meters) in diameter. When the Canal was built the tunnels were the same size as the tunnels under the Hudson River in New York that were built to bring the railroad into New York City.

Cross-section of Lock Chamber and Walls, Panama Canal

A section across the width of the locks, showing the culverts for filling and draining the chambers. One side is shown; the other is the same.

From the main culvert there are 14 lateral culverts running underneath the lock floor. In the floor of the lock there are 70 holes, each about 4 feet (1.2 meters) wide. These many holes allow the lock chamber to either fill or empty with minimal turbulence. It all happens so smoothly you hardly even know the ship is being lifted until you happen to look at a ship in the next chamber or a point on shore.

The water from the highest lock, makes its way to the next lock, then on to the lowest lock, and finally it is emptied out flushing into the approach and out to sea.

---

[6] GNU Free Documentation License, Version 1.2

Since all the equipment of the locks is operated electrically, the whole process of locking a ship up or down is controlled from a central control room located on the center wall of the upper flight of locks. The controls are designed to minimize the chances of operator error so there is an actual model of the locks with moving components that mirror the actual state of the locks. An operator can see at a glance exactly the position of all locks and valves. Interlocks are built into the controls so that no component can be moved if another is not in the right position.

There are walkways across the lock gates that allow Canal workers to pass from one side of the lock chamber to the other. When the gates are closed and about to open a bell warns workers and the rails collapse into the gate. Sometimes you will see the red lights flashing on the center wall and hear a siren. This is a warning that hazardous cargo is on the ships and no open flames, smoking or electrical tools are permitted.

Collapsible walkways allow workers to pass across closed gates

While we are in the second chamber of Miraflores, if you look aft in the distance you will see Ancon Hill, a 654 foot (199.2 meter) hill overlooking Panama City on the other side of the hill. On top of the hill are a giant Panamanian flag and an overlook where you get a fantastic view of the city. I've sometimes stayed at a little bed and breakfast up on Ancon Hill. Because the hill was never developed in the US Canal Zone days, monkeys still come to eat bananas off your balcony, and you see brightly colored toucans. When I've stayed there I've gotten up early to hike to the top of Ancon Hill and watch the sun rise over the Pacific. The view of Panama City and the Bay of Panama is breathtaking.

---

[7] Ibid

Once the mansion of Ferdinand de Lesseps, the house was moved to Ancon Hill and serves as the residence of the Administrator of the ACP

Just down the hill is a series of tunnels built by the US during the World War II. The tunnels have wooden floors that were designed to prevent an enemy from listening. There are dorm rooms, a hospital, chapel, cafeteria and even a machine to shred loads of documents. Interestingly the present government in Panama has announced plans to remodel these tunnels as an emergency hide out for the President of Panama should Panama or the Canal ever be attacked.

During the US days the lower slopes of Ancon Hill contained residences for officers and Gorgas Hospital. Higher up was the residence of the Governor of the Canal Zone. Originally the Governor's residence was the mansion de Lesseps had built for himself. It was later moved to Ancon Hill and has expanded over the years. Today it is the home of the Administrator of the Panama Canal Authority. On up was the headquarters of the US Southern Army Command. Under US jurisdiction it always irked the Panamanians that the US flag flew over Ancon Hill, so when Panama regained control of the hill, following the 1977 Panama Canal Treaty, one of the first things the country did was fly a large oversized Panamanian flag from the top of Ancon hill. Today the flag flies day and night, lit up at night by spotlights.

7:29 am Medical evacuation complete - passing to the second chamber

* * * *

The most pretentious old public building in Panama is the Panama Canal Headquarters Building on Ancon Hill. If you look over to Ancon Hill while you are still in the locks you can see the Panama Canal Headquarters about halfway up the hill. The building opened in 1914.

Inside are remarkable murals depicting the history and construction of the Canal that were created by William B. Van Ingen of New York. Van Ingen, who had achieved considerable fame for his murals in the Library of Congress, agreed to produce the murals at $25 a square foot. The artist visited Panama twice during the Canal construction and made charcoal sketches. The murals were painted in his New York studio and eventually moved to Panama.

Long before OSHA, this charcoal sketch by William Van Engen illustrates how workers were lifted in and out of the lock chambers

* * * * *

111

The Panama Canal Authority, or ACP, which operates the Canal is an autonomous government legal entity with exclusive charge of the operation, administration, management, preservation, maintenance, and modernization of the Canal so that the Canal may operate in a safe, continuous, efficient, and profitable manner. Because of its importance and uniqueness, the ACP is financially autonomous and has its own, non-political hiring and operational authority. An Administrator is appointed for a seven-year term, and may be re-elected for an additional term. There is an eleven-member board of directors, nine appointed by the president and one by the legislature. An advisory board is composed representatives from the world's largest shipping firms and representatives from the biggest customers.

* * * *

Because of the extreme tides on the Pacific it was decided to split the lock complexes on the Pacific side with one chamber at Pedro Miguel and two chambers at Miraflores. The drop from Miraflores Lake to the Pacific approach varies due to the tidal differences on the Pacific, between 43 feet (13.1 meters) at extreme high tide and 64.5 feet (19.7 meters) at extreme low tide.

8:10 am Gates opened and left Miraflores Locks, passing into Miraflores Lake

Miraflores Lake is a small, man made lake that serves only as a 1.3 mile (2 kilometer) connection between the single lock at Pedro Miguel and the double locks at Miraflores, and is 54 feet (16.5 meters) above sea level.

* * * *

The image and expectation that many people have is that as they transit the Canal they will see wildlife and birds along the shoreline. Although Panama is one of the most bio-diverse areas in the world, and the rainforests you will see along the sides of the Canal have an amazing diversity of birds and animals, don't expect to see much. Unless you have really good eyes and a great pair of binoculars the Canal channels are too far from shore to see much more than spectacular foliage. And we are transiting during the middle of the day when most respectable animals are napping. But they are there! Anteaters, jaguars, cougars, monkeys, deer, agouti, parrots, toucans, sloths, snakes, hundreds of butterflies including the iridescent blue Morpho . . . they're all there. All of this giving you a great reason to come back and visit Panama and stay a while!

What you can look for are crocs! The Canal has American crocodile as well as caiman. Although often locally called "alligators", they are in fact crocodiles. How I remember: "canal" and "crocodile" both start with "C". Crocodiles like to hang out near the entrance to Gatun Locks. Some of these guys have been here since before the Canal was built and some are huge! These big suckers can be very aggressive so Canal workers have to be very cautious when doing maintenance work in this area. Look on the banks . . . or watch in the water. The tip off is what looks like a log . . . moving in the wrong direction or against the current. And yes, both the crocodiles and caiman have attacked and killed people. Caiman grow as large 12 to 15 feet (3.7 to 4.6 meters), and crocodiles can get as large as 18 feet (5.5 meters) and weigh as much as a ton. People have been killed in this area, in Gatun Lake and around the entrance channel to Gatun Locks. Since it is common for the animal to take its victim and hide the body underwater, the bodies of those attacked are usually never found. So keep your hands and feet inside the ship!

People always ask about the large birds with the forked tails. These are frigates, and you see lots of them around the Canal. Panama has 940 bird species, but unfortunately you aren't going to see a lot from the middle of the Canal. You may hear first, then see, some flocks of the little green parrots we have . . . noisy buggers. You'll probably see them in the tops of the trees along the Canal.

* * * *

What astounds me every time I go through the Canal is that here is something that was built almost 100 years ago, and it still works exactly the same way it was designed to work. We live in a throw-away society. How long does a toaster last? One or two years if you're lucky. Every few years you dump your old computer. Your printer is broken: it's cheaper to throw it away and buy a new one than try to fix it. But here is this engineering marvel, still working after almost 100 years . . . working 24 hours a day, 365 days a year.

* * * *

Looking over to the right or starboard side of the ship as we leave Miraflores locks you will see a large complex of buildings that was Fort Clayton during the US occupation of the Canal Zone. Today it is known as the "City of Knowledge" and is home to a number of large high tech and computer operations, call centers, and university buildings. There are hotels and housing developments and the gigantic, sprawling US Embassy.

* * * *

The average depth of the Canal channel is 43 feet (13 meters) and the minimum depth is 41 feet (12.5 meters), although these numbers are changing as the Canal is deepened as part of the Canal Expansion program.

* * * *

The width varies from 500 to 1,000 ft (150 to 300 meters), and again this is increasing as the Canal is enlarged with the expansion.

* * * *

Approximately 35-40 ships a day pass through the canal.

* * * *

The top customers of the Canal are the US, People's Republic of China, Chile, Japan and Korea.

* * * *

The average time to pass from ocean to ocean is about 10 hours, down from the 12.5 hours just a few years ago. Panamax ships, such as MV JUST CRUISING, generally take 10 to 12 hours. Often cargo ships have to tie up for periods at several spots along the Canal or anchor for a while in Gatun Lake in order to maximize traffic flow. Cruise ships generally get a priority transit.

* * * *

Since the turnover of the Canal Panama is on an economic roll, on track to become what is already being called "The Singapore of the Americas". When the US started closing down bases and pulling out of Panama after the 1977 Treaty times were tough for Panama. All those US jobs suddenly disappeared. In the 86 years the US operated the Canal in Panama it had paid the original $10 million, plus $250,000 per year after the first nine years, or a total of $29.25 million. In the *first year* of Panama's ownership and stewardship of the Canal, the Canal made a direct transfer to the national treasury of $252 million!

During the *first four years* of Panamanian made direct contributions to the national treasury of $1.1 billion plus all the additional indirect contributions to the national economy such as salaries, taxes, procurement and local business.

Today the Canal writes an annual direct check to the government of Panama for about $400 million. It's estimated that by the time the Canal expansion is finished in 2015 that amount will be $1.25 billion a year.

There were a lot of doomsayers who predicted Panama couldn't manage the Canal, and that it would fall apart once the Turnover took place. The reality is that the Canal is doing better than ever!

So how has Panama done?

There has been a 35% decrease in waiting time, granted assisted slightly by lower demand.

Transit time has been decreased by 25%.

There has been a 30% reduction in accidents.

There has been continuing upgrading and maintenance of items the US delayed prior to the Turnover at a cost of $1.3 billion.

The Americans ran the Canal as a federally operated service with tolls just covering operating costs: the Panamanians run it as a very profitable business.

The Canal now generates $2 billion a year.

The Canal is being expanded to accommodate larger vessels at a cost of $5.2 billion to be completed by 2014.

Of the $5.25 billion expansion, $3 billion will come from retained earnings, and the rest from bilateral and multilateral lenders, led by the Japan Bank for International Cooperation, European Investment Bank and the Inter-American Development Bank.

* * * *

9:00 am Connected to mules and entering Pedro Miguel Locks

Pedro Miguel, like the other locks, is named after one of the little towns that were flooded during the construction of the Canal. Pedro Miguel has only one chamber which will raise the vessel 29 feet (8.9 meters) from Miraflores Lake up to the level of Gatun Lake for our transit across the Isthmus.

The bulk of Canal traffic is freight – Less than 2% is passenger ships

* * * *

One safety concern always has been the failure of the lock gates, perhaps caused by a runaway ship hitting a gate. This could not only unleash a flood, but drain the entire lock system and even Gatun Lake.

Originally the locks had chain barriers stretched across the lock to prevent a ship from ramming a gate. These were lowered into the lock floor when it was time for the ship to pass. These "fender chains" were designed to stop ships up to 10,000 tons, but with ships getting much larger and the expense of maintaining the chains they were removed in 1980.

Extra safety against flooding the system and emptying Gatun Lake is provided by an extra set of gates at both ends of the upper chambers on both sides providing four gates that would all have to fail to create a Canal disaster. The additional gates are 70 feet (21 meters) from the operating gates.

* * * *

On the starboard side you will see a parking area where folks who live here like to bring visitors to see ships in the Canal. There aren't always ships actually in the locks, so sometimes you have to try a couple of spots if you want your friends to see more than an empty lock.

* * * *

As you make your way through the Canal you will see a number of navigational lights, as well as 19 different lighthouses in the Canal designed originally as navigational lights.

Lighthouse at Gatun

3C - Gaillard Cut

9:40 am Vessel exits Pedro Miguel – Line handlers and first pilot disembark, second pilot on board

From Pedro Miguel to Gamboa you enter into one of the most interesting sections of the Canal, and the most challenging to construct. Gaillard Cut, originally known as Culebra Cut, passes through what was once nine miles of solid rock including what was known as Culebra Mountain. The mountain was cut in half to allow the Canal to pass through.

* * * *

Ferdinand de Lesseps 1805 - 1894

Ferdinand de Lesseps is often called "the great engineer" even although he was a promoter and not an engineer. De Lesseps was riding high after his incredible achievement in building the Suez Canal. The French viewed themselves as the "great engineers" of the world and, being French, quite invincible.

The creation of the Suez Canal was a phenomenal achievement, in its day the equivalent of landing a man on the moon. But Suez had been a sea level canal. It involved excavating a channel for water across a desert. Panama would prove quite different.

As we mentioned the idea of a canal across Panama had been around since the earliest Spanish explorers. Riding on the success of Suez, and sensing the time was right for a canal across Panama, in 1876 the French sent over a preliminary exploration team. Their report recommended a canal design that would include locks and a series tunnels. De Lesseps, already committed to a sea level canal, didn't like this idea and so sent over a second team in 1877. This team basically mapped out the route along the original Panama Railroad, which is somewhat the route the Canal follows today. They called for just one tunnel through the Continental Divide at Culebra.

Meanwhile, a concession to build a canal was negotiated by the French with Colombia, since Panama was then part of Colombia. The concession gave the French a 99-year lease without paying any compensation to Colombia and at the end of the lease the canal would revert to Colombia.

Sometimes people say, "I thought the US had a 99-year lease", confusing the French agreement with Colombia with the agreement the US would make with the newly minted Republic of Panama.

An International Congress was held in Paris to consider fourteen plans that had been offered for consideration. Only one of the engineers had any construction experience in the tropics, and he urged a canal that using locks. But de Lesseps, at the time called "the greatest Frenchman who ever lived", had organized the conference with only one purpose and that was to have his plan rubber-stamped. Before the final vote half of the committee walked out in disgust, but de Lesseps popularity managed to carry the day.

The resolution for a sea level canal passed with only eight of the remaining delegates opposed. The "no" votes included the engineer with the tropical experience who always said a sea level Canal wouldn't work and Alexandre Gustave Eiffel, of Eiffel tower fame. Of those voting in favor, only one, Pedro Sosa of Panama, had ever been in Central America.

* * * *

The French were big on ceremony and festivities, and so with great celebration the canal construction was begun. As de Lesseps was a trained diplomat and not an engineer, his son Charles took on the task of supervising the daily work. De Lesseps himself handled the important work of promoting and raising money for the project from private subscription. His boundless confidence and enthusiasm for the project and his consummate faith in the miracles of technology attracted investors.

* * * *

French equipment at work

The French had no concept of what they faced in the tropics. Disease such as malaria and yellow fever was rampant and nobody understood the disease or the cause. When the French came they loved all the palm trees and indoor foliage that was the decorating rage in Europe. So they decorated their homes with palm trees sitting in saucers of standing water, without knowing that mosquitoes were the cause of their illnesses. If you went into hospital you had a 75% chance of being carried out in a coffin. In hospitals in order to keep ants from invading patients' beds, the four posts of the beds were placed in bowls of water creating the ideal breeding ground for mosquitoes.

Machinery came from many quarters -- France, the US and Belgium. Equipment was constantly being modified and used in experimental combinations. A growing accumulation of discarded, inoperative equipment along the canal route testified to earlier mistakes. But most importantly, the technology simply didn't exist.

Each of five excavators working on the Atlantic side could remove 392 cubic yards (300 cubic meters) each day, but lack of spoil trains defeated their work. The equipment wasn't the right type, and was too small and too light. French bucket-chain excavators got caught and halted by stones and rock.

* * * * *

The Chagres could rise and flood in an hour, sweeping away men and materials. Isthmus is one of the wettest places on earth where rain can fall at what would be an hourly rate of 4 inches (10.2 centimeters) per hour. The French had no idea what to do with all the water flowing from the Chagres River. The US would come along and wisely utilize all of this water . . . and even to this day, it is the water generated by the Chagres River that allows the Canal to function.

It was becoming clear to nearly everyone except Ferdinand de Lesseps that a sea level canal would not work. Eventually and reluctantly he agreed to change, but . . . suddenly, there was no more money. The company was broke . . . 20,000 had died . . . and there was no canal.

The French failed because they were ahead of their time. The medical understanding and technology needed to conquer the Isthmus just did not exist.

* * * *

A "new" Panama Canal Company was organized, but with insufficient working capital, and a public that had soured on the idea of a canal, the idea was abandoned and the rights to build a canal were eventually sold to the Americans.

* * * *

Abandoned French machinery rusting away

California and Oregon had achieved statehood and there still wasn't a transcontinental railroad, so the US had an economic need for a canal. Additionally, President Teddy Roosevelt was trying to establish a US naval supremacy that would support an expansionist policy. A naval base had been established in Cuba in the Spanish-American War. When the battleship MAINE was blown up in Cuba, the nearest battleship was the OREGON up in San Francisco. It took the OREGON 67 days to steam from San Francisco to Cuba, just about the time the war was over. The experience clearly showed the military significance of an Isthmian canal.

Philippe Bunau-Varilla, chief engineer for de Lesseps, had managed to get his hands on shares of the new company and became a kind of spokesperson for a Panama canal. Congress was arguing between canal routes through Nicaragua or Panama, Just before the vote Bunau-Varilla mailed a letter to every Congressman enclosing a one-centavo Nicaraguan stamp showing Nicaragua's famous Momotombo volcano in full eruption. The stamp clearly pointed out the differences between the two countries; one with active volcanoes, the other comparatively stable.

On June 19, 1902, the Senate vote favored a Panama canal route by just eight votes.

* * * *

Once a route was decided, the US needed to get a concession from Colombia. US Secretary of state John Hay negotiated a treaty with the Colombian charge d'affaires, but this was turned down by the Colombian legislature.

Impatient to build the canal, Roosevelt supported Panama's independence movement. He dispatched warships to both sides of the Isthmus blocking sea approaches, conveniently just in time for Panama to declare independence from Colombia on November 3, 1903.

Philippe Bunau-Varilla, the guy who was now representing the French concession and at the same time claiming to be the official ambassador of this newly minted country, negotiated a treaty giving the US full rights and sovereignty over a 10 mile (16 kilometer) wide Canal Zone that split Panama in two. The new country of Panama had the choice to accept the treaty or have all US support for their new country withdrawn.

* * * *

If the Americans were to be successful, they had to control disease and death. Chief Sanitary Officer of the US Army Corps of Engineers, Dr. William Crawford Gorgas and his staff set up operations. Dr. Walter Reed, Gorgas' commanding officer, had identified the mosquito as the disease-carrying culprit. Gorgas, who himself had survived yellow fever and was now immune, knew that he needed to eradicate mosquitoes on the Isthmus before new workers arrived, became infected, and died.

Previously unscreened offices and houses got window screens and screen doors. Mosquito nets were distributed. Fumigation brigades, like the one shown below, went house-to-house spaying against mosquitoes in homes, cisterns and cesspools.

Clean running water was introduced to do away with the need for standing water containers in homes that could breed mosquitoes. Thanks to Gorgas yellow fever was completely wiped out in Panama with the last reported case in 1905.

Sanitation brigade in what is today Casco Viejo

Often when people are planning a cruise through the Canal they visit their local public health office or seek out a tropical medicine specialist. Then they come on the ship laden down with malaria pills and having received yellow fever shots . . . and gotten stuck with a $500 medical bill. Pay your money and take your choice, but yellow fever is not a problem in Panama and hasn't been since 1905. Malaria? Unless you are planning to visit a remote part of the Darien jungle, and I have no idea why you would want to do this unless are going to break bread with Colombian FARC rebels or visit the jungle lab of a Colombian drug lord, you don't have to worry about malaria. If you get malaria in most cases it is readily cured by the same pills you would take to prevent it. Hear out your doctor and make your own decision. But $500 is $500 and might be better spent on Panama tours or Embera Indian basketry.

The greater problem today in Panama and in South and Central America and the islands of the Caribbean is dengue fever for which there is no preventative pill or cure. So Panama is very concerned about controlling mosquitoes. But on the ship . . . in the Canal . . . you're not going to need any bug spray. The wind alone will keep you bug-free.

Do as you wish, and of course listen to your physician, but as for me, I wouldn't even think about taking malaria pills . . . and I live in Panama!

Malaria, unlike yellow fever, does not confer immunity, so you can get it again. Malaria was the cause of more deaths during the French and US construction periods than yellow fever. During the first year of the American effort, 1905, nearly everyone, including Gorgas, had contracted malaria.

Gorgas said, "If we cannot control malaria, I feel very little anxiety about other diseases. If we do not control malaria our mortality is going to be heavy."

Gorgas said that getting rid of the mosquito that carried yellow fever carrier was like "making war on the family cat," while a campaign against the malaria-carrying mosquito was "like fighting all the beasts of the jungle."

The task to eradicate disease-carrying mosquitoes from the Isthmus was almost as big as the task of building the Canal itself. Vegetation around houses and buildings was removed. More than 100 square miles of swamp was drained. Ditches were installed so water would not pool. Thousands of minnows were hatched and released and spiders, ants and lizards were bred and released to feed on adult insects. A mixture of carbolic acid, resin and oil was sprayed monthly in areas where standing water might collect. It was said by tourists who came to Panama to observe the Canal construction that the entire Isthmus smelled like an oil refinery.

Dr. William Gorgas   John Frank Stevens   George Washington Goethals

* * * *

John Wallace was the first man in charge of the US effort. Wallace tried picking up where the French had left off, but without a lot of support was frustrated and resigned.

Teddy Roosevelt's famous remark regarding the canal effort, after the US-supported, sudden creation of the Republic of Panama, was, "Let the dirt fly!"

The man who actually made the "dirt fly" was John F. Stevens, the second man in charge of the American effort. Steven's background was as a railroad engineer and his ability to design a railroad was critical. Virtually none of the equipment the French had left was useable. Everything that was needed for Canal construction had to be brought to the Isthmus and distributed efficiently along the construction line. Stevens completely overhauled the Panama Railroad, which would not only carry workers, materials and supplies, but also move the dirt and rock.

Later Stevens would comment, "This is no reflection on the French, but I cannot conceive how they did the work they did with the plant they had." Stevens built an efficient railroad operation to support the construction effort, in essence building a railroad from scratch with everything needing to be imported, including experienced railroaders. The size of the work force tripled in six months. To support this rapidly growing workforce Stevens built entire communities including housing, mess halls, YMCAs, hospitals, hotels, schools, churches, laundries and cafeterias. Communities were designed from scratch. Complex schedules were devised so that the work never stopped and trains carrying the spoil of rock and dirt were at the right place at the right time.

By comparison to the Americans, the French had used a primitive rail system. Stevens developed a complex system of railroad tracks at different levels within the Culebra Cut that would enable the spoil to be removed. The tracks could be moved as necessary so that the spoil trains kept pace with the excavation, thus enabling the giant Bucyrus steam shovels to keep working continuously.

It was Stevens who pushed for a lock canal rather than a sea level canal. Congress voted approval by a narrow margin, the margin being the difference between US success and a repeat of the French failure.

With all systems "go" and work proceeding efficiently and on schedule, in 1907 Stevens suddenly retired without giving any explanation other than that it was "personal."

* * * *

Frustrated by the loss of Stevens, Roosevelt decided to go to Panama himself to survey the situation on the ground.

President Roosevelt and party viewing Canal construction first hand

In 1907 Roosevelt went to Panama, the first president in history to leave the US while in office. He chose November, the worst time of year to visit, at the height of the rainy season, because he wanted to see Panama at its worst and understand the challenges faced. He visited the construction sites, talked to the workers and even had an early presidential "photo op" sitting at the controls of a steam shovel in Culebra cut which, ironically popularized the "Panama Hat" which were made in Ecuador!

Roosevelt came to view the building of the Canal as a mighty battle, pitting the US against the unbelievable challenge of building the path between the seas.

* * * *

Determined not to lose another capable leader, Roosevelt appointed someone who could not resign, then Lieutenant Colonel George Washington Goethals of the US Army Corps of Engineers, an Army man used to taking orders. Determined to give Goethals what he needed to get the job done, the President gave Goethals absolute authority, answerable only to the Secretary of War and the President himself.

Accepting the challenge, Goethals said, "I am no longer a commander in the US Army. I now consider that I am commanding the Army of Panama, and that the enemy we are going to combat is the Culebra Cut and the locks and dams at both ends of the Canal, and any man here on the work who does his duty will never have any cause to complain of militarism."

Goethals would never wear a military uniform in Panama, but in the end would become *General* George Washington Goethals. He was a West Point graduate who had previous experience not only with organization and command but with the "nuts and bolts" of locks and dams.

* * * *

The Isthmus of Panama lacked a population large enough to provide laborers for such a vast project, so Goethals assigned recruiting agents to scour the world for people to work on the canal. The US may have thought it was building the canal, but generally there were no more than 5,000 Americans employed. Almost all of the down and dirty workers came from the rest of the world. Like the French, the Americans looked to the nearest source of cheap labor, the Caribbean. Almost 20,000 laborers came from Barbados, representing about 30 to 40 percent of the adult men of Barbados.

Workers from Barbados arrive on the SS ANCON

Canal workers were paid in either gold or silver. US, mostly white, workers were paid in gold, and everyone else was paid in silver. (Any US citizen today would love to be paid in either gold or silver!) The pay car had separate windows for people being paid in gold and in silver. Thus began the distinction that ruled life in the Canal Zone and became a euphemism for racism, a highly stratified system to "Gold" and "Silver." Signs on toilets, drinking fountains, shops, and railway cars noted "Gold" or "Silver" which effectively was a nice way of saying "white" or "colored." Those paid in gold were all white Americans, and those paid in silver were all persons of color, including local Panamanians. A stated goal of life within the Canal Zone was to prevent "intermingling of the races". Most Panamanians working within the Zone were people of color who had menial jobs and quite naturally came to resent not only the system, but the US and the Canal Zone occupation.

Long after the signs were pulled down the attitudes within the Canal Zone remained. We have friends, neighbors, who have been in Panama for years. He is Panamanian, went to the US for college and fell in love with beautiful gal from Iowa. They married and came back to Panama where both worked for the US Army. Both are US citizens, but she is a white, blond-haired, blue-eyed, Dutch girl from Iowa and he is a Panamanian. Up until the 1977 treaty, if they went to shop in the "PX" or military store in the Canal Zone, she was allowed in, but he was not, even although they were married and both worked for the US Army. Problem was that he was a person of color, number one, and a Panamanian, number two.

That gives you some idea of the feelings of resentment that Panamanians felt about the Canal Zone. And it helps you understand what was behind US President Jimmy Carter's statement, at the turnover of the Canal at the turn of the Century,

"We didn't understand clearly enough the feeling of many Panamanians that the arrangement implied an element of colonialism and subjugation and not an equal representation . . ."

* * * *

SS ANCON making the first Panama Canal Transit

The Panama Canal cost Americans around $375 million, including the $10 million paid to Panama and the $40 million paid to the French company. It was the single most expensive construction project in US history to that time. Amazingly, unlike any other such project on record, the American canal had cost less than estimated, with the final figure some $23 million below the 1907 estimate, in spite of landslides and a design change to a wider canal.

Goethals watched the first transit from his private train along the shoreline

Plans for a grand celebration of the opening of the Panama Canal were abruptly put on hold by World War I. A tug boat festooned with flags made its way through the Canal, and then on August 15, 1914 the Canal opened with the ANCON making the first official transit.

Unlike any other government project, the Canal finished under budget, ahead of schedule, and without scandal.

By July 1, 1914, a total of 238.8 million cubic yards (about 36.5 million cubic meters) had been excavated during the American construction era. Together with some 30 million cubic yards (about 4.6 million cubic meters) excavated by the French, this gives a total of around 268.8 cubic yards (about 41.1. million cubic meters) or more than four times the volume originally estimated for de Lesseps' sea level canal. It is said that if de Lesseps had pursued his original idea of a sea level canal, he would still be digging!

The greater cost was in the cost of human lives. Hospital records during the US construction era record 5,609 lives were lost from disease and accident. The estimate for the French era is 20,000, although because people were dying so rapidly accurate records weren't kept. It is likely that the number of people who died during the 10 years of the French effort far exceeds the estimate of 20,000. Adding deaths during the French and the US eras brings the total to over 25,000. However, the true number is probably far greater since the French only recorded the deaths that occurred in hospital.

As you make your way through the Canal a sober fact to ponder is that almost 500 people died for every mile of the Panama Canal.

Engraved in the rotunda of the Panama Canal Administration building are these words of Theodore Roosevelt:

"It is not the critic who counts, not the man who points out how the strong man stumbled, or where the doer of deeds could have done them better. The credit belongs to the man who is actually in the arena; whose face is marred by dust and sweat and blood; who strives valiantly, who errs and comes short again and again; who knows the great enthusiasms, the great devotions, and spends himself in a worthy cause; who, at the best, knows in the end the triumph of high achievement; and who, at the worst, if he fails, at least fails while daring greatly, so that his place shall never be with those cold and timid souls who know neither victory nor defeat."

David McCullough in his book THE PATH BETWEEN THE SEAS writes:

"The creation of a water passage across Panama was one of the supreme human achievements of all time, the culmination of a heroic dream of over four hundred years and of more than twenty years of phenomenal effort and sacrifice . . . Primarily the canal is an expression of that old and noble desire to bridge the divide, to bring people together. It is a work of civilization."[8]

* * * *

9:55 am Cruising Gaillard Cut and Gatun Lake

The biggest challenge of building a Canal was getting ships through the continental divide in the middle of the Isthmus of Panama. The lowest point was a "saddle" between what is now called Gold Hill on the east and Contractors Hill on the west. To complete the Canal it was necessary to somehow get over, under or through this mountain.

The Canal builders decided to cut an 8.75 mile (14.1 kilometer) stretch through the Continental Divide from Gamboa to the little town of Pedro Miguel on the South. Ships would be lifted up to the level of a newly created lake and then sail across the Isthmus 85 feet (26 meters) above sea level. To get the ships through the Continental Divide the cut through the mountain would have to take it from 210 feet (64 meters) to 40 feet (12.2 meters) above sea level.

Holes were drilled and filled with explosives to loosen the dirt and rock. Gigantic steam shovels would pile the spoil on railroad cars that would haul it away to fill or dump sites. This is where the railroad system designed by John L. Stevens would prove essential. Wooden flatcars, each carrying 19 cubic yards (69.6 cubic meters) of spoil, would be pulled by long trains to the designated dump sites. Stevens had designed a unique rail car where the sides could be dropped and a huge scoop dragged along the line of cars that efficiently pushed the spoil off both sides as it was winched along.

---

[8] David McCullough, THE PATH BETWEEN THE SEAS.

Canal workers pause for a photograph

More than 100 million cubic yards (about 76.5 million cubic meters) of spoil had to be hauled away from the excavation site and dumped. Part of the spoil was used to link four small islands on the Pacific side to create a breakwater which is today known as the Amador Peninsula running over three miles out into the Pacific. Spoil was also used as fill to create the town of Balboa and what became the Fort Amador military reservation.

* * * * *

The unstable nature of the geology of Culebra and the frequency of heavy rains in Panama made earth slides a constant threat to Canal builders. During the French era land slides would sweep away both machinery and people burying both under tons of earth. On October 4, 1907 after several days of heavy rain 500,000 cubic yards (382,277 cubic meters) of material slid into the cut and the slide continued for ten days moving an average of 14 feet (4.3 meters) every 24 hours.

The worst slide happened on the east side of Gold Hill when the mountain slid covering a 75-acre (30.4 hectare) area, destroying buildings in Culebra village and requiring the removal of some 10 million cubic yards (7,645,540 cubic meters) of material. Another Gold Hill slide required removal of some 7 million cubic yards (5,351,884 cubic meters) of material.

The genius behind the massive Culebra excavation was a young engineer, David Gaillard, a graduate of the United States Military Academy at West Point. Goethals brought Gaillard with him and put the young engineer in charge of the Culebra Cut excavation.

The cut was the most difficult part of the construction taking nine years to excavate, during which 100 million tons of rock were removed and the mountain was cut down from 210 feet (64 meters) to 40 feet (12.2 meters)

Gaillard was evacuated from Panama in 1913 with what was thought to be nervous exhaustion. In fact it was a brain tumor and Gaillard died nine months before the opening of the Panama Canal. In recognition of his achievement Culebra Cut was renamed in his honor.

Outside the Miraflores Visitor Center is a memorial plaque to David Gaillard and the men who did the "impossible".

Memorial plaque outside Miraflores Visitor Center

* * * *

Centennial Bridge, built to celebrate the 100th anniversary of the Republic of Panama, was dedicated in 2004. It is the second bridge across the Panama Canal joining the continents. The bridge crosses Gaillard Cut just before the Pedro Miguel locks. The opening of the bridge to traffic was delayed until 2005 while the US and Panama argued about who was responsible to clean up the cache of poisonous gas canisters and other weapons that the US had left buried near the bridge site.

Centennial is a cable-stayed bridge with a total span of 3,451 feet (1,052 meters). The main span is 1,051 feet (320 meters) and clears the canal by 262 feet (80 meters). The supporting towers are 604 feet (184 meters) high. The bridge clears the Canal by 262 feet (80 meters), allowing large vessels and even "Titan", Hitler's giant floating crane, to pass under the bridge.

The west tower of the bridge is set back about 164 feet (50 meters) to allow for future widening of the Canal.

Passing underneath Centennial Bridge

* * * *

The two remaining parts of Culebra Mountain are now called, on the starboard or right side, Gold Hill, and on the port or left side, Contractor's Hill.

You will see what is left of Gold Hill rising 662 feet (201.8 meters) above sea level atop a sheer cliff, its side blasted away for the Canal. Gradually over the years to control erosion and slides the hill has been whittled away.

Why "gold" hill? Turns out the overeager and over optimistic writer of a prospectus for the French Canal Company lured investors by saying "this mountain is full of gold and it is believed that the ore from this place alone will be worth more than will be the total cost of the canal construction." Well the prospectus was full of something . . . because there never was any gold. Not an ounce of gold was ever found but the name stuck.

Moving a mountain . . . cutting through Gold Hill

3D - Gamboa & Gatun Lake

On the starboard or right of the ship is a small bridge crossing the Chagres River. The bridge carries the Panama Canal Railway and one lane of traffic at a time.

One-way bridge where Panama Railway and highway cross the entry of the Chagres River into Gatun Lake

This river and its many tributaries upstream is the source of the water in Gatun Lake and the fresh water necessary to run the Panama Canal.

Upstream is another dam called Madden Dam that created Alajuela Lake. The lake is an important part of the Canal water system and is 250 feet (76.2 meters) above sea level. It can store one third of the Canal's annual need. Madden Dam prevents the possible torrential flow of the Chagres river into the navigational route of Lake Gatun. The water is also used to generate hydroelectric power, and to supply Panama City's freshwater. Its upper basin is covered by dense tropical forests and to protect it Panama created Chagres National Park in 1985.

* * * *

One of the fantastic opportunities when you visit Panama is the chance to actually go up into Chagres National Park and visit the Indigenous group of Embera Indians who live in the Chagres. To visit my Embera Indian friends who live in a tiny village on Rio San Juan de Pequini that feeds into Alajuela Lake, you go to Alajuela Lake where the Embera will meet you with a dug out canoe. You travel across the lake, then up the river through dense jungle for 45 minutes to visit their village. It's a fantastic, once-in-a-lifetime experience.

* * * *

Just after the tiny bridge across the entrance of the Chagres River is the entrance to Gamboa Rainforest Resort, a luxury destination resort located on the Panama Canal, in the heart of the Panamanian rainforest. The Gamboa Rainforest Resort is designed to provide a variety of educational and adventure experiences in addition to a luxury resort vacation.

The Gamboa Aerial Tram is a popular shore excursion and Gatun Lake fishing and kayaking tours depart from the Gamboa Resort.

* * * *.

When you drive from Panama City to Chagres you go through Soberania National Park, just 15 miles (24 kilometers) from downtown Panama City. The park was established in 1980 and is a strip bordering much of the eastern side of the Canal. In the protected area there are 105 species of mammals, 525 species of birds, 79 reptiles, 55 amphibious and 36 species of fresh water fish, so the park is an important wildlife refuge.

Among the mammals you can find jaguar, the white-tailed deer, neques, raccoons, sloths, ant eaters, herds of wild pigs and various species of monkeys.

Along that same road you come to a hillside cemetery beside the road called the Mount Hope Cemetery or the French Cemetery. This is the resting place of some of the workers of the Panama Canal from the French period, many of whom came from Martinique, Jamaica and St. Lucia. It is estimated that 20,000 workers died during the French era, but nobody knows for sure. The French recorded only people who died in hospitals, but people were dying so fast that many never made it to hospital.

A West Indian worker named Alfred Dottin recalled,

"Death was our constant companion. I shall never forget the trainloads of dead men being carted away, daily, as if they were just so much lumber. Malaria with all its horrible meaning those days was just a household word. I saw mosquitoes, I say this, without fear of exaggerating, by the thousands attack one man. There were days when we could only work a few hours because of the high fever racking our bodies – it was a living hell."[9]

Workers wrote their wills before leaving for Panama: a few had the foresight to bring their coffins with them from France.

* * * *

Gamboa is a stretch of the Canal where you will usually get to see the Panama Canal Railway in operation. Many cruise passengers opting for a shore excursion riding the rails of the Panama Canal Railway assume that they are following the route of the original Panama Railroad and will wind their way along the Panama Canal. One cruise line even hyped this excursion on their Internet site by saying that as you rode along you could "watch for monkeys and toucans."

First, the original route of the Panama Railroad is different than the route of the current Panama Canal Railway.

Second, the current Panama Canal Railway exists primarily to move shipping containers across the Isthmus and, although it occasionally provides glimpses of the Canal, runs mostly through jungle and not next to the Canal.

Third, about that rain forest and those "monkeys and toucans" . . . Yes, the animals are there, but being self-respectable animals they are not hanging around next to the railroad tracks and, even if they were, the train is whizzing along at 40 mph. You can "watch for monkeys and toucans" all you want, but don't expect to see any from the train.

The Panama Canal Railway runs over a little bridge that spans the Chagres River so often you will see a train on the starboard side of the ship as you pass where the Chagres flows into Gatun Lake.

---

[9] Matthew Parker, PANAMA FEVER, p. xxi.

William Aspinwall's initial plan was to combine his existing wooden paddle-wheel steamships with the Panama railroad as a way to get mail across the US before the days of a transcontinental railroad. But all that changed when gold was discovered in California. With a concession from Colombia to build a railroad, Aspinwall seized this golden opportunity and began work on the project.

The Panama Railroad would become one of the most expensive railroads ever built. With only 7 miles (11.3 kilometers) of track laid, the railroad was already doing a brisk business with prospectors climbing aboard the partially completed railroad. The stock soared on Wall Street providing $4 million to push construction ahead through the jungle.

The completed railroad was only a single railroad track running 47 miles (75.6 kilometers) following the Chagres River across the Isthmus of Panama, but when it opened in January 1855 it was the first transoceanic railroad sometimes enthusiastically referred to as a transcontinental railroad.

Although the railroad had cost $6.5 million, over $137,000 per mile, it turned almost an instant profit carrying prospectors and gold across the Isthmus. Over $700 million in gold was carried on the railroad between 1855 and 1867. But when the Gold Rush petered out and the first transcontinental railroad opened in the US, the bottom fell out for the Panama Railroad. Share price plummeted from $369 to a low of $52.

When de Lesseps arrived he snapped up the failing railroad at inflated prices up to $250 per share. The French paid $25 million for the railroad. When the US bought the French rights to build a canal they got the railroad rights as well. Since the canal followed the route of the railroad along the Chagres, it cost the US $9 million to relocate the railroad.

When the Carter-Torrijos Treaty turned what remained of the Panama Railroad over to Panama, the railroad was in poor repair and losing $4 million a year. Panama's aggressive process of privatizing many of the assets it acquired with the Canal turnover included the railroad.

Today the Panama Canal Railway is a very profitable operation moving containers across the Isthmus. Panama is the only place in the world where it is possible to transship containers in-bond from the Atlantic to the Pacific in under four hours. Often container ships have containers stacked too high to meet Canal restrictions, and so they can offload extra containers at one end of the Canal and by the time they reach the other end the containers are waiting to be reloaded. Because containers can be transshipped in bond, they can be sent from the Pacific port to the gigantic Colon Free Zone on the other side of the Isthmus.

A tiny part of the railroad operation is the one passenger train that runs in the morning from Panama City to Colon and in the evening from Colon to Panama City, mainly to transport business men who are doing business at the Colon Free Zone. When cruise ships are in port, the passenger train operates during the day as a shore excursion for cruise ship visitors. All of the rolling stock of the present railroad is refurbished old engines and cars brought in from the US.

Cruise passenger train staff singing for Dome Car passengers

* * * *

Dredging is a continuing operation in the Canal with routine dredging maintenance before the expansion program running about $150 million annually. Now, with the expansion, there is major additional dredging going on as part of the Canal expansion. As you pass by the little old Canal Zone town of Gamboa, on the left or port side of the ship, you will see the Panama Canal Dredging Division.

The lock leaves or gates for the Canal are made of steel and each weighs from 390 to 730 tons. The gates are hollow so that they can be floated out for repair. Nice, but . . . how do you pick up a 390-730 ton steel gate to be able to float it out?

Enter the cranes. The Panama Canal has had two giant cranes, the largest, which you see is named "Titan", and the smaller one, "Hercules".

The Titan floating crane is among the largest and strongest in the world. It was originally built by Hitler's Germany and claimed by the US as war booty. Titan spent 50 years in Long Beach, California before being moved to Panama in 1999. The crane can be floated into the locks of the Panama Canal and is used for the heavy lifting required to maintain the doors of the locks of the canal. It can lift 350 metric tons and is one of the "strongest" cranes in the world.

If the cranes are not in use elsewhere in the Canal they are docked at the Dredging Division.

Titan, the giant floating crane built by Hitler's Germany

* * * *

Just after the Dredging Division is a small dock used by the Smithsonian Tropical Research Institute. The Smithsonian Tropical Research Institution (STRI) in Panama is a bureau of the Smithsonian Institution founded in 1923.

A boat leaves here each morning to take day workers on the forty minute ride out to the island of Barro Colorado, where STRI maintains an international research center. Each afternoon the boat brings the day workers back to Gamboa.

Barro Colorado is one of the most interesting islands in Gatun Lake. Barro Colorado provides a unique opportunity for long-term ecological studies in the tropics. Every year the island is used by visiting scientists from academic and research institutions in the US and around the world. Additionally 38 resident staff scientists are encouraged to pursue their own research priorities.

* * * *

This afternoon we will be cruising about 23 miles (37 kilometers) miles across Gatun Lake to the entrance of the Gatun Lock complex.

At the time it was built, Gatun Lake was the largest man-made lake in the world. Today, Gatun Lake doesn't even make the top-thirty list man-made bodies of water. Gatun Lake has an area of 164 square miles (425 square kilometers) at its normal level. The lake stores 4,200,000 acre feet of water (5.2 cubic kilometers) which is about as much water as comes down the Chagres River during an average year. Which means if you emptied Gatun Lake, it would only take an average year's rainfall to refill the lake, which gives you some idea of the enormous amount of rain that falls in this area of Panama, something like 200 inches (5 meters) a year! So my usual weather forecast for the Panama Canal is that sometime, it's going to rain, even if just a few sprinkles.

One of the reasons why de Lesseps' plan for a sea level canal would not have worked was the tremendous amount of water that comes down through the Chagres River. Look at all this water! And you're only going to see a tiny part of Gatun Lake: remember it moves off into lots of little coves behind the islands. When it rains here . . . folks, it rains! Sometimes when it really decides to rain in Panama it's like someone in the heavens is emptying out oil barrels full of water.

What de Lesseps' sea level canal plan never anticipated was how to handle this enormous flow of water, rushing through his canal into the sea. Creating Gatun Lake not only solved the problem of not having to dig all the way through the Continental Divide, but it created a positive solution to the Chagres River water problem!

* * * *

Gatun Lake has a 1,100 mile (1,770 kilometer) shoreline. The lake is about 85 feet (25.9 meters) deep, but, as part of the Canal Expansion program with the new locks, the Canal will require more water, so Gatun Lake needs to be increased. One way, raise the dam, but . . . oops . . . the existing locks are then eight feet (2.4 meters) under water . . . so they are increasing the water in Gatun Lake by deepening the lake. And you will see as we go through the Canal work in progress as they are dynamiting the bottom of the lake and dredging to increase the depth. That will increase the volume of water as well as enable ships with deeper draft to get through the Canal.

One of the tours offered on cruises that stop in Panama is Peacock Bass fishing on Gatun Lake. Peacock Bass are not native to Panama but originate in the Rio Negro river basin in the Amazon. A renowned Panamanian aquarist and doctor was raising the fish in a pond for sale as an aquarium fish. In 1958 a flood wiped out his pond and the Peacock Bass accidentally got into Gatun Lake. The Peacock Bass have flourished and have become the dominant game fish in the Panama Canal. I've done the fishing tour and I've caught fish. Nothing like the 32 pound record, but it was fun.

Another tour offered on cruises that stop in Panama is a tour where you take a small motor boat and explore some of the little islands and many coves along the shoreline. In some of these coves the monkeys come down and jump on the boat for grapes. The guy who conducts one of these tours lives on a houseboat on Gatun Lake, so you go to his houseboat for a Panamanian lunch!

What you see as islands in Gatun Lake today are actually the tops of mountains that used to be here before the lake was flooded.

Many of these islands have been pretty much undisturbed for almost 100 years because of the Canal's policy, both during the US Canal days and today with Panama running the show, that all of the area around the Canal needs to been preserved as protected area to protect the rain forest and watershed that provide the fresh water necessary to operate the Canal.

* * * *

In our post 9/11 world Canal Security is a major concern. Whereas in the past the Canal's neutrality and usefulness avoided conventional threats, since 9/11 the "rules of engagement" are different. Now you have fanatical groups who aren't afraid to hurt themselves or to die in the process and are looking for spectacular targets of particular interest and concern to the US.

There are several avenues of protection for the Panama Canal.

First, Panama is neutral country and the Panama Canal is open to everyone.

Part of Panama's defense is the famous "Swiss strategy", a take-off of the phrase, "If you have them by the balls, their hearts and minds will follow." In this case, "If you have them by their money, their hearts and minds will follow." It worked for Switzerland and it is working for Panama.

Panama's second line of defense is the US. Many people do not realize that there were actually two treaties signed in 1977. The first treaty turned the Canal over to Panama. In the second treaty the US agreed to protect the neutrality of the Canal in perpetuity. Panama abolished the army after the dictatorship. It doesn't need an army.

The Canal uses an Electronic Data Collection System that requires all pre-arrival information to be submitted to the Canal in advance so that a risk assessment can be made and to insure that all international security regulations are followed. Cargo manifests, crew and passenger lists are carefully monitored and checked against US security databases.

Each year the US sponsors and finances "Operation Panamax", a security exercise that simulates an attack on the Canal. The exercise involves as many as fifteen countries in addition to Panama. Additionally it provides the US an opportunity to showcase military hardware for sale to friendly countries.

3E - The Atlantic Locks

1:15 pm Approaching Gatun Locks

Looking to the right or starboard side of the ship as we approach Gatun Locks you will see the massive construction project building the new Atlantic lock complex and approach channel.

As ships have gotten bigger the Panama Canal Authority has realized the necessity of enlarging the Canal. This is nothing new. The US began a program to enlarge the Canal and in effect build a "third lane" back in 1939. They started and actually dug channels which will become a part of the new expansion program, but WWII came along and the project had to be abandoned. The current Expansion or Amplification of the Canal is once again a "third lane" concept. The program consists of the construction of two new sets of locks - one on the Pacific and one on the Atlantic side of the Canal. Each lock will have three chambers and each chamber will have three water reutilization basins.

The Gatun Lock control house

The program also entails the widening and deepening of existing navigational channels in Gatun Lake and Gaillard Cut.

If you look to the starboard side you will see one of the major construction sites of new lock construction. The new locks will be large enough to accommodate even larger container ships than those now on the drawing boards.

The Canal Authority is not building a new Canal that will parallel the existing Canal, but another lane with the necessary approach channels. The present locks will continue to be used, but the new lock complexes will allow for larger vessels. All traffic will feed into the existing Canal route which is being enlarged and deepened as part of the expansion project.

1:55 pm Another team of lines men and another pilot is boarded

The new locks will be different not only in size but also in operation. Instead of the existing swing or miter gates, the new locks will have rolling gates which are easier to maintain. And the new locks will feature water saving basins that will recycle 60% of the fresh water.

For generations electric locomotives have been used to assist ships through the locks, but the size of the new locks would have required 12 to 16 mules. So . . . the mules will disappear in the new lock chambers. The size of the new locks makes it possible to use two of the existing tug boats, one at each end of the ship, allowing for a more efficient transit.

The existing chambers will continue to be used for smaller vessels.

The cost of the expansion program is $5.25 billion and it is scheduled to be completed by 2014 at the beginning of the Canal's second century.

* * * *

Since MV JUST CRUISING is 105 feet (32 meters) wide and the locks are 110 feet (33.5 meters) wide we have only a 2.5 foot (about .8 meter) clearance on either side of the ship.

Gatun is the last of the Canal lock complexes and consists of three chambers. The ship will be lowered 85 feet (26 meters) back down to sea level. By now you are an expert and know to watch for the row boat, the "bumpers", and understand the role of the locomotives and how water flows through the lock system and eventually out to sea.

2:00 pm Connecting to the mules

When it was built the concrete construction of the Panama Canal was the largest ever undertaken and the record remained until the construction of the Hoover Dam in the 1930s. Pedro Miguel was the first lock complex, completed in 1911, and Miraflores was finished in 1913.

Since much of the concrete in the Canal is now almost 100 years old, the Canal Authority spends a great deal of money to repair and replace deteriorating concrete. It is believed that within the Canal walls there are pockets of concrete which still have not completely dried.

Can you find the two little guys in the lower left hand corner?

If you look carefully at the picture above you can make out several figures in the lower left hand corner. The main culverts are 18 feet (5.5 meters) in diameter, the same size of the tunnels that carried the railroad lines under the Hudson River into New York City.

2:32 pm Inside first lock chamber and gate closed

By now you also understand why there are two sets of locks for the chambers that connect directly into Gatun Lake. In some catastrophic event where a ship's engines failed and the locomotives were unable to stop the forward motion, the second set of locks would prevent Gatun Lake from emptying.

* * * *

3:10 pm Passing to the second lock chamber

While in the second chamber if you look to the left or port side of the ship, in the distance, you will see Gatun Dam and the hydroelectric plant that generates electricity.

Gatun Dam is an earthen dam built across the Chagres River, constructed between 1907 and 1913. The dam creates the large artificial Gatun Lake that allows ships, once they are lifted by the Gatun Locks up 85 feet (26 meters) above sea level, to sail across the Isthmus of Panama. The dam, lake and locks are all named the honor the town of Gatun which was flooded in order to create the Canal.

Construction of the dam was itself a stunning engineering achievement, eclipsed only by the simultaneous excavation of the Gaillard Cut. When it was completed Gatun Dam was the largest earth dam in the world and Lake Gatun was the largest man-made lake in the world.

Originally there was a gap in the hills around the Chagres Valley of about 1.2 miles (2 kilometers). This gap was filled with material excavated from Culebra Cut and the Gatun lock site to create a dam 2,100 feet (640 meters) thick at the bottom, 7,500 feet (2,300 meters) long along the top and 98 feet (30 meters) thick at the top. At the normal level of Gatun Lake the top of the dam is 30 feet (9 meters) above the lake level.

To create the dam two parallel walls of stone were built and then clay dredged out of the river base of the Chagres River was pumped into the center of the walls to create, in effect, a solid core of natural material within the dam.

As you look to the port or left side what you see primarily is the spillway which regulates the flow of water from Gatun Lake down a concrete channel. The crest of the spillway dam is 16 feet (4.9 meters) below the normal lake level. The spillway dam has 14 electrically operated gates, each 46 feet (14 meters) wide by 20 feet (6 meters) high. These gates are used to control the flow of water and the height of water in Gatun Lake. The capacity of the spillway is 140,000 cubic feet (4,100 cubic meters) of water per second which is more than the maximum flow of the Chagres River.

Sometimes during the rainy season so much water is pouring into Gatun Lake that the lake needs to be lowered and the spillway gates are opened, which is a spectacular sight that always draws locals to watch. Should this not be sufficient to lower the lake, the culverts in the locks can theoretically release an additional 49,000 cubic feet (1,400 cubic meters) of excess water per second.

The dam contains some 22 million cubic yards (17 million cubic meters) of material, and weighs some 30 million short tons (27 million long tons). It covers 290 acres (1.17 square kilometers) of ground, and contains enough earth and rock to build a wall almost 5 feet high (1.5 meters) and a foot thick (.3 meters) all the way around the earth at the Equator!

A hydroelectric power plant at the dam produces power that in the US Canal days was just used for the operation of the Canal. Today the plant provides enough electricity for the Canal as well as additional power which is sold onto the Panama grid. Under Panamanian operation, the Canal generates significant revenue from the sale of surplus electricity.

* * * *

3:40 pm Passing to the third lock chamber

There are three places along the Canal where locals and visitors can get a good view of the action. Earlier we saw the Miraflores Visitor Center and the parking area by Pedro Miguel. Now on the starboard or right side is the Gatun Lock Observation Center.

If you look down on the starboard side of the last chamber, just after the observation center, you will see one of the huge old gears that were used to open the lock gates. Today the lock gates or individual lock "leaves" are opened by hydraulic arms each operated by a 15 horsepower motor.

Just below the steps that to the observation platform you can see one of the early locomotives built by General Electric.

* * * *

Transiting the Canal is more fun if there is another ship in the lock chamber next to your vessel, and it is the most fun when the vessel in the next lock chamber is another giant cruise ship.

Two giant cruise ships side-by-side in Gatun Lock

3F - Colon & Limon Bay

4:25 pm Exiting Gatun Locks – line handlers disembarked

As we make our way out of the channel, this is an excellent time to keep your eyes pealed along the banks and in the water for crocodiles. There are a number of huge crocs that hang out in this area that we frequently see from the ship. Canal workers going out into this area must be very careful!

Along the way you will see two very interesting channels branching off our main channel. On the port or left side of the vessel you will see the French Passage.

This tiny inlet is all that remains from the original French attempt to dig the Panama Canal, an attempt that cost over 20,000 lives.

On the right or starboard side of the ship, now bustling with construction activity, is the access channel for the new Atlantic Lock complex, formerly known as the US Channel. The Canal opened in 1914 but rather quickly folks began to realize that it wasn't large enough to handle all the larger and larger military ships. As we said, in 1939 the US began an ambitious program to expand the Canal, enlarging it and building a "third lane" of larger locks . . . very similar in concept to the huge expansion project now being undertaken by Panama. The US project began in 1939 but the effort was abandoned when the US entered World War II. The idea was revisited periodically but with price tags in the billions of dollars nothing happened. The US Channel is what remains of that attempt.

But the work isn't going to go to waste since the original US Channel is being used as part of the entrance channel to the new set locks.

* * * *

The huge port off the starboard or right side of the ship is operated by the Panama Ports Company, part of Hutchison Port Holdings, which operates 255 berths in 44 ports across the world. Hutchinson in turn is owned by the Cheung Kong Group, one of Hong Kong's leading multi-national conglomerates. This company also operates a port on the other end of the Canal at Balboa. And this has led to one of those crazy rumors, rampant in some places, including the US, that the People's Republic of China is running the Canal. Not so. Panama, not China, owns and runs the Canal. If you work in Panama you have to be Panamanian. But the People's Republic recognizes what hopefully are good investments, things like investing in US Treasury bonds . . . and investing in Panama's port infrastructure.

Keeping a sharp lookout on the bridge in the Canal

* * * *

There are two places cruise ships dock in Colon. Colon 2000 is a terminal used by a lot of Carnival Corporation companies. Home Port is used mostly by Royal Caribbean and has its own terminal designed to handle thousands of passengers embarking and disembarking.

Royal Caribbean has done very well home porting ships in Panama. Guests from Asia, Europe and Central and South America and even Canada can avoid the hassles of US immigration that they would encounter sailing from Florida. Guests from the US can begin their cruise right in the heart of the Caribbean and enjoy more of the southern Caribbean area. I predict in coming years you will see more cruise lines home porting vessels in Panama using Colon on the Atlantic side and Amador on the Pacific.

There used to be another port facility called Cristobal or Pier 6. This was a charming old port building that was built by the US in 1916 and used as a coal refueling station. Unfortunately containerized cargo is more profitable than cruise ship terminals, so Pier 6 was razed in 2010.

* * * *

The city of Colon is the second largest city in Panama. Colon was a very important area during the US Canal occupation and home to several major US military operations that provided a lot of local revenue and employment. Today Colon is home to the Colon Free Zone, the second largest free port in the world, second only to Hong Kong. It's not "duty free shopping" in the cruise-port sense, but a port where goods can be assembled, purchased wholesale and distributed by container loads around the world. Location at the "crossroads of the Americas" is one of the main keys to the enormous success of the Colon Free Zone.

Other than the Free Zone, and a few new hotel and shopping complexes, the center of Colon is a pretty depressed area. It was actually used in the James Bond film "Quantum of Solace" to represent Haiti . . . it's that bad. Although much of the city was burned during a Colombian civil war in 1885, and again in a massive fire in 1915, many of the surviving buildings still reflect the French style architecture of the Canal construction days. With some government investment and employment projects for locals, downtown Colon could be developed into a real tourist center.

* * * *

From King Charles V of Spain (1534) onward, many people have looked longingly at the idea of a Canal across Central America. Benjamin Franklin, one of the founding fathers of the US, was entranced by the idea of a canal. When Thomas Jefferson became US ambassador to France, he was interested in seeing a canal in Panama. Simon Bolivar chose Panama City as the site for his Latin American Congress claiming that if the world would have a capital, it would be Panama. Bolivar was passionately in favor of a canal.

At the time Panama was a poor region of Colombia, largely neglected by the mother country, except when Colombia needed to conscript troops. But Panama wasn't the only canal option. The Dutch were looking at Nicaragua as a potential site for a canal. Britain was also in the game. And the French had managed to wrest a concession from Colombia for a railway across Panama. But the French syndicate failed to raise sufficient funds for the railway and the concession was taken over by a New York businessman by the name of William Aspinwall. Aspinwall was already running a steamship service between Panama and San Francisco and a canal across Panama would greatly enhance his operation.

When gold was discovered in California there was a rush for people to get to California to make their fortune in gold. There were three ways to get to California: the plains across, the Cape around, or across the Isthmus of Panama. The Panama route was the quickest, but also the most expensive. Boats would come from New Orleans to Panama and men would get off at the little village of Chagres, located up the Chagres River, and fight their way across the Isthmus to Panama City where they would board a steamship for California. There was nothing more than a 21-mile muddy trail across the Isthmus. Chagres quickly became known as "American Chagres" loaded down with bars and brothels. It was the American Wild West in Panama. There was no law enforcement so everyone packed their own gun. More than a hundred prostitutes worked the tent town and drinks in the saloon in Chagres cost more than they did in New York City.

It was an ideal opportunity for Aspinwall to build his railroad. After looking at several options for the western terminus, he settled on a swampy island just off Limon Bay called Manzanillo. As work began on the railroad Manzanillo began to sprout a small town, which the company named Aspinwall after the company president. Fortunately the locals would have none of this, so a law was passed calling the town Colon, after Christopher Columbus. During the days of the US Canal Zone the area of the city within the Zone was named Cristobal (Christopher) and the old Panamanian area was called Colon (Columbus).

Colon in the day

* * * *

4:55 pm pilot disembarked and ship headed out to sea

As we sail past Colon toward the breakwater we bid farewell to our Panama Canal pilots.

Getting off with the pilots and the Ship's Agent in Colon can be "interesting"

The Bay of Limon is the huge natural harbor, 4.5 miles (7 kilometers) and 2.5 miles (4 kilometers) wide, that provides anchorage for ships awaiting transit.

The breakwaters that extend from the west and east sides of the Bay of Limon are themselves a great engineering achievement - 6 miles (9.6 kilometers) long, and 425 feet (130 meters) wide at the base.

The breakwaters were originally built to protect the Canal from torpedoes. When a ship enters from the Atlantic and passes through the breakwater it is headed due south, and if it is clear and the right time of year you can see the Southern Cross near the horizon dead ahead. Once a Southbound ship is inside the breakwater the vessel turns southeast to the entrance of Gatun Locks. Torpedoes went straight ahead, so if one was fired from outside the breakwater it would miss the Canal entrance.

Today the breakwaters serve a useful function of protecting the inner harbor against storms and protecting the Canal channel from silting and surf.

The mast lights marking the entrance to the breakwater are among the tallest in the world.

From Gatun Locks to the outer breakwater is 5.4 miles (7.2 kilometers).

Way off on the port side, in the distance there is a navigation light that marks where the former US Fort Sherman was located. And off to the starboard side, around the end of the breakwater, was another US installation called Coco Solo.

During the US Canal period there were 12-16 military forts and operations in the Canal Zone, including a jungle survival school where Indigenous Embera Indians were used to train troops, including the first US astronauts.

4 - Cruising Panama

If you are just in the planning stages for cruising to Panama and the Panama Canal, you should be aware that there are basically five different types of cruises to Panama.

1. **Cruises that only call at a Panamanian port**, either on the Pacific side at Amador (a/k/a "Fuerte Amador"), or on the Atlantic/Caribbean side at Colon or Cristobal. These ships do not go through the Canal or into Canal waters. There are options for a variety of shore excursions that will allow you to get off the ship and experience some of Panama, including taking a small ferry through the Canal.

2. **Southern Caribbean Cruises** that enter and turn around in the Canal, generally round trip from Florida. These enter from the Caribbean through Gatun Locks, doing a partial transit, discharge guests for shore excursions, then retrace their route through Gatun Locks to the port at Colon to pick up guests who were on shore excursions and allow guests who remained on board a brief stop at the port.

3. **Ships that homeport in Panama**, that is you embark and disembark the ship in Panama. Royal Caribbean's ENCHANTMENT OF THE SEAS was the first to do this, sailing roundtrip from Colon to Cartagena, Colombia; Santa Marta, Colombia; Oranjestad, Aruba; Willemstad, Curacao; and Kralendijk, Bonaire. I predict that additional cruise lines will offer this option in the future. Guests on this type of cruise can book pre or post cruise stays in Panama or stay independently in order to experience the Canal and some of what Panama has to offer.

4. **Ships transiting the Panama Canal** that just go through the Canal but do not actually stop in Panama or allow their guests to get off and experience Panama. Most of the spring and fall repositioning cruises that move ships from Alaska to the Caribbean just transit the Canal. Most of the big cruise lines operating in Alaska and the Caribbean have ships doing this itinerary.

5. **Ships transiting the Canal that stop in Panama**. Happily more and more itineraries are including the chance to actually see something of Panama. There are a lot of itineraries offering a full day in Panama either before or after the Canal transit day.

Now the dreaded "Which is best?" question . . . People ask, "Richard, which is the best itinerary?" And generally there is no "best". . It all depends on you and what you want out of your experience.

I wouldn't make the decision on cruise line loyalty alone. I'd study the itineraries carefully and see what itinerary really matches your interests. Almost all cruise ships transit the Canal during the day, so "daylight transit" is exactly what you'd expect from everyone. Look carefully at the kind support that is offered on board to provide you with background information that's more than just talking about tours and preferred shops, i.e. folks who do what I do.

I wouldn't make the decision based on price alone. A transit of the Panama Canal is the "trip of a lifetime" for most people, different from a week-long Caribbean get-away for sun and fun. Although price is obviously a factor, it shouldn't be the determining factor.

* * * *

The Panama Ports

Colon 2000 Pier

Amador or "Fuerte Amador" - Amador is the causeway created at the Pacific entrance to the Panama Canal, a long strip of land created by joining together a number of small islands. Although a dock is in the plan, at the present time ships anchor out and you tender to shore. The causeway divides the Bay of Panama from the Canal so offers fantastic views of the new Panama City across the Bay. A military installation during the US Canal Zone days, today the Amador Causeway is a favorite place for locals to jog, ride bikes, walk dogs, or just sit and enjoy the views. There are shops, restaurants, discos, a big new convention center, marinas, an outpost of the Smithsonian Tropical Research Institute, and the new Bridge of Life Museum of Biodiversity designed by Frank Gehry. It is about a twenty minute cab ride from Amador to downtown Panama City or the old French part of the city, Casco Viejo.

Balboa - Primarily a commercial container port on the Pacific side. Seldom used by cruise ships. It is about a twenty minute cab ride to downtown Panama City or Casco Viejo.

Cristobal - During the days of the US Canal Zone Colon (Columbus) was the Panamanian section and Cristobal (Christopher) was the US Canal Zone section. For many years cruise ships stopped at Pier 6, called "Cristobal". Pier 6 was an old, traditional pier, like ones you used to find in New York, and San Francisco. It was built by the US in 1919 as a coaling station. Unfortunately, since containerized shipping is more profitable for a port than cruise traffic, Pier 6 was demolished in 2010.

Colon – There are two piers used by cruise ships in Colon; Colon 2000 and Home Port. Colon 2000 is favored by cruise lines owned by Carnival Corporation. It offers some local shops and souvenir stores. In the same complex is a very nice Radisson hotel and Super 99, a big Panamanian grocery store chain owned by the current President of Panama. Home Port is a very new, functional terminal favored by Royal Caribbean and designed to embark and disembark several thousand people at once. Royal Caribbean homeports one Royal Caribbean ship and a vessel from its Spanish subsidiary in Colon.

Colon is not a city to walk around in and explore on your own. There is a lot of poverty and the accompanying problem of street crime. And there isn't anything to see in Colon. All the interesting stuff in Panama is an hour to two hour ride away from Colon. The easiest, safest and most efficient way is to take a ship's tour.

Colon is a commercial city, home to the world's second largest free port, the Colon Free Zone which does $21.6 billion a year in trade and exchanging wholesale goods. The Colon Free Zone is not a "duty free" shopping area for tourists. Colon is not designed for cruise tourism and even Panamanians don't consider it a safe city in which to wander about. Ships advise that you remain within the confines of the terminal facilities.

Hopefully the Panamanian government will get its tourist act together, get more jobs into Colon and use the locals to clean up the place and at the same time raise the standard of living in Colon. With remnants of French architecture from the French Canal era, Colon could be a charming tourist attraction if it were cleaned up. As it is, the James Bond movie "Quantum of Solace" used it as a Haitian look-a-like. What kind of "recommendation" is that?

* * * *

"Get off the Dam ship!"

This worked well when I lectured on Holland America. I even wanted Holland America to print up T-shirts reading "Get off the Dam ship!" You've come all this way, so why not see some of Panama?

There are about three major tour companies, and a few smaller ones, that serve the cruise industry in Panama. The name of the tour may vary from cruise line to cruise line, but most ships offer a similar selection of tours in Panama. Unfortunately few ships remain in Panama overnight, so generally you've got one day and a lot of fantastic tour opportunities. Folks always ask, "What is the best tour?" I generally answer that it depends on you and your interests: unfortunately you can't do them all.

* * * *

Here are some of my favorites . . .

If you are interested in CULTURE . . . definitely the **"AUTHENTIC EMBERA INDIAN VILLAGE TOUR."**

OK, this is hands-down my favorite tour. Why? The Embera village experience is so different, so unique and special to Panama.

The Embera people inhabited a wide swath of what is today Panama, Colombia and Ecuador long before Europeans arrived. Visiting the Embera Village at Rio San Juan de Pequini has been described as "something right out of NATIONAL GEOGRAPHIC."

The "best" and most "authentic" village in my opinion is Embera Puru which requires riding a 45-minute trip by dug out canoe (with required life jackets) across Alejuela Lake and up the Rio San Juan de Pequini to the remote village

Tour companies use about six different villages. This helps spread the "wealth" around while not overwhelming any one village. River levels vary depending on the season, so some villages up river are only available during the wet season. Each village has developed its own traditions, and while some may be more "authentic" than others, this is not a "show." These are real Embera people who live and work in the villages and are committed to preserving their culture.

These are warm, friendly, intelligent people who are committed to preserving a traditional lifestyle in a "second world" country that is rapidly moving toward "first world" status. After the Canal turnover much of the area that had been Canal Zone was turned into a National Park in order to preserve the rain forest which is essential to providing the water supply necessary to keep the Canal operating. Suddenly the Embera people living in this area where no longer able to practice their traditional subsistence way of life since, as a National Park, hunting and agriculture are outlawed. Today they make their living by sharing their culture with visitors and selling crafts.

Katarina and Erito – Erito has at various times served as "chief" at Embera Puru and directs their tourism program

Usually the chief of the village will give a welcome, translated by your guide, and explain about their history and culture. There will be traditional dances and music and the opportunity to sample traditional food such as delicious, freshly caught fried tilapia fish, fried plantains, and incredibly fresh fruit. You can wander around the village and view each family's selection of crafts for sale. The men carve a very hard tropical wood called *cocobolo*, and make beautiful animal carvings from a nut called a *"tagua"*, sometimes known as vegetable ivory. When *tagua* dries it is very hard and so is used to make buttons for clothes. The women make beautiful baskets from palm fibers with all natural dies.

When I lecture on ships I always hesitate to "oversell" this tour, but I can tell you that again and again that people come back from this tour, sometimes wet and muddy, and say things like, "Richard, that was the best shore excursion ever" or "That was the best experience of my life."

There are a couple of things to remember if you take this tour. First, take along enough money. You will see spectacular baskets and carvings at reasonable prices. Indians don't cash traveler's checks and they don't take credit cards. Second, by request of the Embera village chiefs, do not take anything for the children. No pens, pencils, notebooks, no quarters or dollar bills. If you want to help the family, purchase some craft items. The Embera want their children to know the Embera tradition of hospitality and not to become little beggars.

The Embera children will capture your heart

If you'd like to take some educational supplies, which *are* needed and appreciated, give them to the chief who will pass them on to the village school teacher.

If you buy a craft item from the artisan, I suggest having you picture taken with the artist. It will make the souvenir of your visit even more meaningful.

Anne Gordon is a former Hollywood animal wrangler who came to Panama to film a movie that was in part filmed at Embera Puru. She fell in love with one of the Embera men, married and they live in Panama City and do private tours to visit their families at Embera Puru. You can contact Anne through EmberaVillageTours.com.

* * * *

If you are interested in the HISTORY OF PANAMA . . . **"THE SHAPING OF PANAMA"** . . . or similarly named tour.

One of the challenges for cruise ship tourists in Panama coming from Colon is that it requires about an hour to drive across the Isthmus. The post-European history starts when Columbus arrived in 1503, stopping near the Bay of Limon and later up in the area of Bocas del Toro to repair his ships. In 1510 Balboa founded the first settlement on the mainland of the Americas at Darien in Panama. At the site of the original city of Panama, "Old Panama" or "Panama Viejo", there is a bridge, still in use, called "The Bridge of The King" that dates back to 1619.

Typically this tour travels from Colon across the Isthmus to Amador Peninsula, the peninsula joining several little islands that was created with earth from the Canal excavations. On the one side of Amador Peninsula is the Canal and on the other side is the Bay of Panama with incredible views of the towering skyline of the current, modern Panama City. There is usually a nice lunch at a restaurant in Amador before venturing to "Casco Viejo", the old French quarter of Panama City dating back to the French Canal days. Generally there is a 40 minute walking tour around Casco Viejo led by your tour guide. The tour moves on to Balboa, the heart of the old US Canal Zone, and usually stops at an Indian craft market behind the old Balboa YMCA, before returning back to the ship in Colon.

* * * *

If you are interested in PIRACY AND SPANISH TREASURE FLEETS . . . **"PORTOBELO"**.

Portobelo was founded in 1597 and was an important silver-exporting port and one of the ports on the route of the Spanish treasure fleets.

In spite of all the fortifications, many still standing, in 1668 the pirate Henry Morgan captured and plundered Portobelo.

Portobelo is also home to the statue of the Black Christ and its rich tradition which is celebrated annually by thousands of pilgrims.

The area around Portobelo is dominated by a West Indian culture and there is a lot of poverty. Sometimes cruise passengers complain when they see poverty or "trash in the streets". The reality is that not everyone in the world can live the same way folks do who take luxury cruises, and not everyone in the world is so compulsive about trash as North Americans and Europeans.

* * * *

THE FORT AT SAN LORENZO is another great tour for history buffs! Now a UNESCO World Heritage site Fort San Lorenzo is an outstanding example of Spanish colonial military architecture guarding the mouth of the Chagres River. Fort San Lorenzo was abandoned by Spain in 1821 when Panama became independent. During the California Gold Rush in 1849 it served as a camping ground for adventurers, particularly on the old town of Chagres below the fort and on the west bank of the Chagres River.

Unfortunately the fortifications at Portobelo and San Lorenzo are in poor repair, but it is hoped with the patronage of UNESCO that eventually they will be restored.

* * * *

If you are interested in the PANAMA CANAL . . . and can't get enough of the Canal . . . **"THE PANAMA CANAL EXPERIENCE"**.

This is particularly valuable for people who are just calling at Panama, either in Amador or Colon and otherwise would not have any experience actually *in* the Canal. It is also good for folks on a cruise that is going to enter the Canal and turn around without making a complete transit. You board a small ferry boat at the midway point of the Canal and continue through Gaillard Cut, under the Centennial Bridge, through Pedro Miguel and Miraflores locks, under the Bridge of the Americas and out to Amador Peninsula where a bus picks you up to take you back to your ship.

On the Panama Canal Experience tour you can reach out and touch the Canal walls

Going through the locks in a small boat is very different than on a giant cruise ship! You get a whole different perspective and really sense the immensity of the locks. You can actually reach out and touch the sides of the Canal from the ferry boat. The ferry is a ferry: it's not a luxury cruise ship by any means! They have narration, free soft drinks and water, local for purchase (Atlas, Soberana and Panama - Panama is my favorite!), and a simple, but good Panamanian lunch . . . definitely not like the buffet on board, but good.

* * * *

If you want to see WILDLIFE . . . the **"GATUN LAKE SAFARI"**. This tour is operated by a "gringo" (not an offensive term in Panama, just descriptive of expats) who actually lives on a houseboat on Gatun Lake. This tour used to be offered through the cruise lines. Now you have to book it independently and directly with Captain Carl at JungleLandPanama.com.

About 20 guests ride in small boats across Gatun Lake into some of the many little eddies and bays. This guy knows where the troops of monkeys hang out. When I did the tour we saw five of the six different types of monkeys and in several places the monkeys came right on the boat to eat grapes out of our hands. We saw caiman, iguana and sloths as well as monkeys. It is the one tour where I can almost guarantee you will actually see some of the abundance of wildlife living in the protected area that surrounds Gatun Lake. Lunch is served on Captain Carl's houseboat and if you like you can view and hold some of his pet animals.

Monkeys come right down onto the boat and eat out of your hand

The cruise lines are offering some similar tours with names like "Monkey Island" and the like. Gatun Lake offers a great opportunity to explore the rain forest along the shoreline and experience a little of Panama's wildlife.

* * * *

If you are a RAILROAD buff . . . the **"PANAMA CANAL RAILWAY"**.

The original Panama Railroad was opened in 1855 primarily to meet the needs of folks crossing the Isthmus for the California Gold Rush. It cost $25 in gold to take the train across Panama, or, if you couldn't afford that, $5 in gold to walk along the tracks. The railway pretty much followed along the Chagres River. When the Chagres was dammed to create Gatun Lake much of the original route of the Panama Railroad ended up under water. What you have today is a lineal descendant of that original railway. Today's railway exists solely to move cargo containers from one side of Panama to the other and is a joint venture between the Kansas City Southern Railroad and privately held Lanigan Holdings. Old Amtrak engines provide the power.

Dome car on the Panama Canal Railway

There is one passenger train that makes one run a day for locals and when cruise ships are in port provides tours for the ships. Cars are restored '60s Pullman cars and there is one dome car from 1938.

The run between Colon and Balboa takes about an hour, unless the tourist train has to pull over to allow freight trains priority. The route passes through stretches of rain forest (but forget seeing wildlife at 40 mph!), catches glimpses of the Panama Canal and some of the old Canal Zone buildings. If you are a railroad buff, or just want a relaxing glimpse of a little of Panama this may be a good choice.

Some cruise lines offer you the opportunity to ride in the glass-domed observation car. There is only one of these cars and it is usually sold out online long before the cruise departs. And the dome car is usually a lot more expensive. Is it worth it? It depends. In my opinion the view is the same from the dome car as from the regular cars. And it is a glass dome car in the tropics so it is often hotter in the dome car. Funny thing, people pay a whole lot extra to sit in the dome car and then complain that there are no shades to pull down to keep the sun from shining in!

Regular car on the Panama Canal Railway

So, unless you are looking for bragging rights or the other components of the dome car tour are significantly different, I wouldn't worry if you are unable to book a seat in the dome car.

There, I just saved you a whole lot more than the price of this book!

Be aware that this trip is usually sold as one way on the train and one way by bus. Since there only is one passenger train doing a one way trip allows more cruise visitors the opportunity of riding the rails in Panama.

* * * *

This is not to say the other tours aren't good or worth your investment, but these are the highlights and some of my favorites in various areas of interest. You will want to talk with the shore excursion people on your particular cruise for specific details applicable to your voyage.

Here are a few comments on several other tours that are often offered in addition to those above. The names of these tours may vary with cruise lines making the names sound more sexy and adventurous, but this will give you an idea.

"Fishing on Gatun Lake" – You generally go to Gamboa Resort, which is a lovely, luxury resort on the Panama Canal. You board a small fishing boat with generally four or five people and you have a delightful cruise around Gatun Lake in and out of little coves, often seeing birds, monkeys and iguanas. They will try and find a few spots where you can catch the famed Peacock Bass that entered Gatun Lake by accident during the US Canal Zone period. Usually a few people catch some fish which are then released. Ships won't allow you to bring your catch back on board. If you are a serious fisherman you won't like this tour, bit if you just want some time in a little boat along the shores of a beautiful lake, it's great.

"Gamboa Aerial Tram" - The area along the Canal where Gamboa Resort is located is part of the 55,000-acre Soberania National Park. The Gamboa Resort bills itself as an ecological experience and has a butterfly exhibit and even a demonstration little Embera village display.

The Aerial Tram takes you through the treetops up a hill to a viewing platform from which you get a spectacular view of the Panama Canal snaking its way through the jungle. You need to climb stairs to get to the viewing platform . . . think taking the stairs from Deck 5 to Deck 12 . . . so if you aren't prepared for the climb, you might pass on this tour. I've seen monkeys, agouti, coati, parakeets, Amazon parrots and toucans, but of course wildlife is wild and there are no guarantees.

"Kayaking on Gatun Lake" – Yet another tour that generally departs from Gamboa Resort. If you enjoy sit-on-top kayaking and just want a day enjoying the beauty of Gatun Lake and are looking for some exercise, this may be the thing. It is a group tour, so you will be with a group, and most cruise lines require operators to make you to wear a life jacket.

If your tour is departing from Gamboa Resort, there usually are some vendors selling various crafts including Embera baskets and carvings and Kuna molas in the lobby area of the Gamboa reception building.

"Rainforest Hikes" – There are a number of variations offered but generally these are relatively easy walks on relatively open pathways through the rain forest with a knowledgeable guide who will introduce you to the rain forest and point out various plants, including plants that are used for medicinal purposes.

The tour brochure narrative will read something like this, "Look for coati iguanas, sloth's, monkeys and other birds and animal life." The operative word here is "look" . . . not "see". You can look all you want, and you will probably see birds and you may see some wildlife. However, because most ship tours are going to be in the middle of the day, most self-respecting wild animals are curled up taking naps and not prowling around the jungle looking for tourists.

That being said, the tropical rain forest is an amazing ecosystem and Panama is one of the best places in the world to experience the rain forest first hand.

* * * *

I know I really shouldn't tell you this story, and not to in any way discourage you from taking a guided walk through the rain forest, and this really is an aberration, but . . . it's just too good to pass up!

When I talk about Panama on ships, and take questions, someone always asks about snakes. And, yes, we do have a lot of snakes, 127 varieties to be exact. But, not to worry, only twenty are poisonous. However, those twenty include some of the most venomous snakes in the world, including the fer de lance. Most of the really dangerous snakes stay away from populated areas, except, unfortunately, the fer de lance. The fer de lance can outrun a horse on an open beach and is an aggressive snake, known to even lie in wait in an area frequented by warm blooded animals.

When people ask about snakes I always tell them that you will be very lucky to even see a snake in Panama and your chances of getting bitten by a poisonous snake are less than your chances of getting struck by lightening. In most of Panama you are within 45 minutes of a government hospital that has antivenin so your chances of actually dying are nil.

After one talk a lady from Milwaukee came up to me and said, "Richard, I was bitten by fer de lance in Panama and lived to tell about it." I was dumbfounded!

"Really! How?"

You didn't hear this from me, but, the lady from Milwaukee took this rain forest walk. She was at the end of the line of guests when they stopped to hear the guide explain a particular plant. She felt something snap at her ankle, looked down, and didn't see anything but two tiny marks, which she assumed might have been insect bites. She mentioned it to the guide who told her she probably had just stepped on a twig.

By the time she got back to the ship her ankle was feeling sore and a little discolored so she went to the medical center. The ship doctor told her she probably had stepped on a twig, gave her some aspirin and charged her account for an office visit. By the next morning she was feeling worse and went back to the doctor, who charged her for another visit, gave her some more aspirin and told her she would feel better the next day. That evening, feeling worse and with the discoloration spreading, she went back to the ship's doctor for yet another office call. By this time she says, "He was looking at me like I was some kind of hypochondriac, gave me some more aspirin and said I'd feel better in the morning."

By the next morning her leg was discolored, the discoloration was spreading to her arms, and she had blood in her urine. She went back to the ship doctor, insistent that something was wrong and she was not leaving until he took notice. Finally, they did some blood tests (which they should have done in the first place), video conferenced with their medical people in the US and with the Centers For Disease Control and it was determined that she had been bitten by a fer de lance. At this point the ship diverted to a port where they had a medical jet standing by to evacuate the lady to Miami where she was in the hospital for two months recovering.

Wow! The woman was young, athletic in good physical shape, in her 30s, all of which contributed to her successful recovery. So it is possible to get struck by lightening, get bitten by a fer de lance, or even win the lottery! All very unlikely, but possible.

Sorry! It's still a great tour if you've never had opportunity to walk through a rain forest! I know some of you would love to see any snake in the wild, but that is very unlikely. Even herpetologists who visit Panama looking for snakes have a hard time finding them!

* * * *

"Old Canal Zone" – Generally refers to Balboa, which was the "downtown" of the old US Canal Zone, Ancon Hill which is where the officers lived, and some of the housing areas around what used to be Fort Clayton. Most of these places are now private residences, or offices, but it does give you the idea of how life was in the Zone.

The heart of the old US Canal Zone: Balboa Union Church, the only church founded by act of Congress; building donated by John D. Rockefeller

On this tour you usually drive by the Panama Canal Headquarters building and the residence of the head of the Panama Canal Authority that was once de Lesseps' mansion. This tour will usually stop at the craft market behind the old YMCA which is a very good place to buy Embera baskets and carvings and Kuna molas at pretty good prices.

* * * *

"Lock Tours & Observation Centers" – If you are transiting the Canal you, and not the folks at the two observation centers, will have the best view. There is no "behind the scenes" tour at the Canal: what you see is what you get.
The Miraflores Visitor Center has restaurants, a gift shop and a small museum. The better museum is the Interoceanic Canal Museum located in what was a luxury hotel built during the French canal effort, but unfortunately, no tours seem to go to that museum. The observation "center" at Gatun is just a raised platform. Frankly, if you are on a cruise that is actually transiting the Canal, you are paying top dollar for the best seat in the house, so I don't see the reason to pay more to go on a lock and observation center tour where the view won't compare.

View from Gatun Locks observation platform

If you're just stopping in Panama and won't see the Canal operation otherwise, and can't get a space on the Panama Canal Experience tour, this is a good choice.

* * * *

"El Valle" or El Valle de Anton is a mountain town about two hours from Panama City that is actually nestled in the second largest volcano crater in the world. Unlike the humid, hot climate of Panama City, El Valle has a spring-like climate year round with jagged mountains, lush forest and lots of flowers. Although I don't think it's as nice as Boquete, which is where I live, it does have the advantage of being closer to Panama City, so a lot of expats and retirees from North America have settled in El Valle. If you want to get a glimpse of another side of Panama, a trip to "El Valle" is a good choice.
* * * *

Quickie stops . . .

Some ships stop and only spend an evening in Panama. Frankly, it really doesn't give you much opportunity to do much of anything.

If your port call is just at **night in Colon**, good luck. Colon is not a city in which to wander around at night! Panama City is too far away. The highlight of a night in Colon at Colon 2000 Pier is a visit to a Super 99 supermarket, a chain incidentally owned by the current President of Panama, Ricardo Martinelli.

Amador is a tender port and the tender ride it at night can give you a beautiful view of downtown. **Amador, or Fuerte Amador** as some cruise lines like to call it, is an area of Panama City, but main part of downtown Panama or Albrook Mall are about a 20 minute cab ride. Casco Viejo, the old French area, is also about a 20 minute cab ride away, but can be an "iffy" area at night, despite the of clubs and restaurants that are springing up.

The Amador Peninsula itself can be a happening area at night particularly on weekends. But most of the clubs open late and run until the early morning hours. There are some restaurants with great nighttime views of the city. A favorite activity in Panama City is to stroll along the Peninsula at dusk and watch the city lights come on. The view of Panama City from Amador Peninsula is fantastic. The **"Panama City by Night"** tours typically give you a bus tour of a big, busy bustling city at night which I suppose is better than nothing and you do get a chance to see some of Panama City.

"Colonial Panama by Night" or the "Casco Viejo" – What is called "Casco Viejo" today was the Panama City of the French Canal era and the areas that weren't damaged in the US Invasion still have a French architectural feel almost like old New Orleans. The area is being preserved and restored and there are boutique hotels, craft stores, boutiques and trendy restaurants and bars. It's a wonderful place to visit and while it may not be an area for the uninitiated to walk around alone at night, if you are going with a tour you will be fine.

"Miraflores Locks by Night" is the chance to see the locks in operation at night. There aren't always ships actually in the locks, so it may just be the locks and Canal lit up. There is a lot of work going on the new lock complex at Miraflores and this work generally goes on around the clock with the construction areas lit up by huge lights. But if you are actually transiting the Canal, you will get the best view from your ship.

* * * *

Advance booking on line . . .

More and more cruise lines encourage you to book your shore excursions on line in advance of your cruise. This makes a lot of sense since you don't have to stand in long lines while on your cruise. However, sometimes tour information has changed between the time you booked on line and when you are actually on the ship. Sometimes the folks writing the Internet copy haven't a clue what the trip is really like. A lot of cruise lines now include video clips of the actual tour which is a big help and some offer a way for guests to rate the tour, assuming the legitimacy of the rating game.

Go ahead and book your tours online, but before the final closing date, the date after which there is no refund, attend the port talks and the shore excursion lectures and find out the latest information.

Most lines allow you to cancel or change up until the final closing date with no penalty. Some cruise lines even allow you to book more than one tour for the same time period. I think it's a flaw in some systems and often I've seen guests book three or four tours with the idea that they will wait until they get on board and then decide which reservations to keep and which to let go. So even if the tour you really want is showing "Sold Out", go ahead and ask to be put on a waiting list.

* * * *

And if you're the independent sort . . .

Yes, you can do your own thing, hire a taxi for $25-30 an hour, and be independent. It works well for some people and in some ports. But Panama being Panama, I think most people will do best booking one of the shore excursions from the ship. There are a lot of adventures available and a limited time. The tour operators are vetted by the cruise lines, quality controlled, are required to have insurance and operate safely and, important in an area like Panama City with tons of unpredictable traffic, the ship isn't going to leave until the last ship tour bus has returned.

If you do wish to book your own tours in advance work the Internet. There are several bulletin board sites for frequent cruisers (like CruiseCritic.com) where people share their experiences and recommend independent tour operators that they have used. There are lots of independent adventure tour operators who may be able to provide you with a more unique experience.

There are actually three "Panama Cities". Old Panama was the first Panama City. It was the richest city in the Americas until it was looted by the privateer Henry Morgan. In the fighting the old city burned and the citizens decided they would relocate and build a new city. Old Panama is a UNESCO World Heritage site and a very interesting place to visit. Unfortunately I don't know of a ship tour that visits Old Panama.

The ship tours do visit the second Panama City, known as Casco Viejo or sometimes "Colonial Panama." This is the picturesque city of the French Canal era is home of the president's residence known as the House of the Herons, the old opera house and the Ministry of the Exterior which houses the actual little house where Simon Bolivar called the Congress of Latin American presidents in 1826. The Church of St Joseph is located here where Panama's famous altar of solid gold is located. Most ship tours just drive past the church and I don't know of any who give you time to actually go inside and see the gold altar.

The Interoceanic Canal Museum is located in Casco Viejo. Great museum and again, a visit inside isn't usually on the ship tours.

The third "Panama City" is the contemporary city with its Singapore-like skyline of high rise towers and notably the new Trump Ocean Plaza with its sail-like profile reminiscent of Dubai's Al Arab Hotel and the Revolution Tower, derisively named "Screw Tower", which looks like a giant pile of CD jewel cases twisted askew and ready to fall.

Briant Dominici is a trained botanist, fluent in English, who does a variety of nature tours around Panama City. Briant does full and half day tours, and if you are embarking or disembarking your cruise in Panama, even offers a 9 hour tour to the San Blas Islands. [PanamaTravelTours.com] We've had several friends, including groups, that have used Briant. And Briant promptly responds to emails!

Anne Gordon, whom I mentioned earlier in addition to independent tours of her husband's Embera Village, also offers Whale Watching tours in season. [WhaleWatchingPanama.com and EmberaVillageTours.com]

There is a Hop On Hop Off bus in Panama City if you enjoy that kind of independent tour and you can book tickets online as well as pay on the bus. [City-Sightseeing.com]

If you are really twisted you could always just do your own shopping tour of Panama City's giant shopping malls, each trying to outdo the other.

Independent is fine . . . just be sure your driver or operator gets you back to the ship on time.

* * * *

Stuff to be aware of . . .

Accessibility - Please note outside of the US, Canada and the EU the concept of "accessibility" is virtually unknown. If you have specific mobility issues you will need to discuss those with the shore excursion folks on your ship. Most tours are not going to be suitable for wheelchairs or scooters.

Activity levels - For your own enjoyment and in consideration of your fellow guests pay particular attention to the tour descriptions and the amounts of walking and climbing involved. *Every tour is not for every body.* Know and respect your body and limitations. While others may admire your "can do" attitude, even when you suspect you can't, no one likes to have a tour held up or compromised by people who shouldn't have booked the tour in the first place. If you have physical challenges you may do best to book an independent tour: just be sure to inform the operator in advance of your situation.

Buses – The buses used by tour operators are good and often air conditioned, but may not be up to the standard you might expect in Europe or North America. Don't expect rest rooms on buses. (An important tip: don't always expect toilet paper in public rest rooms!)

Roads – Can be bumpy, particularly on the road out to where you board the canoes for the Embera Village Tour.

Guides - Panamanians often speak English like they speak Spanish . . . fast. So if your guide's rapid-fire Spanish-accented English is difficult to understand, just ask him or her to speak more slowly.

Rain – Panama is in the rain forest. It will usually rain sometime, so go prepared. It will be warm rain and it probably won't last all day, but it's a good idea to take along a plastic poncho. Incredibly the gift shops on most ships don't sell plastic ponchos even although the ship is visiting rain forest ports, so it's a good idea to pack an inexpensive poncho. If it rains your footwear may get muddy.

Mosquitoes and pests – The rain forest has more bugs than anyplace else on earth. Keep your eyes open and you will be amazed at the variety of insects. Sometimes there are mosquitoes although not nearly what you would expect. Yellow fever was eradicated in Panama during the US era of Canal construction and malaria isn't a problem except in some remote areas like the Darien and Bocas which you won't be visiting. What is a problem in the Caribbean, Central and South America is dengue fever. I recommend bringing bug repellant along but using it only as needed. Again, incredibly, the shops on ships generally either don't sell bug repellant or are sold out. Go figure!

Safety – Generally Panama is a very safe country. Like any city of 2 million people there are a few places in Panama City where you need to be careful. Colon is, in my opinion, not a city where tourists should walk around. As in any place in the world there are a few *"maleantes"* (good Spanish word for crooks) who prey on tourists. You can help by dressing down, leaving the crown jewels and Rolex watches (including the fake Rolexes since a potential thief may not note the difference at first glance) in your stateroom safe, and not flashing excessive amounts of money.

Sometimes tour buses will have police escorts. This is primarily to get tour buses through traffic and back to the ship on time. And sometimes a tourist police officer will ride along with the group on the Embera village tour (usually to talk with the girls!). Panama's special tourist police officers generally speak only Spanish . . . go figure!

Visitors always comment on the bars you see on windows. Yes, this keeps out burglars, but it is also a cultural thing throughout Latin America. It's a style, but it also makes a statement. Having bars on your windows implies that you have accumulated lots of valuable stuff . . . even if you haven't. In North America we stick up real, or fake, security service signs and put in security systems linked to the police department. In Panama and most of Latin America you put up bars or barbed wire.

Taxis – By law official licensed taxis must be painted yellow with a horizontal checkered stripe. Lots of folks with cars will make extra money carting folks around and maybe even offering tours, but only the yellow taxis are licensed. Panama is experimenting with metering taxis, but most are not metered and operate on a zone fare system. Like anywhere else in the world there are "local" rates and tourist rates. A local may take a taxi within the same zone for $2 and you may pay $5 to $10 for the same trip. Taxi drivers are the same the world over. Keep in mind that the hourly rate for a taxi in Panama City is about $25-30 per hour.

Trash – What amazes me all over the world is that North American and European cruise passengers may take tours to some of the most exciting and famous places in the world, and when they come back to the ship . . . they talk trash!

Culturally people's attitudes about trash differ. I have been in villages along the Amazon where are guests are focused on trash along the trail while the people who live there are focused on finding food for that night's dinner. Not everyone has the luxury of worrying about trash in the streets.

Cleanliness, neatness and order are very important cultural values in Europe and North America. What makes traveling the world interesting is that not everyone has the same cultural values. The reason why you visit far off places is to experience different cultures with at times different values.

You will see trash in some areas of Panama. Panama is aware of it and working on it, but it takes time to alter attitudes and traditions.

Unfinished houses – People often comment on all the little houses that are in various stages of construction. Most Panamanians build what they can afford and finish the project as they can afford it, building what they can't afford instead of taking out a loan and spending a lifetime paying off the bank.

The Canal from the Panama Canal Railway

5 - Panama 101

Twenty million years ago there was no Isthmus of Panama. The gap between the continents allowed the waters of the Atlantic and Pacific oceans to flow freely together.

Scientists theorize that around 250 million years ago there was a land mass supercontinent which they call Pangea. The theory is this supercontinent gradually drifted apart to form the continents we know today. This left the North and South American continents separated from one another.

The earth's crust is believed to be broken up into various tectonic plates which shift in relation to one another, shifting we feel as earthquakes. This shifting underground creates friction and heat melting the earth and producing magma which can escape upward creating volcanoes.

In the area in the Pacific, just off Panama you have three tectonic plates coming together, part of what today is called the Pacific "Ring of Fire." It's why we have earthquakes and volcanoes all around this Pacific "Ring of Fire."

---

[10] US Geological Survey

As the Pacific plates slowly pushed under the Caribbean plate submarine volcanoes were formed and some 15 million years ago these submarine volcanoes began to push above the ocean surface and became islands. Over millions more years the ocean flow carried mud, sand and sediment to fill in the gaps between the islands and an isthmus had formed between North and South America.

The Isthmus of Panama which joins together the North and South American continents became the "bridge of life". Scientists believe the formation of the Isthmus of Panama is one of the most important geologic events to happen on Earth in the last 69 million years. This bridge of life played a major role in the biodiversity of the world making it possible for animals and plants to migrate between the continents.

* * * *

When I lecture on ships I always ask the audience, "When I say 'Panama' what comes to mind?"

Generally I get the same set of answers:

Malaria
Yellow fever
Mosquitoes
Snakes
Money laundering
Drugs
Panama Canal
Noriega
Panama hats

It really sounds like a place you'd like to visit!

People labor under a lot of misconceptions.

For example, take **Panama hats**. Panama hats were popularized when Teddy Roosevelt, the first US President to leave the country while in office, came to Panama to see for himself the Canal construction. He wore a Panama hat in numerous photo ops which instantly made the hat a popular fashion accessory.

Only one problem: Panama hats are made in Ecuador, not Panama.

Noriega is a sick old man and ancient history. Noriega was arrested by the US over twenty years ago. We will talk about that period of Panama's history later, but Noriega, after serving his prison sentence in the US was extradited to France to serve a prison sentence for money laundering. In December 2012 he was extradited from France to Panama and currently resides in El Renacer Prison (interestingly meaning "rebirth") which is located right beside the Panama Canal just South of where the Chagres River flows into the Canal. It is a simple, nondescript Panamanian prison and Noriega has a simple cell with some accommodation made due to his poor health and to protect his security. Some of his friends and family would like to see him under house arrest due to his age and infirmity, but that is unlikely since he faces additional very serious charges and sentences already handed down for multiple murders, kidnapping, and corruption.

Panama Canal – Good! Especially for folks are plunking down thousands of dollars to cruise through the Panama Canal!

Drugs - Yes, a problem. Panama borders Colombia and has 1,547 miles (2,490 kilometers) of coastline and is right in the path between Colombia and the US which is the world's largest consumer of illicit drugs. This will continue to be a problem in Panama, Mexico and elsewhere in the world as long as the US continues its failed drug prohibition that provides the drug cartels with financial wealth sufficient to buy off almost anyone.

Money laundering is no more a problem in Panama than Miami or Los Angeles. It is far more difficult to open a bank account in Panama than it is in North America.

Snakes: we have a few. As mentioned when I was encouraging you to take a walk through the rainforest, 127 to be exact, but only twenty of these are poisonous. You have a better chance of getting struck by lightening in Panama than getting bitten by a poisonous snake. If you live in Panama the "snakes in the grass" you need to look out for are dishonest contractors and Americans on the lam from the law. Count yourself fortunate if you even see a snake in the wild. Of course it's the ones you don't see that can be problematic.

You always want to be the first person in the line walking through the jungle. First person, fer de lance snake thinks, "Damn it, here they come again!" Second person, "I'm really getting tired of this!" Third person . . . bam!

Mosquitoes: we have some, but not what you might think. This is not Alaska or Wisconsin in the summertime! If you are coming from a country where yellow fever is present, Panama requires you to have a yellow fever vaccination. Unless you are leaving the typical tourist areas and heading off deep into the jungles of the Darien or Bocas del Toro, neither yellow fever nor malaria is of concern. What is of concern is dengue fever which is a problem throughout the Caribbean, Latin and South America. Dengue is transmitted by mosquitoes and for this reason Panama is vigilant in controlling mosquitoes.

* * * *

Panama has been described as the "crossroads of the Americas" and even due to the Panama Canal, the "crossroads of the world."

Simon Bolivar was the great liberator of Latin America who is sometimes referred to as the "George Washington of South America". In 1826, at the height of his power, he convened a congress of Latin American republics in Panama City. The building where the congress was convened is enshrined in the Ministry of The Exterior in Panama City. Long before the construction of the Canal, Bolivar said, "If ever the world were to have a capital it would be Panama."

So what is in Panama?

940 bird species
10,000 species of plants
200 species of mammals
Mountain from which you can see two oceans
Rivers where you ride twenty sets of rapids in an afternoon
Greatest number of deep-sea fishing records in the world
Seven Indigenous Indian cultures
125 animal species found nowhere else in the world
Almost 1,500 miles of coastline

* * * *

Panama City from Ancon Hill

The Republic of Panama is a constitutional democracy with an elected president and national assembly, both serving five-year terms. As a result of its experience with dictatorship, both the president and vice president must sit out two additional terms (ten years) before becoming eligible for reelection.

The military was abolished after Noriega. Panama has no need for a military since in the second 1977 treaty turning over control of the Canal to Panama the US agreed to protect the neutrality of the Canal and ipso facto Panama, in perpetuity.

The National Police do have field uniforms that look like military fatigues, but they are police, not military.

Although called the Balboa, the Panamanian currency is in fact the US dollar. In 1941 Panama briefly, seven days briefly, printed its own currency. Subsequently these notes were burned and now are only collector items. Panama does mint its own coins which are identical in size and weight to US coins, and so US and Panamanian coins are used interchangeably. If you end up with Panamanian coins, not to worry, they work fine in US vending machines! Because of the short life span of paper dollar bills and the high cost of shipping old currency back to the US, the Panamanian government has issued a one Balboa coin that is equal to the US dollar.

Because Panama's currency is the US dollar it has been very attractive to investors who like the security of the US dollar. There are over 100 international banks in Panama. 70% of the economy is service based, which includes the Panama Canal. Panama is second only to Hong Kong in the number of offshore registered companies. The Colon Free Zone is the second largest free zone in the world.

Tocumen International Airport is the busiest airport in Central America and one of the most modern and technologically advanced airports in Central and South America. The airport is the home of Panama's Copa Airlines, and is a hub for flights to the Caribbean, North and South America, and, increasingly, Europe. International travelers discouraged by security delays in the US, are increasingly choosing to connect through Panama.

Panama is increasingly being called the "Singapore of Latin America" and has enjoyed a booming economy with GDP growth of 8-12% a year before the world economic collapse. Even post-collapse, Panama has had 5-12% GDP growth when some countries were having negative GDP growth. While the ratings of other countries' bonds have been lowered, the rating of Panama's bonds has been increasing.

The current President is a tough-talking, non-nonsense businessman who owns the major supermarket chain in Panama. In his inaugural address, US-educated President Ricardo Martinelli said, "In my administration it's OK to put your foot in your mouth, but not to put your hand in the till." Quite a change in Panama! When a shirt-tail relative was arrested in another Central American country in a drug sting, Martinelli personally met the plane at the airport to put on the handcuffs.

With a $5.25 billion Panama Canal expansion underway, numerous Dubai-like towers, a new subway system under construction, a total traffic redesign underway, a proposed $4 billion copper mining project and the possibility of a $9 billion Qatar oil refinery in Chiriqui province, Panama is on an economic roll. All of this has happened since the overthrow of Noriega. And all of this in a country of 3.3 million people, 2 million of whom live in and around Panama City.

Additionally Panama has become one of the top international retirement destinations in the world. Baby boomer retires are lured by a lush, tropical environment, low cost of living, easy access to the rest of the world, easy permanent residence for pensioners, the US dollar, and a neutral country with warm relations with the US and the rest of the world.

* * * *

One of the great things about Panama is that there are seven living Indigenous cultures who have been here since before Columbus arrived. It's estimated that there may have been over 1 million Indigenous inhabitants at the time the Spanish arrived.

East of what is the Panama Canal the Kuna lived on the San Blas islands and along the Caribbean coast. The Chocoes, more correctly known as the Embera and Wounaan, lived in the jungles stretching into what is today as Panama, Colombia and Ecuador. To the west were the Guaymies, or as they prefer to be known today the Ngobe Bugle, and the smaller groups of Teribes and Bokotas.

Traditionally in Panama the Indigenous were at the bottom of the totem pole, looked down on by the white European conquerors and their ancestors. Military strongman Omar Torrijos empowered the Indigenous and today both the Ngobe Bugle and Kuna control their traditional lands as autonomous territories and are a political force with which to be reckoned.

The Embera and Wounaan by nature live in small communities stretched out over immense rainforests stretching today over three countries. There is a movement amongst the Embera and Wounaan to achieve more autonomy and political clout.

Fortunately today the Indigenous in Panama have been discovered by tourists and the result is that the country as a whole is learning to appreciate Indigenous people and their contributions and working to aid them in preserving their lifestyles.

* * * *

The Kuna people live primarily along the Caribbean coast of Panama east of the Canal and on the low-lying San Blas Islands. Many live and work in Panama City and the women are easily recognizable because of their unique costumes and the rows of beads they wear on their forearms and legs.

Kuna Yala has its own political organization and the flag of Kuna Yala, with its swastika-like symbol of good luck, was around long before Hitler was born. The Kuna are monogamous. Their traditional beliefs have been mixed into religions like Christianity that were brought in by various missionary groups.

Few cruise ships actually call in the San Blas Islands due to the fact that the powerful Kuna General Congress feared that their traditional society and culture was being negatively influenced by all of the cruise ships and, maybe more importantly, the Kuna chiefs felt they weren't getting a share of the pie.

Subsistence agriculture and fishing has traditionally been the base of the Kuna economy. Today many are involved in producing the beautiful and colorful molas for tourists.

Kuna woman displays her molas

"Mola" in Kuna means "cloth", so a mola can be any piece of cloth. Traditionally the Kuna have made brightly colored and complex designs out of cloth. The cloth is not cut with scissors, but ripped, and then turned under and sewn into the pattern. You will find Kuna molas for sale all over Panama City and maybe even by the shops on board. Like any piece of artwork, prices vary wildly according to the beauty, complexity and quality of the work. When shopping for a mola you want to turn it over and look at the quality of the hand stitchery on the back side of the piece.

* * * *

The other groups you are likely to meet around Panama City are the Embera and Wounaan, particularly if you opt to take the Embera Village shore excursion.

---

[11] GNU Free Documentation License, Version 1.2

Both the Embera and Wounaan come from the same genetic stock, but have developed different languages and slightly different cultural traditions over the centuries. Most of the Choco people you meet will be Embera.

Embera villages are small, generally under 150 people, and are usually grouped around one or two main families. If there is discord in a village the odd man out simply leaves and goes off to form another village.

Zueleka, Katerina and Erito, our Embera friends from Embera Puru in front of their house – Erito has a lot fewer problems with his house than I do with mine!

Traditionally the Embera are hunters and gatherers, hunting in the jungle using blow guns, fishing underwater with spears, and growing basic crops such as corn, rice and yucca. Typically villages are located near rivers and the *piragua* or *cayuco* boats made from hollowed out logs provide transportation. Embera are monogamous with young people traditionally finding mates from other nearby villages. Many are nominally Catholic with heavy intermixing of native beliefs.

Houses are raised for protection from jungle animals and flooding rivers and are made of palm and natural fibers. The sides are usually wide open except during the windy season.

Traditionally Embera women wore only a bright colored skirt that originally was made from tree bark. Today the Embera tribe sends traditional designs to Japan to be made into special fabric for dresses. These are, in effect, limited editions, so if when you visit a village and you see a woman with a rack of brightly colored cloth in her house, she is showing off her collection of limited editions.

Traditionally men wore loin clothes, but today, except when there are visitors with whom they want to share their traditions, the guys just wear shorts. Older women dress in the accepted, traditional Embera way, i.e. "topless." Young, rebellious women may dress more Western wearing tops.

It's all cultural folks!

People always ask me how I came to live in Panama and "Why Panama?" If you want the complete answer you'll have to go to Amazon and get my book ESCAPE TO PARADISE: LIVING AND RETIRING IN PANAMA.

The short version is I was on a cruise nine years ago that stopped in Gatun Lake. My wife wanted to take the Embera Village tour but I opted just to go ashore at the "Gatun Lake Yacht Club", which as long as I've been doing the Canal has never had any kind of boat, let alone a "yacht." But I met these Embera guys whose wives were selling baskets. One of these, Erito, and I got talking so I started buying beer . . . four hours of beer drinking later, when my wife returned from the village tour, Erito, his brothers and I were old friends. They kept telling me they wanted me to visit their village and so when I went back to California I scoured the Web for information on the Embera and in the process discovered all of the benefits of retiring in Panama . . . and here we are!

What does this all have to do about "topless" Embera women? During our beer drinking, Erito's younger brother gave me the gift of a bead necklace. With nothing else to give him, I gave him the T-shirt off my back, whereupon he said, "I can't wait to get back to the village so I can put my girlfriend (a beautiful, bare-breasted 16-year-old standing nearby) in the T-shirt so she will look sexy like American girls." Pity me: I had to explain that in America we try to get the T-shirt *off* the girl!

Like I said, it's all cultural!

The Embera are fantastic artisans fashioning beautiful baskets using all natural palm fibers and natural dies. The women make the baskets and the men are the carvers. Beautiful carvings are made out of the super hard *cocobolo* wood. The *tagua* nut, known as vegetable ivory, is carved into forms of frogs, birds, fish and animals.

The Embera are warm and wonderful people and if you have the opportunity pay them a visit. If you visit the village and want to help, buy some craft work. At the request of the village elders, please do not give anything (money, pencils, candy, etc.) to the children. The Embera chiefs want the children to learn to be gracious hosts and not beggars.

* * * *

The largest Indigenous group is the Guaymies or, as they prefer to be called, Ngobe Bugle. They are the only group in Panama who were able to fight off the early Spanish explorers and settlers.

Today the Ngobe Bugle are most heavily concentrated in Chiriqui, Veraguas and Bocas. They are an agricultural people growing rice, corn, bananas, yucca, fruits and breeding domestic animals like cattle, pigs and poultry. They are the backbone of Panama's agricultural economy.

Traditionally the Ngobe Bugle have been polygamous with the man as the very strong head of the household. (Although increasingly many of the men I talk to assure me that one wife is "more than enough.") In some traditional Ngobe Bugle families, although the husband spoke both the native language and Spanish, the women were not allowed to learn Spanish. The influence of European Panamanian culture and very fluid family structure is leading more to a kind of serial monogamy of sorts (like in North America and Europe) where the children are looked upon almost as the children of "the village".

Our Ngobe Bugle neighbors – Melida has picked coffee for us as long as we've had our coffee farm

The Ngobe Bugle have been heavily influenced by Christianity in this officially Roman Catholic country, but their Christianity is often an interesting mix of Indigenous tradition, Christianity and spiritualism.

The Ngobe Bugle women dress in traditional, bright-colored, hand sewn dresses. They use a various plant fibers died with vegetable dies to create *"chacaras"* or bags which are used for everything from purses to baby bags. The *"chaquira"* is an elaborate wide bead necklace with multicolored geometric designs that is made by the women, traditionally for the men to wear on ceremonial occasions.

* * * *

The Bokatas, Bibi and Teribes are very small Indigenous tribal groups living mostly in the area around Bocas del Toro on the westernmost end of Panama.

* * * *

Panama's greatest treasure is her people. Panama historically has been the "crossroads of the world" and so people have come and settled in Panama from all over, resulting in an interesting mix of cultures, races and traditions and widespread tolerance and acceptance.

6. The Big Ditch

In 1847 William H. Aspinwall and a group of investors acquired rights to transport mail for the US from the Isthmus of Panama to California. They founded the Pacific Mail Steamship Company and constructed boats for this purpose, as well as to transport agricultural goods between Panama and California.

Although they didn't know it at the time, their timing couldn't have been better.

In 1847 gold was discovered at Sutter's Mill in Colima, California and the rush was on. Over the next seven years some 300,000 people flocked to California seeking their fortune. Of that 300,000 half would arrived by sea with most of those by sea coming by way of Panama.

There were three ways to get to California:

"The Plains Across" – the exhausting and at times dangerous journey across the American continent;

"The Horn Around" – the long, arduous journey by boat around the Southern tip of South America;

"The Isthmus Over" – by boat to Chagres, Panama, then slog across the Isthmus and board a boat in Panama City bound for San Francisco.

Although it was the more expensive way, "The Isthmus Over" was the fastest way, and this was, after all a Gold RUSH.

Rather than spend 112 days sailing "Around The Horn" people opted to sail to Chagres, which almost overnight became a rowdy shanty boom town. From Chagres they would have to follow the same path the Spaniards and pirates had used across the Continental Divide to reach Panama City where they would board another ship bound for San Francisco. It could take a week or more to slog through the jungle across the Isthmus.

Aspinwall's first ship, the CALIFORNIA, was launched in 1848 and made it's way down around the Horn to Panama City intending to carry mail and supplies from Panama to San Francisco. When it arrived in Panama it was mobbed by about 700 gold-seekers willing to pay any price to get to California. She finally sailed overloaded with 400 lucky would-be gold millionaires. When she reached San Francisco her entire crew, except for the captain, elected to jump ship and go off to look for gold. The ship was stuck for almost four months in San Francisco while a new, and more expensive, crew was located.

Aspinwall's first mail ship

Intending to move the mail across Panama by railroad, Aspinwall had secured a concession from Colombia to build a railroad across its Panamanian territory. Construction began in May 1850 but quickly bogged down. Gold seekers willingly paid just to be able to walk along the partially cleared railroad route. The Panama Railroad would turn out to be one of the most costly railroads ever built. By July 1852 they had finished 23 miles (37 kilometers) of track and reached the Chagres River where a massive bridge had to be built across the river.

In January 1854, excavation began at the summit of the Continental Divide to cut the mountain down 40 feet (12.2 meters).

Meanwhile workers were building the route from Panama City. When the cut at Culebra was finally completed in January 1855 the first railroad from sea to sea was completed.

Panama Railroad at Culebra Summit

By 1855 the rush was over. Most of the easy-to-get-at gold was gone and what gold remained had to be extracted from difficult locations. Before the Gold Rush petered out, the Panama Railroad carried over $700 million dollars worth of gold across the Isthmus.

William Aspinwall's Panama Railroad played a significant role in moving people and supplies and in the growth of San Francisco.

Many of those returning from the Gold Rush without finding gold were broke and disillusioned, and many just ended up staying in Panama. Panama had survived the first US invasion.

* * * *

California became a state 1850 and Oregon in 1859. The Trans-Continental railroad in the US wasn't opened until 1869, so there was demand to link the oceans together and to provide a cheaper and easier connection between US states and with the rest of the world.

A Frenchman, dubbed "the greatest Frenchman who ever lived", named Ferdinand de Lesseps saw a great opportunity and seized it.

De Lesseps, sometimes also called "the great engineer" even although he was a promoter and not an engineer, was riding high after his triumph in creating the Suez Canal.

Until you've sailed across the Suez and spent the day gazing out at mile upon mile of sand, you really can't appreciate what a phenomenal achievement it was to link the Mediterranean with the Red Sea. When the Suez Canal opened in 1869 it was like when the first man landed on the moon! It was a fantastic achievement of French engineering. The French were called "the great engineers" and all across Europe they were building fantastic bridges and structures.

De Lesseps pitching his plan for a Suez Canal

Although ancient Egyptian canals had been built, they had long since been covered over by shifting sands. De Lesseps, who for most of his life had been a diplomat, was able to parlay his connection with S'aid Pasha of Egypt to obtain permission for his French company to construct a sea level canal.

Riding high after Suez, a canal across Central America seemed the next logical step. There were two possible routes, one across Nicaragua and the other across Panama. Nicaragua was the longer route, but it was able to use the vast expanse of Lake Nicaragua in the middle of the country.

France wasn't the only player. The US, realizing the need for a Canal to support the expanding West, had sent several surveying expeditions to look at routes across both Nicaragua and Panama and even Mexico. The US had been quietly negotiating with both Colombia, for Panama, and Nicaragua. Great Britain was also talking about a possible Canal.

Matthew Parker, in PANAMA FEVER:

"Paris in the spring of 1879 was awash with financial speculation. Money was more plentiful and mobile than ever before. . . Penalties for debt and bankruptcy had been eased, and restrictions on lifting shares had been lifted. In the Paris bourse, young stockbrokers noisily wheeled and dealed betting on pretty much anything and often making huge sums for themselves."[12]

It was a ready made environment for a promoter like de Lesseps.

"Greatness" was the operative word for the French. The Franco Prussian War in 1870 had crushed France both militarily and emotionally. The Second French Empire was replaced by the Third French Republic. France was determined to be great once again, this time not by war, but through the greatness of engineering achievement that had been evidenced by the opening of Suez, just a year before the crushing Franco Prussian War.

Cartoon of the day: the Great Frenchman who could accomplish anything

---

[12] Mathew Parker, PANAMA FEVER, p. 49

De Lesseps could have retired after his triumph in Suez, but the time and the conditions were right for de Lesseps to lead another French engineering triumph. De Lesseps was not an engineer nor had he ever been to Panama or the tropics, but the idea of building yet another grand canal captivated him. Several survey teams were dispatched and if they returned with less than favorable reports, de Lesseps simply sent out another group of surveyors. Quietly de Lesseps and associates negotiated with Colombia rights to build the Canal across Panama.

In 1897 De Lesseps called the *"Congres International d'Etudes du Canal Interocéanique"* in Paris to consider a Canal across Central America, knowing in advance what he planned to do and looking for an official endorsement. Instead of getting a quick rubber stamp to his plan he got a heated debate.

Proposals included several requiring tunnels through mountains and lock systems, but de Lesseps was determined to build a sea level canal, just as he had in Suez. One of the fourteen plans was from an English group and was almost the same as the Canal eventually built by the Americans. Only one of the engineers had any construction experience in the tropics, and he urged a canal using locks. Before the final vote half of the Committee walked out in disgust, but de Lesseps popularity managed to carry the day.

The resolution for a sea level canal passed with only eight of the remaining delegates opposed. The "no" votes included the engineer with tropical experience who always said a sea level canal wouldn't work and Alexandre Gustave Eiffel, of Eiffel tower fame. Of those voting in favor, only one, Pedro Sosa, knew anything about Panama.

With his plan now "approved" de Lesseps set about doing what he did best: selling, promoting and raising money. The concept excited the French and eagerly they snapped up stock offerings investing their pensions and life savings in the promise of a canal in Panama.

Back in the US it looked like the US would finally get a canal, only one built and controlled by the French.

Celebrating the start of the French Canal

The French arrived in Panama in 1881 with one local paper enthusiastically comparing de Lesseps plan to link the oceans with Columbus' discovery of America. The French arrival was celebrated with great pomp, ceremony and celebration. Lavish state dinners and balls were held with de Lesseps, already 75 years old, dancing through the night.

Confidence and optimism prevailed; after all, all they had to do was move mountains and dig a canal. De Lesseps declared that Panama would be easier than Suez. Before they even began to dig, the French ordered 150,000 kerosene torches sent to Panama to be used in the grand midnight parade that would celebrate the completion of the canal.

* * * * *

With the Monroe Doctrine in hand, the US looked askance at the French moving ahead with a canal the US had intended to build on what US President Rutherford Hayes considered to be "virtually part of the coast line of the United States." Reluctantly viewing the French Panama project as a private and not a state project, the US choose to sit back, watch, and criticize. De Lesseps dismissed American opposition as "a phantom and a bugbear."

After inaugurating the construction project, de Lesseps returned, via the US, to France to do what he did best, raise money. The French enthusiastically bought into the project snapping up shares of the company demanding to buy more shares than were available.

Before leaving Panama, de Lesseps made some decisions which might have caused those enthusiastic purchasers of shares in the Panama project to question the "grand Frenchman's" management. At stockholder expense he built himself a grand house for $100,000, a summer house at La Boca for $150,000 and ordered a private rail car for him to travel around Panama for $42,000.

Fiscal mismanagement would haunt the French effort as ultimately, unable to meet the challenges of Panama, the French would run out of money.

Willis Fletcher Johnson, writing of FOUR CENTURIES OF THE PANAMA CANAL (1906) describes the mismanagement:

"When a $50,000 building was needed, a $100,000 building was erected, at a corrupt cost of $200,000."[13]

One of de Lesseps early acts was to order thousands of snow shovels from France. Johnson recalls seeing, after the French had left, warehouses full of "thousands of snow shovels."

"Apparently, agents were sent all over France, asking manufacturers if they had any surplus stocks of goods of which they wished to rid. If the answer was affirmative, as of course it usually was, they were told to ship the goods to Panama. But they were nothing that was wanted or could be used there. no matter; ship them along. So they sent cargo after cargo, of the most useless things, from hairpins to grand pianos. Almost every week the men at Colon were surprised by the arrival of a ship load of things they had not ordered, did not want, and could not use." [14]

The French, although they did not know it, were doomed from the start.

It was not just fiscal mismanagement. Fundamentally, de Lesseps plan for a sea level canal was impossible. It is said that if the French had continued in their efforts to dig a sea level canal that they would still be digging.

---

[13] Willis Fletcher Johnson, FOUR CENTURIES OF THE PANAMA CANAL (1906), p. 100

[14] Ibid, p. 101.

Near the end, de Lesseps reluctantly accepted the necessity of a canal using locks and Gustave Eiffel, of Eiffel tower fame, received the contract to build the locks. Unfortunately for Eiffel, this would embroil him in the great controversy of "The Panama Affair" that followed the French Failure.

French machinery at work

'The real reasons for the French failure were first, they knew nothing about the tropics, and second, the equipment and technology for such a Herculean construction project did not exist.

It rains in the rain forest. The area around Chagres can get up to 16.7 feet (5.1 meters) of rain a year and an incredible amount of rain can come down in a very short time. The French never came up with a plan of what to do with all the water roaring down the Chagres River, or of a tropical river than can rise 12 feet (3.7 meters) in a matter of hours. All of that rain, plus all of the excavation equals mud and standing water, the perfect breeding ground for disease-carrying mosquitoes. Only the French simply did not understand the tropical diseases they would face. Medicine had only vague theories of how diseases like malaria and yellow fever were spread. They thought it perhaps the diseases was spread through some kind of swamp vapors: no one had made the connection with mosquitoes.

Stylish Victorian interiors featured rooms overloaded with furniture and palm trees giving the space a colonial touch. Now the French came to Panama with all of these beautiful folliage everywhere, so they decorated their houses and porches with beautiful palms in pots standing in saucers of water. Ooops! To control the occasional plague of ants that is common in Panama, and keep the ants out of patient beds, in hospitals they put bowls of standing water under the four posts of the beds. Those who were admitted to hospital for any reason had a 75% chance of dying.

By disease and accident over 20,000 people died in ten years. Since the French only recorded the deaths of those who died in hospital, the actual death toll was much higher.

Whole towns were thrown up without adequate sanitation. The rain pooled everywhere. Shanty towns sprang up without any form of public order. There was little for workers to do in their off hours but drink and fornicate. Colon had over 150 bars, and one street, "Bottle Alley", was nothing but 40 bars. Workers who got sick were simply terminated so the subcontractors didn't have to pay for hospitalization. Men who died on the job were sometimes just rolled down the hill and buried under tons of spoil.

Life in Panama was hell.

Mismanagement plagued the operation and not just in terms of fiscal mismanagement. The machinery available to do the job was simply too light weight. It was not standardized and was shipped without replacement parts. Every kind of machine available was being used, so there was no standardization and many machines ended up being unusable and simply sat rusting in the jungle. Machines were jerry-rigged, improvised, or created on the spot.

Contracts were let in the same random way in which supplies were ordered. Over 200 different firms were contracted without any coordination.

Not surprisingly the French effort ended in dismal failure. Probably as many as 25,000 had died. The money had run out. Except for the recriminations and trials that would consume France over the next several years, the grand French Panama adventure had ended.

French locomotive found in the muck of the present Canal during dredging

The stock was worthless. Millions of French investors had lost everything. For years to come in France the French canal effort would simply be referred to as "The Panama Affair."

The trail of the French canal promoters

De Lesseps and his son and Eiffel were tried and sentenced to prison. In the end it was decided that although the canal was plagued by mismanagement that there was no malfeasance or intent to defraud and the so principals never actually went to jail.

De Lesseps would retire from public eye and eventually become a senile old man, maybe still dreaming of his years of glory, maybe not.

* * * *

The TV show "Survivor" was one of the productions that led to a revolution in television and introduced a whole string of "reality" shows, if you can call being marooned on a deserted island with a dozen or so supposedly "normal" self-obsessed characters selected for their "eye candy" appeal along with a full Hollywood production crew any sort of reality. But the show was a hit, and the first shows were filmed on the Pearl Islands of Panama. Contestants sought to outdo one another to "outwit, outplay, outlast" and be the ultimate "Survivor" who walks away with the money.

Philippe Bunau-Varilla 1859 - 1940

If there was any "survivor" of the French Canal effort it was de Lesseps' chief engineer, Philippe Bunau-Varilla who not only managed to avoid being convicted and sentenced in France, but also eventually managed to acquire stock in a new French Canal company and exercise some control of the French rights to build a canal in Panama.

The Frenchman, Bunau-Varilla, would be a key player in not only in selling the French rights to the US, but in writing the treaty which gave away a swath across Panama that would be known as the US Panama Canal Zone.

* * * *

Since the US from the beginning had been angling to build and control a canal across Central America they weren't saddened by the French failure.

California (1850) and Oregon (1859) had both become states, so there was a need in the US to move material and people across the country. The transcontinental railroad in the US wouldn't be completed until 1869. The Spanish American War in 1898 had shown the US a military need for a Canal. When the battleship MAINE was blown up in Havana Harbor the nearest battleship was the OREGON in San Francisco. It took 67 days to bring the OREGON around the Horn to from San Francisco. As the war came to a close the US acquired the Philippines, Guam, Puerto Rico and a permanent US Naval base at Guantánamo Bay. The US had also thrown out the Hawaiian monarch and annexed the Hawaiian Islands.

As the US "empire" grew, there was clearly the need for a strong US Navy and the need for a canal for the navy to conveniently and quickly move between the Atlantic and Pacific to protect US interests.

The US had always had a sense of entitlement to any future Canal, based on a broad interpretation of the Monroe Doctrine. So when US President Rutherford Hayes said that he considered Panama to be "virtually part of the coast line of the United States" he was simple expressing the US party line.

* * * *

US President William McKinley was assassinated by an anarchist in 1901 and his popular Vice President Theodore Roosevelt became president.

Roosevelt returning from Panama

Roosevelt was born with a silver spoon in his mouth and was a sickly child. But as a federal bureaucrat, later no-nonsense Commissioner of Police in New York City, then Assistant Secretary of the Navy, and finally Vice President, Roosevelt had carefully cultivated his image. When the Spanish American War broke out, Roosevelt had resigned his Navy position to go to war leading a voluntary US Calvary regent the newspapers nicknamed the "Rough Riders."

Rudyard Kipling wrote of Theodore Roosevelt, "The universe seemed to be spinning around and Theodore was the spinner."

Roosevelt expanded the Monroe Doctrine in what is called "The Roosevelt Corollary to the Monroe Doctrine" which stated,

"All that this country desires is to see the neighboring countries stable, orderly, and prosperous. Any country whose people conduct themselves well can count upon our hearty friendship. If a nation shows that it knows how to act with reasonable efficiency and decency in social and political matters, if it keeps order and pays its obligations, it need fear no interference from the United States. Chronic wrong doing or an impotence which results in a general loosening of the ties of civilized society . . . may force the United States, however reluctantly, in flagrant cases of such wrongdoing or impotence, to the exercise of an international police power."

The big question in the US wasn't whether or not to build a canal, but where the canal should be built. Nicaragua or Panama?

Political cartoon of the day: both sides of the trough looked inviting

The issue was hotly debated in Washington, throughout the country, and in scientific circles

There were those in government and who influenced government who had vested interests in both countries and lobbied accordingly. Both countries had their advocates and the same arguments that were present before the French attempt were still in play. Panama was shorter but would require considerable effort to get over the Continental Divide and would have to use a lock system. Nicaragua, although a longer route, could take advantage of Lake Nicaragua and could be a sea level canal.

Unfortunately Nicaragua had decided to start celebrating its live volcanoes by putting them on their postage stamps.

As the debate in Congress raged on, and just days before the Senate was scheduled to vote on the route the canal should take, Bunau-Varilla remembered the Nicaraguan stamps!

"Rushing about to every stamp dealer in Washington he managed to purchase ninety all together, one for each senator. He pasted the precious stamps on sheets of paper and below each typed out: 'An official witness of the volcanic activity on the isthmus of Nicaragua.' The stamp arrived at the office of every member of the Senate with the morning mail on Monday, June 16, three days before the deciding vote."[15]

Of course Panama had volcanoes then, and now; I live on one. But the "stamp lobby" successfully created fear and doubt and proved to be an inexpensive and effective lobbying effort. On June 19, 1902 the Senate voted 42 to 34 in favor of Panama.

* * * *

Now that Panama had been decided on as a location, all the remained was for the US to get Colombia to give up a swath across the middle of its Panamanian territory.

Roosevelt assigned his Secretary of State, John Hay to negotiate a treaty with Colombia that would give the US rights to build a canal across its Panamanian territory. The Hay-Haran Treaty was approved by the US Senate on January 22, 1903. But when the Colombian charge d'affaires, Dr. Tomás Herran, took the treaty home to be ratified, the Colombian legislature took one look at it they unanimously said, "No way Jose!"

---

[15] David McCullough, THE PATH BETWEEN THE SEAS, p. 323

Meanwhile, the Frenchman Bunau-Varilla was hustling around Washington peddling his shares in the New French Canal Company that he controlled, first asking $109 million, and then cutting his price to a fire-sale, bargain basement price of $40 million.

When Panama had joined Bolivar's Grand Colombia it had never intended to be part of Colombia but that's what happened when Grand Colombia dissolved. Since then Panama's relations with Colombia deteriorated. The Thousand Days War between factions in Colombia raged on from 1899 to 1903. Colombia had been looking to Panama to conscript even boy soldiers to fight a war in which Panamanians had no interest. Panamanians began asking, "Why?" and a revolt began brewing. In September 1902 the US had already sent US troops to Panama to protect the US-owned Panama Railroad.

* * * *

Things moved quickly in Washington. Buneau-Varilla and company had actually prepared a "new country kit" to share with their connections in Panama which included, amongst other things a suggested constitution and a silk flag for the new country! Thankfully the Panamanians threw it all in the dump.

Meanwhile, in the fast-moving world of international politics and intrigue . . .

On October 10, 1903 Philippe Bunau-Varilla met with Roosevelt to warn him of imminent rebellion in Panama.

On November 3, 1903 with the US NASHVILLE conveniently standing by in Panama and Bunau-Varilla standing by in Washington, Panama proclaimed independence from Colombia. The only casualties were a shopkeeper and a donkey

On November 6 there was an official declaration of independence from Colombia and on November 7 the US officially recognized the Republic of Panama.

Twelve days later, claiming to represent the newly created Republic of Panama, the Frenchman Bunau-Varilla granted the US a strip of land across Panama and the rights to build the canal and in return the US agreed to protect the new country

" . . . the high contracting parties have resolved for that purpose to conclude a convention and have accordingly appointed as their plenipotentiaries - The President of the United States of America, John Hay, Secretary of State, and The Government of the Republic of Panama, Philippe Bunau-Varilla, Envoy Extraordinary and Minister Plenipotentiary of the Republic of Panama, thereunto specially empowered by said government . . ."

On November 18th the Hay-Bunau-Varilla Treaty was signed and called for:

US to maintain the independence of Panama;

US to have use, occupation and control of zone 10 miles wide dividing Panama;

US to pay Panama $10 million initially and after nine years pay $250,000 per year with Panama having no future share in profits.

It is important to note that *no Panamanian signed the Treaty*. The treaty was ratified despite Panamanian complaints.

Political cartoon of the day calling into question the convenient birthing of this new country nicknamed the "Banana Republic"

Lest those of us accustomed to US manipulation of international affairs just assume Panama was solely created at the convenience of Washington, R. M. Koster and Guillermo Sanchez point out,

"Panama was always a separate national entity [and] was never organically integrated into Colombia. The chief reason why was that Panama achieved independence from Spain on her own. The authors of this independence, perhaps frightened by their own audacity, then began to fear a Spanish reconquest of the isthmus . . . Panama was both small and thinly populated, with no troops and few weapons. That is when the idea came up for Panama to join with a larger nation . . . [Colombia] then governed by Simón Bolívar in a confederation called Gran Colombia. Bolivar was almost a mythological figure, almost a divinity. His prestige drew Panama into a union with Colombia. In no one's mind in Panama, however, was this union intended to be permanent. When the danger of Spanish reconquest was over, Panama would return to independence."[16]

"By the time Bunau-Varilla . . . and Teddy Roosevelt came on the scene, a revolutionary conspiracy was already in progress. But those directing it were realists. They knew Panama's weakness and the strength of Colombia's veteran army. They seized the moment when a coincidence of interests presented the best chance for independence. Here it is that Panama's national aspirations became bound up with the irresistible expansionism of the United States, the political ambitions of Theodore Roosevelt, and the turbulent intriguing of Bunau-Varilla. But the principal separatist impulse came from within Panama . . . [Other countries had achieved their independence with help from other nations] And Panama's founding fathers were no less brave, generous, far-seeing, or fallible than those of any other country."[17]

On February 3, 1904 US Marines clashed with Colombian troops attempting to re-establish Colombian sovereignty in Panama. Twenty days later the US paid Panama $10 million for the Canal Zone. US "Gunboat Diplomacy" insured that Panama remained independent.

Colombia did not recognize the Republic of Panama until 1921 when the US paid Colombia $21 million in "compensation" to buy a kind of Colombian recognition of legitimacy. The US would continue to intervene in Panama's political affairs until 1936 when the US agreed to limit the use of its troops to the Canal Zone and the annual rent on the Canal was increased.

In later years when Roosevelt was criticized over US actions in Panama he famously replied, "I took Panama while Congress talked about it."

---

[16] R.M. Koster and Guillermon Sanchez, IN THE TIME OF THE TYRANTS: PANAMA 1968-1990 New York, W.W. Nortonn & Company, 1990. p 390

[17] pp. 390-391

* * * *

The first order of business in constructing the canal was for the US to evaluate what the French had done and see what French equipment could be used. It turned out that most of the French equipment was rusted and useless and about the only thing that could be used were some of the French buildings.

If the US was to have any chance of success it had to address the disease issues. In 1904 Dr. William Gorgas took over as the Chief Sanitary officer for the canal project.

Gorgas was able to build on the work of Dr. Walter Reed, who had developed insights of a Cuban doctor, Dr. Carlos Finlay, to prove that yellow fever was transmitted by mosquitoes. First in Florida, then in Cuba, Gorgas had attacked yellow fever. Gorgas instituted sanitation programs across Panama, drained swamps, installed screens and mosquito netting. Much of the Canal Zone was sprayed with a mixture of carbolic acid, resin and caustic soda. Oil was placed on standing water to prevent mosquitoes from breeding. Workers were required to take daily doses of quinine.

Without Gorgas the Canal would never have been possible.
* * * *

The popular image was that the US was digging the Canal, but the truth is almost the whole world was involved. Panama and the US alone couldn't provide all the "grunt" labor to dig the canal, so the US began recruiting and importing laborers from all over. They came by the thousands from Greece and Europe, from China and Asia, and from the islands of the Caribbean. Almost forty percent of the adult male population of Barbados came to Panama to work on the canal.

Keeping such a diverse, transient, mostly male population relatively healthy and controlled required the Canal Zone from the start to be a highly ordered and regulated society.

* * * *

The French effort had been compromised by scores of independent contractors who were poorly coordinated and by inadequate machinery that wasn't standardized. The US had one contractor: the US Army Corps of Engineers. The fact that the equipment left behind by the French was unusable proved to be a blessing for the US. The US simply had to build its own equipment.

The first patent for a steam shovel was acquired by William Otis, a Philadelphia engineer, in 1839. The "steam" shovel proved to be a boon to railroad construction. Two companies in the US, Marion Steam Shovel Company and Bucyrus-Erie Shovel Company were building machines that would be instrumental in the construction of the Canal.

One hundred and two shovels were used in the Canal construction, two–thirds of these built by Bucyrus and the others by Marion.

The Bucyrus shovels each weighed 95 US tons (86 metric tons) and could lift up to 30,000 pounds (13,608 kilograms) of rock.

* * * *

Another essential component of success that the French had lacked was a railroad capable of moving 232 million US tons (210 metric tons) of spoil. Just as William Gorgas had been the key to success in controlling tropical diseases, John Frank Stevens, the second man in charge of the Canal construction, was the key to creating the infrastructure that made the Canal possible.

Stevens had been chief engineer for the Great Northern Railroad and had built over a thousand miles of railroad before becoming Vice president of the Chicago, Rock Island and Pacific Railroad. In 1905 he was tapped by Roosevelt to become chief engineer for the Panama Canal.

Stevens immediately saw the need for a railway capable of removing the enormous volume of rock and dirt that would need to be excavated. He rebuilt the Panama Railway from the ground up and developed special cars that could be loaded and unloaded quickly. He oversaw the construction necessary to create in essence the Panama Canal Zone, in effect a new city requiring worker housing, sanitation, and all manner of services.

John Frank Stevens 1853 -1943

When Stevens unexpectedly resigned without stating any public reason, Roosevelt appointed someone who could not resign, US Army Corps of Engineers Lieutenant Colonel George Washington Goethals. It was Goethals who saw the Canal project to completion.

* * * *

While the Americans dug away, there was an underlying resentment building amongst Panamanians. Whereas the French, being French, and convinced that they were the all-knowing engineers of the world, kept to themselves, many Panamanians expected something different from the US effort. After all, the creation and security of Panamanian independence from Colombia had been somewhat of a joint effort, so Panama expected to have more of a role in the US Canal project. They expected a piece of the pie. What they got instead was a self-governed ten-mile swath across their country that was totally controlled and administered by the US without Panamanian participation.

In addition to the Canal the US was building a colonial out post that mirrored as much as possible life back in the US to the exclusion of Panamanians.

* * * *

George Washington Goethals 1858 - 1928

The Panama Canal incredibly was completed ahead of schedule, under budget and without any corruption or scandal.

David McCullough writes of the completion of the Panama Canal,

"Its cost had been enormous. No single construction effort in American history had exacted such a price in dollars or in human life. Dollar expenditures since 1904 totaled $352 million . . . By present standards this does not seem a great deal, but it was more than four times what Suez had cost . . . and so much more than anything before ever built by the Unites States government as to be beyond compare. Taken together, the French and American expenditures came to about $639 million."[18]

In addition to the 20,000 to 25,000 French lives lost, there were 5,600 additional lives lost during the American effort, roughly 500 lives lost for every mile of the Canal.

Again, McCullough,

"The total volume of excavation accomplished since 1904 was 232,440,945 cubic yards and this added to the approximately 30, million cubic yards of useful excavation by the French gave a grand total, in round numbers, of 262 million cubic yards, more than four times the volume originally estimated by Ferdinand de Lesseps for a canal at sea level and nearly three times the excavation at Suez."[19]

---

[18] David McCullough, THE PATH BETWEEN THE SEAS, P. 610

[19] Ibid, p. 611

* * * *

The two truly momentous events in the life of the Panama Canal happened without fanfare.

On August 15, 1914, with the world preoccupied by a World War, the ANCON carrying cement made the first official crossing westbound from the Atlantic to the Pacific

On September 4, 2010, a Chinese freighter, FORTUNE PLUM carrying steel became the one millionth ship to transit the Canal going from the Pacific to the Atlantic, three years ahead of the 100th Anniversary. For whatever reason the Panama Canal Authority wasn't paying attention and missed the historic event! It was weeks before someone noticed that the millionth ship had passed through the Canal without pictures or fanfare. The ACP had to chase down the FORTUNE PLUM to arrange to present a plaque commemorating the historic event!

7 - A Complicated Marriage of Sorts

The relationship between Panama and the US is almost like a complicated marriage of convenience with moments of cooperation and mutual support, an eruption into a brutal divorce, and then, finally, bound by historic ties, evolving into a relationship of mutual respect and friendship.

Would the Republic of Panama exist without the US?

Undoubtedly independence from Colombia would have happened eventually. Panama had signed up to be part of Bolivar's Grand Colombia not part of Colombia. Panama was separated from the mother country not only emotionally but also physically. Panama was the "spout" on the "teapot" that was Colombia, separated geographically by the enormous and impenetrable Darien. Colombia was leaning on Panama conscripting troops to fight essentially Colombian, not Panamanian, wars, without giving anything back in return. So a split was probably inevitable, but had it occurred without US encouragement and backing, it would have taken longer and come at great cost in terms of human life.

The US had one interest in the newly minted Republic of Panama: a canal. Panama's interest in the US was the security of their independence and the economic benefit the canal construction would bring. Whereas the French had come in as the glorious French engineers who "knew it all", ignored the local wisdom and failed miserably, Panamanians expected that the US would build a canal with more of a sense of partnership with the locals with opportunities for jobs, contracts, and supplying food and materials.

The Hay-Bunau-Varilla Treaty provided that the US would have a zone ten miles wide in which to build a canal and that within that zone the US would act "as if it were sovereign." In fact the US took over the ten-mile zone and established it *as* sovereign US territory (no "if"), dividing Panama into two parts. A Panamanian could only pass from one part of his country to another with the good graces of the US which occupied the strip dividing the country.

Obviously the partners in this marriage had entered into it with vastly different expectations. And as the century wore on American dominance in the relationship would become a major issue.

The Roosevelt Corollary to the Monroe Doctrine

The US created a Canal Zone which although physically in Central America could have been a township anywhere in the Midwestern US, just picked up and dropped down in Panama. The Canal Zone had its own shopping areas, with all food and goods shipped in from the US without any tax going to Panama, its own hospitals, post office, police department, laws, courts, railroads, schools, fire departments, sewage, churches, theaters, recreation, values, life-style . . . you name it! Totally separate and totally unequal. For the most part, Panama's piece of this pie was low wage, menial jobs.

You could live your entire life in the Zone without ever leaving . . . or going into Panama! And some people did. Obviously not everyone, since there are loads of Panamanians today that have dual citizenship because one parent or the other lived in the Zone or was a US citizen stationed in the Zone.

Once the Canal was completed, life was good in the Zone. Things were cheap, even although everything had to be imported from the States. Things were subsidized. There were great financial benefits to Canal Zone postings including yearly vacations at government expense back to the States or elsewhere in the world. Gardening and maintenance were covered. You had life as in the US only without snow. Multiple generational families lived in the Zone. Some of these US children of the Zone and ex US military or Canal people who choose to remain and retire in Panama are known as "Zonians."

Hotel Tivoli, Ancon

The US had 12-16 military installations in the Canal Zone depending on when and how you counted. These provided jobs and despite the containment of the Zone, contributed to the local economy, sometimes in ways less desirable than other ways. All those jobs gave ordinary Panamanians a way to see the way others lived and the benefits these "*extranjeros*" enjoyed in a part of their country to which they were denied access.

The Zone had been built on a not-to-subtle form of discrimination between "Gold", usually American and usually white, and "Silver", usually other nationalities and people of color.

* * * *

In January 1963, President John F. Kennedy recognizing a deteriorating situation in Panama and aware of the sensitivities of many Panamanians who resented all the US flags being flown in the Canal Zone, issued an Executive Order that on non-military bases in the Zone wherever a US flag was flown, a Panamanian flag should also be flown.

The Zonians bitterly resented Kennedy's policy and his meddling in their paradise and sued in the Canal Zone's Federal District Court, which reluctantly and unhappily upheld the presidential order. Before the policy could be carried out, Kennedy was assassinated in Dallas, and the federally appointed Canal Zone governor immediately took it upon himself to rescind a presidential order.

Thus began the Panamanian "Flag Wars", a series of confrontations, mainly between young people, over which flag would fly where.

Meanwhile back in the States, as Bob Dylan would note, the times were "a'changin'". Forced integration had come to an end in bastions of the Confederacy. 200,000 people led by Dr. Martin Luther King, Jr. had marched on Washington. The Civil Rights Movement in the US was in full swing. But back in the Canal Zone things were as they always had been.

Life had changed internationally as well. Colonialism was out: new countries were emerging with the freedom to control their own destinies. Yet back in Panama the Canal Zone was still part of the US colonial empire.

The Flag Wars came to a head on January 9, 1964 when a group of students from Panama City's most prestigious high school went to the entrance of the Canal Zone, climbed to the top of a light pole and planted an historically significant Panamanian flag. Someone, presumably US soldiers, opened fire and the boy on the top of the pole was killed and two other boys were injured. In response rioting broke out all across Panama wherever the Canal Zone joined the Republic, with Panamanians tearing holes in the "Fence of Shame" that separated the Canal Zone from the Republic of Panama.

The next day, as rioting continued, Panama broke off relations with the US. When all was said and done, 21 Panamanians including six teenagers, and four US soldiers were dead, and as many as 500 civilians were injured. To this day in Panama January 9 is a national holiday, and celebrated as the Day Of The Martyrs.

Panama celebrates two independence days as national holidays, smart people these Panamanians, the first celebrating independence from Spain and the other independence from Colombia. If there were an "Independence From The US" day, it would be January 9th. It was a day when three teenagers led an entire country in standing up for their sovereignty. It might also be called the day when Panama stood up and demanded to control its destiny.

A photographer from LIFE magazine happened to catch the moment as the boy who later died, reached the top of the light pole and planted the Panamanian flag. That picture was chosen as the cover of the very popular LIFE magazine and inside was a story about the deteriorating situation in Panama. Most Americans were totally unaware of life in the Zone, let alone the feelings of Panamanians, and the Zonians preferred it that way, lest someone rattle their cage. Suddenly ordinary US citizens realized that all was not well in Panama. This incident, and the outrage it provoked in the US as well as Panama, was a precursor to the decision to transfer the Canal Zone back to Panama.

As late as 1987 the US was still calling the road between the former Canal Zone and Panama City "4th of July Avenue" while the Panamanians called it "Avenue Of The Martyrs". Today, if you drive into Panama City coming across the Bridge of the Americas, as you drive along the Avenue of the Martyrs you will pass by an ordinary looking street light post, with three teenagers immortalized in bronze climbing the pole and at the top flies a Panamanian flag.

* * * *

Panama has a very ugly black bird with a huge wingspan that you often see flying in groups high in the sky. We call them "The Panamanian Air Force", but they are actually turkey vultures that perform the very valuable task of cleaning up road kill and disposing of dead animals. In Panama they have a saying that "Politicians are like vultures: during the day they fight over the same road kill, but at night they all go home to the same tree to roost." So many of the politicians during the day fight over this and that, but they intermarry, and all belong to the same clubs, go to the same parties and hang out together.

One notable Panamanian politician was Arnulfo Arias, notable because he was elected president three times, yet he never finished a term in office because he was always thrown out by a military coup.

[At the age of 63 Arias married an 18-year-old interior decorator, Mireya Moscoso, who would later serve as president from 1999–2004. In 1984 at the age of 83 Arias ran again for president and although polls showed a substantial lead, election results were manipulated by Noriega so that Noriega's hand-picked man was elected. Arias fled to Florida, where his widow, Mireya Moscoso still spends part of her time.]

In 1968 Arias was overthrown by the National Guard in a military coup led by General Omar Torrijos. Although Torrijos never assumed the role of president, preferring the title "Maximum Leader of the Panamanian Revolution", Torrijos ran the country from 1968-1981 as a military strongman. To this day, Omar Torrijos is the most popular figure ever to live in Panama. Torrijos was a social reformist, a populist who empowered the Indigenous, redistributed wealth, opened universities formerly reserved for the privileged few families to all Panamanians, and in spite of being a military strongman opened up government.

Omar Torrijos, Maximum Leader of the Panamanian Revolution 1929-1981

Omar Torrijos liked to parade around with ordinary people and Indians in his battle fatigues smoking a big cigar like another Latin American military strongman, Fidel Castro. All of this made the US nervous and the CIA needed an insider to keep an eye on Torrijos. They already had just the man surreptitiously on the CIA payroll, a young officer named Manuel Noriega.

Noriega was born in Panama City, raised by his grandparents and ended up in Chiriqui province. He was a career soldier having been educated at military school in Peru, trained at the US School of the Americas in the Canal Zone, as well as at Fort Bragg in the US.

Noriega was commissioned in the Panama National guard and in 1968 was made a Lieutenant. Nobody is quite sure how or why Noriega came to the attention of Torrijos, but Torrijos took the young Lieutenant under his wing. Sometime in the late '50s Noriega started working for the CIA. He provided the ideal CIA "insider" to keep an eye on General Torrijos.

It was Omar Torrijos who negotiated the US withdrawal from Panama and the turnover of the Canal Zone and the Panama Canal with US President Jimmy Carter. Torrijos had the reputation as a "man's man" who liked hard liquor, cigars and women. He established a friendship with a stereotypical "man's man", movie actor John Wayne. It is said that during the negotiation for the treaties, Jimmy Carter used John Wayne to help smooth over some rough spots with Torrijos as well as encouraging his politically conservative friends to support the treaty. In gratitude Omar Torrijos supposedly gave John Wayne the island of Taborcillo off the coast of Panama. The island is now being developed as a resort called "John Wayne Island".

Signing of the Carter-Torrijos Panama Canal Treaties

The Torrijos-Carter Treaties were signed on September 7, 1977.

Supposedly Torrijos had started celebrating early and showed up for the event noticeably drunk for the signing, slurring his speech and needing to brace himself for the photo op that followed.

* * * *

Omar Torrijos died in a small plane crash in 1981. Nobody knows for sure why the crash occurred. Panama, just like the US, has its share of conspiracy theorists. Some claim the crash was caused by the CIA and others say it was engineered by Noriega. Weather conditions for small planes can turn deadly flying over Panama's mountainous interior very rapidly. Most likely Omar Torrijos death was just what it appears of the surface, an unfortunate accident.

Torrijos death left a gaping void in leadership. Noriega, a member of Torrijos party and head of the secret police, managed to leverage his secret police power to close down all opposition, and emerge as Torrijos' successor.

Panamanians don't like to talk about "the dictatorship" just like most Americans don't like to talk about Spiro Agnew, the Nixon presidency and Watergate. It was a dark period when anyone who criticized was likely to be beaten or disappear. You will find that a number of Panamanians will have a four or five-year period of their history where they worked abroad.

There is no doubt that Noriega was a military dictator and a thug who brought a great deal of grief to Panama and in the process robbed the country blind. There also is no doubt that Noriega worked for the CIA, probably as early as the late '50s, and that during some periods of his employ he was being paid more than the president of the US.

Not that Noriega wasn't worth his keep. Noriega maintained friendly relations with Cuba and Fidel Castro and was useful to the US in back-channel communications and negotiation with Cuba. He helped the Reagan administration by sending illegal aid to the Contras in Nicaragua.

Noriega's image in the US was increasingly being portrayed as a drug kingpin. In an effort to "clean up" his image, Noriega sought the support of Oliver North. At one point, according to Congressional testimony, North supposedly said to a meeting of the Reagan administration's Restricted Interagency Group: "I can arrange to have General Noriega execute some insurgent -- some operations there -- sabotage operations in that area. [Nicaragua] It will cost us about $1 million. Do we want to do it?"

North flew to London to meet with Noriega and the two supposedly discussed developing a commando training program for the Contras in Panama, with Israeli support, and of plans to sabotage targets in Nicaragua.

The very idea of such conversations is reprehensible to most Americans. The plans were supposedly aborted when the Iran-Contra scandal came to light in 1986.

Relations with Noriega deteriorated rapidly. Former CIA chief George H. W. Bush was Vice President with an eye on the Oval Office for himself. Noriega would turn out to be a Frankenstein-like monster.

Noriega sought to manipulate the situation to his continued advantage defying and taunting the US in an effort to shore up his deteriorating leadership. The US increasingly portrayed Noriega as a drug mastermind while at the same time the US Department of Justice was investigating the CIA assisting Contras with importing crack cocaine into Los Angeles.

Former CIA spymaster George H. W. Bush, when running for president, attempted to pass off his relationships with Noriega noting that the last seven American administrations had paid off Noriega.

Retired Navy Admiral Stanford Turner, who took over the CIA from George Bush in 1977, paints a different picture:

"Bush is in the government during the Ford administration and Noriega is on the payroll. Bush is out of the government during the Carter years and Noriega is off the payroll. Bush comes back and so does Noriega. Those are the facts, and you have to figure out for yourself what they mean."[20]

Then CIA Director Bush [41] and Manuel Noriega

There were increasing tensions between Panama and the Canal Zone. Although many US assets in Panama had already been turned over, many in Panama believed the now Republican US administration would renege on the deal agreed to by a Democrat administration before the "Grand Prize" of the Panama Canal was scheduled to be awarded in December 1999.

And there was good reason for concern. In 2002 the Texas Republican Party, the party of US President George H. W. Bush, still had the following plank in its platform:

"The Party urges Congress to support HJR 77, the Panama and America Security Act, which declare the Carter-Torrijos Treaty null and void. We support re-establishing United States control over the Canal in order to retain our military bases in Panama, to preserve our right to transit through the Canal, and to prevent the establishment of Chinese missile bases in Panama."

---

[20] Frederick Kemp, DIVORCING THE DICTATOR: AMERICA'S BUNGLED AFFAIR WITH NORIEGA New York, G.P. Putnam's Sons, 1990 p. 29

In February 1988 Panamanian President Eric Arturo Devalle removed Noriega as commander of the National Guard only to be overthrown himself by Noriega. In March Noriega declared a "state of emergency" and took total control. In April 1988 US President Ronald Regan addressed the deteriorating situation in Panama declaring a "national emergency" and freezing all assets.

In May 1889 Noriega called for elections but when voters rejected his hand-picked candidate he nullified the election. In response President George H. W. Bush, in the light of "massive irregularities", called for Noriega to step down, recalled the US ambassador and beefed up US troops in the Canal Zone.

Bush:

"On May 7, the people of Panama, by an overwhelming margin of votes, braved repression, intimidation, and fraud to choose democracy over dictatorship. They sent a clear and unmistakable message. They wanted an end to dictatorship and restoration of elected democratic government. But this act of self-determination was brutally repressed before the eyes of the entire world. Noriega answered the cry of his people with beatings and killings. The candidates chosen by the Panamanian people will not be allowed to take office today, as required by the Panamanian Constitution. Panama is therefore, as of this date, without any legitimate government."

The situation in Panama continued to deteriorate as Noriega foiled an attempted coup and had the leaders executed.

On December 15 the Noriega-dominated legislature used the phrase that a "state of war" existed between the US and Panama, a statement Noriega would later say represented that attitude and actions of the US toward Panama and not vice versa. Even had Panama "declared war" on the US, it would be a little like a flea on the back of an elephant saying, "I'm going to get you Mr. Elephant!" At any rate, for whatever reason, and some believe that it was in reaction to the press image of George H. W. Bush as a "wimp", the US took this declaration of "war" seriously, perhaps with good reason. Although tiny, and although the Canal was at the time under US control, the Canal was actually in Panama. Subsequently it came to light that Noriega did indeed have an actual plan to destroy the Canal; all Noriega had to do was pull the trigger.

Panama was in political and economic shambles. The US had agreed to turnover the Canal just before the Millennium. Panamanians were ready for change and fully expected that eventually the US would negotiate Noriega's retirement. To add to the US embarrassment an unarmed US Marine in civilian clothes was killed by Panamanian soldiers.

* * * *

On December 20 at 12:01 am as Panamanians dreamed of Christmas, the Panama Canal was closed. At 1:00 am at US Fort Clayton in Panama U.S. officials installed Guillermo Endara as Panama's new President in a secret ceremony. Endara would have been president had not Noriega invalidated the electoral results. Almost immediately the US began a massive invasion of the Republic of Panama. For the first time in modern history the US invaded another country without being at war.

Instead of the negotiation Panamanians expected, operation "Just Cause" was launched with 26,000 troops invading tiny Panama, attacking with tanks and aircraft. At least six times as many civilians as Panamanian military died in "Operation Just Cause", according to Physicians for Human Rights. The exact numbers are still being argued, but Physicians for Human Rights estimated 300 civilians and 50 military were killed, another 3,000 injured and 15,000 left homeless. It is said that in this nation of 3.3 million people, where everyone is related, almost everyone has a family member or knows someone who was killed or injured by the US invasion. Most Americans like to think that Panama, like the rest of the countries the US invades, is grateful for US intervention. Although most Panamanians ape any US fashion or brand and genuinely like the US and Americans, and although they were happy to be rid of Noriega, the violence with which it was accomplished remains a sore spot.

Bush:

"General Noriega's reckless threats and attacks upon Americans in Panama created an imminent danger to the 35,000 American citizens in Panama. As President, I have no higher obligation than to safeguard the lives of American citizens. And that is why I directed our Armed Forces to protect the lives of American citizens in Panama and to bring General Noriega to justice in the United States . . .

"Operation Just Cause"

"At this moment, U.S. forces, including forces deployed from the United States last night, are engaged in action in Panama. The United States intends to withdraw the forces newly deployed to Panama as quickly as possible . . . Tragically, some Americans have lost their lives in defense of their fellow citizens, in defense of democracy. And my heart goes out to their families. We also regret and mourn the loss of innocent Panamanians.

"The brave Panamanians elected by the people of Panama in the elections last May, President Guillermo Endara and Vice Presidents Calderon and Ford, have assumed the rightful leadership of their country. You remember those horrible pictures of newly elected [Panamanian] Vice President [Guillermo 'Billy'] Ford, covered head to toe with blood, beaten mercilessly by so-called 'dignity battalions.' Well, the United States today recognizes the democratically elected government of President Endara. I will send our Ambassador back to Panama immediately.

"Key military objectives have been achieved. Most organized resistance has been eliminated, but the operation is not over yet: General Noriega is in hiding. And nevertheless, yesterday a dictator ruled Panama, and today constitutionally elected leaders govern."

Many Panamanians lost everything as a result of the invasion. After the invasion Panama was in chaos; the US had no plan. The old police force was in hiding and there was no law. The US had "liberated" Panama only to bring incredible hardship, chaos, and anarchy in the streets. There was widespread looting. Many small businesses were destroyed. Larger business, unable to collect, went bankrupt.

After the invasion Panama was in chaos; the US had no plan

As his government fell, Noriega moved around hiding out from US forces, eventually taking refuge in the Vatican Embassy, home of the Papal nuncio. Noriega had taken the US Army's Psych Ops training but was now himself the target. The US blasted the residence with rock music day and night until Noriega surrendered.

If they had rap music he would have been out in several hours!

Noriega was arrested and hustled off to prison in Miami as a POW. Originally sentenced to 40 years, the sentence was reduced to 30 years, and with good behavior Noriega ended up serving 17 years. As a POW he was entitled to be addressed as "General" (albeit of an army of one, since Panama had abolished the military). Noriega had a suite of rooms in prison, exercise machines, telephone and was provided with "General" uniforms at US taxpayer expense.

Noriega, after serving his prison sentence in the US was extradited to France to serve a prison sentence for money laundering serving not as a make believe "General" but as just another prisoner. In December 2012 he was extradited from France to Panama and currently resides in a simple, nondescript Panamanian prison and Noriega has an ordinary cell with some accommodation made due to his poor health and to protect his security. Some of his friends, family and old PRD party friends would like to see him under house arrest due to his age and infirmity. But with the PRD out of power it is highly unlikely that Noriega will get house arrest since he faces additional very serious charges and sentences already handed down for multiple murders, kidnapping, and corruption.

News photographers have captured occasional pictures of a fail, old man in a wheelchair being escorted to hospital with high security for treatment. Most Panamanians are much more concerned about inflation, pay raises and the latest fashions in stores at the gigantic Panama City malls. At best, Noriega is an interesting bit history. And it is doubtful that Noriega even recognizes the booming country to which he returned.

* * * *

The role of the US in Panama will always be the topic of discussion and controversy. There are differing opinions amongst Panamanians and Americans even to this day. Some US citizens question why we turned the Canal over to Panama. And there are many criticisms of the US Invasion of Panama.

When I talk on cruises I'm always aware that there will be mixed opinions amongst my usually heavily US audience. On one particular Canal cruise on one side of the theater I had a man who was a career Army officer who had taught at the US War College. He had a definite opinion! On the other side of the room was a "bird colonel", career Army man, graduate of West Point, whose life-long friend and West Point roommate was a General in the US Southern Command who resigned in opposition to the Bush Administration's policy in Panama. He had a very different opinion!

So not everyone agrees, even within the US Army, but the important thing is to look at history and try and learn from it.

Everett Ellis Briggs, US Ambassador to Panama from 1982 to 1986 says, in regard to the US Invasion, "Almost everyone in government, however, shares some of the blame."

While in prison in Miami, Noriega, with the help of Peter Eisner, an American journalist who had covered Panama, wrote his memoirs. About two thirds of the book is Noriega's as-told-to story. It is a measured book, not at all the ramblings of a mad-man dictator, and like the memoirs of every head of state, self-justifying. The other third of the book is Peter Eisner's analysis. Eisner writes,

"The shambles of US actions and responsibility in Panama were the result of the actions of rigid and ruthless ideologues; Noriega was the target, but *the responsibility lies with a country whose citizens should not be so complacent as to fall for the rhetoric.*"[21]

There are amazing parallels between the CIA's involvement with Noriega and the US invasion of Panama and its aftermath and the CIA's involvement with Saddam Hussein and the US invasion of Iraq and the aftermath. Perhaps the US should review history more often and maybe as citizens we should, in Eisner's words, "not be so complacent as to fall for the rhetoric."

* * * *

When the Carter-Torrijos treaty was signed the US almost immediately began withdrawing and gradually turning over Canal operations to Panama, but it was not until December 31, 1999 exactly as the new millennium began that Panama once again achieved full sovereignty over its territory and the Panama Canal.

Following the Invasion, Panama had to deal with the aftermath and destruction of the Invasion as well as the US closure of military bases. Although Panama gained back property, buildings and infrastructure, many jobs were lost hurting the country economically. Combining the war damage and the sudden loss of jobs and revenue, Panama went through some tough economic times. It was not until several years after the Turnover of the Canal that the money started to flow.

---

[21] Peter Eisner in THE MEMOIRS OF MANUEL NORIEGA, AMERICA'S PRISONER, P. 249.

Many people look at the Turnover only in terms of what the US "gave away" or "lost". What they fail to realize is that the US was unloading a lot of liability. The US had operated the Canal as a service, just breaking even. Panama came in and starting operating the Canal as a very profitable business. Had the US hung onto the Canal it would have had to have changed the way it was operated. But there were generations of special interests to deal with. The US turned over to Panama enormous military bases, but the bases in Panama were no longer needed and just a budget drain. The concept of war had changed and the US was now dependent the ability to rapidly deploy a slimmed down military.

On December 14, a few days before the new millennium and the actual Turnover of the Canal, former US President Jimmy Carter joined Panamanian President Mireya Moscoso, King Juan Carlos of Spain, and various Latin American leaders at a ceremony celebrating the Turnover of the Canal. Conspicuously absent were US President Bill Clinton, Vice President Al Gore, and the US Secretary of State, Madeleine Albright.

Carter said,

"We didn't understand clearly enough the feeling of many Panamanians that the arrangement implied an element of colonialism and subjugation and not an equal representation . . ."

Panama and the US moved into the new millennium with a new relationship based on mutual respect, trust and cooperation. Panama and the US are not only linked by historic ties, and the fact that many Panamanians have joint Panamanian-US citizenship, but by the commitments of the Carter-Torrijos Treaty. There were actually two treaties. The first treaty turned over the Canal and the Canal Zone to Panama. In the second treaty the US agreed to defend the neutrality of the Canal in perpetuity

So, far from being over, the relationship has just moved on to a different level. Today the US and Panama relate as neighboring sovereign states each vitally important to the other. Panama has yielded to US bullying to change its long tradition of private banking and allow the US access to Panamanian banking records in order to secure US ratification of a Free Trade Agreement.

8 - Moving Forward

As the clock ticked onward on December 31, 1999 and most of the world was worried about Y2K issues, fearing prison doors flinging open, planes crashing and apocalyptic chaos as our computerized society was confounded with new double-zero digits, Panama was in a mood of national celebration. A huge digital clock at the base of Ancon Hill, just below the Panama Canal Headquarters, ticked off the minutes until the Turnover. The magic moment . . . when the clock reached zero! As the time grew nearer anticipation grew and thousand flocked onto Ancon Hill. It was not only a new millennium, but more importantly for Panama, a symbolic new beginning and actual ownership of its Canal.

A lot of people think that at 11:59 pm on December 31 the last US employee to leave the Canal threw the keys to the Panamanians and said, "Here. Good luck!" The reality was that when the Canal Treaties were signed in 1977 a long process of US disengagement began. Almost immediately the US began unloading military facilities and gradually turning them back to Panama. By the time Panama formally acquired the Canal, Panama had increasingly been involved in its operation for twenty years.

The new millennium signified a new beginning for Panama. The dark days of the dictatorship were over and Panama had survived both the dictatorship and the US Invasion. Panama had lived without an army and in a democracy for ten years. And now the Panama Canal belonged to Panama.

At the time of the turnover Mireya Moscoso was President of Panama. Moscoso, Panama's first woman president, was a former interior decorator who at the age of eighteen had married former President Arnulfo Arias. Her administration has been dogged by accusations of fraud and misuse of funds.

Moscoso was followed by Martin Torrijos, the illegitimate son of former military strongman Omar Torrijos. Being Torrijos illegitimate son carried no censorial weight in Panama: it was a mark of pride for Martin and many believe helped him to secure the Presidency.

Martin Torrijos was raised in the US, worked in Mc Donald's, and graduated from Texas A&M. Torrijos did a lot of the right things: trying to crack down on corruption, which in Panama as in many Latin countries had been the accepted way of doing business, initiating various reforms, and struggling for a strict accounting of money.

It was Martin Torrijos who proposed a plan to expand, or "amplify", the Panama Canal, which his father Omar Torrijos had secured for Panama.

* * * *

Since the Panama Canal was turned over to Panama in 2000, operations have improved significantly. Unlike the US, Panama is running the Canal as a very profitable business venture. The Panama Canal Authority, which oversees the operation, is an independent agency of the government, outside of the government and its tradition of patronage and favoritism to members of the political party in power at the moment.

Since the Turnover major improvements have been made on the Canal infrastructure, deepening and expanding channels, and refurbishing locks and equipment. New equipment has been installed including the latest generation of electric mules. Additionally:

Operating efficiency has improved;

Waiting time has decreased;

Transit times have decreased;

There has been a reduction of accidents;

The Canal is making money – big time!

* * * *

But the Canal faced significant problems.

At the time of the Turnover the Canal had already been in operation for 85 years. The Canal was running for the most part exactly as it had always run, still operating and was still a wonder of the world. But the world had changed. At the time of construction no one could have imagined a ship that could carry 15,000 twenty foot containers!

Traditionally the largest ships were Panamax ships, meaning they were the largest ships that could fit through the Canal. But as technology improved it became more economical to operate larger ships and shipping lines began building Post-Panamax ships that were too large to fit through the Canal. The economies of scale of the Post-Panamax ships were significant enough that it was worth having to make the longer trip around Cape Horn.

The Canal realized that in order to remain competitive and for Panama to continue to be the crossroads of the world, it was necessary to expand the Canal and build larger locks that would be able to accommodate ships now on the drawing boards, and ships yet to be imagineered.

* * * *

On September 1, 2004, Panamanian President Martin Torrijos proposed what was initially projected to be an $8 billion expansion of the Panama Canal. The figure was later revised downward to the present estimate of $5.25 billion.

To proceed Panama needed a national referendum to approve the Canal Expansion. Tabloid-size proposals were distributed all over the country. Arguments were made for and against the Canal Expansion program. The country was covered with posters and flags urging a "Si!" or "No!" vote. The Indian workers on my coffee farm had vigorous discussions about the merits of the proposal. On October 22, 2006 78% of Panamanians voted in favor of the Canal Expansion.

On September 3, 2007, with former US President Jimmy Carter in attendance, work began on the Canal Expansion project.

* * * *

The project was originally scheduled for completion in 2014 during the 100th Anniversary of the Canal. Sometimes called the "Third Lane" project, it involves creating two new sets of locks, one on the Pacific and one on the Atlantic, which will accommodate ships larger than any currently on the drawing boards.

The project includes:

1- Deeping and widening of the Atlantic entrance channel

2 - New approach channel for the Atlantic Post-Panamax locks

3 - Atlantic Post-Panamax locks with three water saving basins per lock chamber

4 - Raising the maximum Gatun Lake operating water level

5 - Widening and deepening of the navigational channel of the Gatun Lake and the Culebra Cut

6 - New approach channel for the Pacific Post-Panamax locks

7 - Pacific Post-Panamax locks with three water saving basins per lock chamber

8 - Deepening and widening of the Pacific entrance channel

* * * *

The new locks will not only be larger than the current locks, but they will operate somewhat differently.

Instead of using the current "swing" or miter gates, they will use rolling gates which are easier to maintain.

Instead of using the traditional "mules" or electric engines to keep the ship centered, the locks will be large enough to accommodate a tug at both ends of the vessel.

The locks will have water saving basins which will allow sixty percent of the water to be recycled.

The "third lane" refers to the construction of the two new lock chambers and approach channels, but does not mean that another entire Canal channel is being dug across Panama.

Most importantly the size of the lock chambers will be increased.

Width: currently 110 feet (33.53 meters) - new 180 feet (55 meters)

Length: currently 1,000 feet (304.8 meters) - new 1,400 ft (427 meters)

Draft: currently 39 feet (12 meters) – new 60 feet (18.3 meters)

* * * *

[22] PanCanal.com

Conceptual Location of the New Pacific Locks

- Culebra Cut
- Pedro Miguel Locks
- Miraflores Lake
- New approach channel
- Miraflores Locks
- New water saving basins
- Corozal
- New three-step Locks
- Current Channel
- New approach channel

[23]

* * * *

The financial impact of the Panama Canal on a country of 3.3 million people is enormous.

In its most recent year the Canal took in $2 billion. $1.3 billion was in tolls and the remainder was primarily from sales of electricity and water.

---

[23] Ibid

In addition to the overall economic contribution of the Canal, in terms of taxes, jobs, support services, contracts, etc., the Canal makes a direct contribution to the government of about $400 million a year. When the Expansion Program is completed in 2015 it is estimated that the direct contribution will be $1.25 billion a year and by 2025 over $6 billion a year.

Panama has proposed creating a Sovereign Fund where eventually $1 billion a year will be sequestered to be used should the country ever face some massive economic or natural disaster.

To work in Panama you must be Panamanian. If no Panamanian is qualified for a particular job, a limited number of foreigners can be employed. Ninety percent of the 6,000 employee Panama Canal workforce is Panamanian.

The $5.25 billion Expansion Project will be financed by gradually increasing tolls originally at an average rate of 3.5% for twenty years, although the Canal announced at the beginning of 2012 a 15% increase. External financing of $3 billion from the World Bank, Japan Bank for International Cooperation and others, will cover the peak construction years between 2009 and 2011.

The Panama Canal Authority and government have been committed to transparency throughout the bidding process and have sought out contractors from around the world with the resources and ability to complete the task.

* * * *

Cruise transits account for very little of the Canal traffic with about 225 cruise ship transits per year out of some 14,600 total transits. The key players in the Panama Canal cruise market, with totals of passengers for a recent year, are:

Princess Cruises 21,881
Celebrity Cruises 21,805
Holland America Line 18,908
Royal Caribbean International 8,308

* * * *

If global warming continues, it is conceivable that the Northwest Passage at some point could provide an alternative route to the Panama Canal. But most experts do not see the Northwest Passage as a viable route for at least the next two decades.

At various times Nicaragua has proposed building a canal along the route that lost out to Panama. In 2006 the Nicaraguan President Enrique Bolanos declared there was sufficient demand for two canals and proposed a $25 billion canal across Nicaragua. The proposal has met strong opposition by environmentalists, but most importantly collided head on with the world financial crisis and reduced demand.

Panama considered this potential competition and decided that even if this scheme or other schemes materialize, there would be sufficient demand for the Panama Canal. And the Expansion Program might just dissuade potential competitors such as Nicaragua.

Cruise ships passing in Gatun Locks

* * * *

In Panama there is a saying, "Panama is the heart of the universe, the bridge of the world." It is location, location, location along with the Panama Canal that combines to make Panama strategic.

Panama is enjoying an economic boom, and is frequently referred to as "the Singapore of Latin America." Despite a world economic downturn Panama's economy continues to grow.

Panama's current President, Ricardo Martinelli, is a no-nonsense businessman who owns the largest chain of supermarkets in the country. Martinelli has a business degree from the University of Arkansas as well as an MBA from the INCAE Business School (founded 1964 by the Central American private sector, Harvard Business School, and USAID). Martinelli still goes back to Arkansas to watch the Razorbacks play.

In his inaugural address Martinelli laid out his no-nonsense approach to governance saying, "In my administration it's OK to put your foot in your mouth, but not to put your hand in the till

Martinelli likes to point out that he has seven CEOs in his cabinet. He's running the country like a business and has made major reforms. Martinelli donates his entire salary to various orphanages and charities, and has already said he won't run again for president since he "can't put up with all this crap." My kind of guy, and since he has a high approval rating, obviously lots of folks agree.

I met him by accident at the tiny airport in David where I had gone to pick up someone. He was an underdog candidate and had just arrived to lead a rag-tag "parade" of supporters and old cars and banners out of the airport. He was on foot with his supporters and I was stuck in my car, waiting for them to get out of the way. He walked over, obviously recognizing me as a gringo who couldn't vote, reached in the window to shake hands and asked in perfect English how we liked Panama and if things were going well for us. Impressed me!

As a result of the lessons learned in "the dictatorship", Panama, like Costa Rica, has abolished the military. Money that was once used for the military is now used for universal education and social programs. Panama has torn a page from the Swiss play book, knowing that if you have their money – and offshore corporations – their hearts and minds will follow and they won't attack you. Of course Panama can afford not to have an army since the US has committed to protect the neutrality of the Panama Canal in perpetuity.

The relationship between Panama and the US strikes me somewhat as the relationship between an older and younger brother. The younger brother obviously wants to strike out on his own and not be ordered about, but if you get in a jam, it's nice to know you have back up from your older brother. This gives Panama a stability that goes beyond its borders and own political system.

Martinelli might well say to Obama, "Mr. President, I have seven CEOs in my Cabinet: how many do you have in yours?"

9 - Questions & Answers

What I really look forward to when I lecture on ships transiting the Canal is the Q&A sessions. If you are in the planning stages for a Panama trip, you obviously have many questions. Based on questions I've answered in the past, maybe I can anticipate some of your concerns.

When is the best time to cruise the Panama Canal?

There is no one "best" time to cruise the Panama Canal or to visit Panama. Since we are about nine degrees off the Equator the weather is pretty much the same all year round. In the Canal area it is always hot and humid, just like you would expect in the Tropics. There is almost no variance in the daytime temperatures and very little in the nighttime temperature.

The Canal is surrounded by Rain Forest and so . . . it rains! No matter when you visit it is likely that sometime during your transit of the Canal you will get some rain, even if it is just a sprinkle.

Usually in Panama there is more rain from May through November, the "green" season, and less rain from December to April, the so-called "dry" season, which in the Canal area just means the "less wet" season.

In Colon the driest months are January, February and March and the wettest are September, October and November.

The rain is warm and usually comes in a rather brief downpour and really doesn't interfere with our enjoyment of the Canal. Stick a cheap plastic poncho in your luggage and you'll do fine.

Most of the Canal cruises you find will be in the September to May period, not because the weather is better, but because during June to September the cruise lines make more money by having their ships positioned in Europe and Alaska.

Month	Mean Temperature °F Daily Minimum	Mean Temperature °F Daily Maximum	Mean Total Rainfall (mm)	Mean Number of Rain Days
Jan	65.3	92.1	29.3	2.9
Feb	65.1	93.6	10.1	1.3
Mar	65.1	94.6	13.1	1.4
Apr	67.1	95.7	64.7	4.9
May	70.0	94.1	225.1	15
Jun	70.3	92.8	235.0	16
Jul	69.8	93.0	168.5	14
Aug	69.6	93.0	219.9	15
Sep	69.8	91.2	253.9	17
Oct	69.4	90.7	330.7	20
Nov	68.5	91.2	252.3	16
Dec	66.6	91.9	104.6	7.5

Temperatures in °F – rain in millimeters – 25 mm is about 1 inch

What is the weather like?

As I said, it's pretty much the same the year round. January to March is a time when we get northerly winds which can make maneuvering the ship into the locks a little more tricky since the ship acts as a giant sail. But with a nice northerly breeze blowing across the decks it makes it feel less hot and humid.

Panama is outside the hurricane zone, although we do sometimes catch the edge of a tropical depression which can make for more rain. While Panama is outside the hurricane zone, you may have to deal with tropical storms in the Caribbean. Usually the ship can avoid the storm itself, but sometimes weather can delay airport traffic in and out of South Florida.

We are getting a balcony, which side of the ship is best?

There is nothing like a balcony stateroom . . . I suppose, since if you are a crew member you are lucky and privileged if you can snag an old fashioned porthole! But from my days as a top-producing travel agency owner I know that there is nothing like sitting on your own balcony in your Jockey shorts or less, sipping wine and watching the sun set.
A balcony is ideal when you are cruising through Gatun Lake. But, you don't want to spend the entire transit on your balcony! You want to move around the ship so you get to see different perspectives of the action.

In the locks it is a crap shoot. There is absolutely no way of knowing whether your ship will be assigned the port or left hand chamber or the right or starboard side chamber. There is no way to psych this out, so either side is great!

Is it safe to do an independent tour in Panama?

The safest way to take a tour is always going to be with the ship. If the tour is late, stuck in traffic, or there is an accident along the way, the ship is going to wait until all the tours are back. If you have booked independently and are delayed you may miss the "boat" and have to find your own way to the next port to catch up with the ship. The tour operators the cruise lines use are vetted; they must have insurance, and are checked for basic safety. They are dependable, and the ship shore excursion office sends along ship "Escorts" who report back on the quality of the tour. Additionally all guest comments are continually reviewed. If an operator doesn't perform, they are out.

In most ports it is easiest, most hassle free, and often most cost-effective to use a ship's tour.

In some ports, like Panama, there is limited availability on things like the Panama Canal Railway and the Canal Ferry Excursion, and guess what? Right! The cruise lines and their big operators book all the space they can get which is generally all the space available.

I work cruises all over the world, including round the world cruises. There are some places in the world where you just want to go ashore and soak up the ambience or there is convenient public transportation and it is easy to do your own thing. Panama is not that kind of place!

So, my best advice, book with the ship!

However, all that being said, there are people who just don't like hanging out in the lounge to be "stickered" and then marched ashore like a group of kindergarteners on a field trip, or delayed by one or two people who shouldn't have booked the tour in the first place. There are folks who just don't want to be with a giant group of "tourists." But, in places like Ephesus, Athens, Rome, Paris, and London, or even exotic places like the Taj Mahal, Angkor Wat and Machu Picchu . . . you may go independently, but you are going to end up at the "sights" surrounded by the same hordes of people and ship tours you sought to avoid.

There are a number of very reliable and excellent smaller tour operators in Panama who work out of both the Pacific and Atlantic ports. If you do your homework, you should end up with a good tour operator and have a fantastic day. Just be sure they allow for traffic and get you back to the ship on time!

How do you find these reliable tour operators? Work the Internet. Browse the cruise bulletin boards. See what others have experienced and who they recommend. It takes a little digging but it will be worth it.

Naturally these independent tour operators are going to expect full or at least partial payment up front. Would you expect anything different? Would you hire and assign guides, and reserve buses just hoping that people might show up as promised? Of course not! Sometimes these independent tour operators will take credit card payments, but because they are small players many times they will want you to use Pay Pal or similar. If you're not comfortable paying in advance book with the ship.

There is also a Hop On Hop Off bus tour available of Panama City [City-Sightseeing.com] which you can book online in advance or just pay when you hop on the bus.

Are there taxis available at the pier that will do tours?

But of course! Regular licensed taxis in Panama must be painted yellow with checkered stripe along the side. There are no meters. Taxis around town are relatively inexpensive, which is why everyone uses them. Traditionally there have been set zones and fares within those zones or if you cross over to another zone, although Panama City is experimenting with taxi meters. All the locals know these rates and of course you don't. Bingo, or as it's known locally, "Gringo Bingo!" Just accept that world-over many taxi drivers are out to take advantage of tourists. If you just accept that, and go with the flow, you will enjoy travelling the world a whole lot more with less frustration. Of course sometimes you are going to get "ripped off"; it's just a part of travel.

There may also be "unofficial" drivers and vans eager to take you on tour. Many of these are just working guys with families eager to make a few extra bucks. They may even take you home to meet their families.

Generally the rate for a licensed taxi is going to run around $25 to $30 an hour.

Are they "safe"? Generally, yes. You pay your money and take your choice. If safety is your primary concern, you stick with the ship.

What kind of vaccines do we need?

If you're from the US, Canada, or Europe generally vaccinations are unnecessary. If you are coming from a country that has yellow fever, you may be required to have a yellow fever vaccination.

Do I need to take malaria pills?

For the Canal and 98% of Panama, no! Your doctor may have a different opinion. Of course your doctor is in the business of . . . well, you know. If you are just transiting the Canal . . . no way!

Do we need a tourist visa?

If you are on a cruise ship transiting the Canal generally not, but the cruise line can advise you of any particular requirement given your citizenship. For North Americans no visa is necessary on a cruise. If you are flying in from North America to pick up a ship in Panama the cost of a tourist visa is included in the cost of your flight.

Watching the Canal go by from the Promenade Deck

Are there lots of mosquitoes?

Sure, we have some mosquitoes, but nothing like Alaska or the mid-western US in the summer. Since the days of the Canal construction controlling the mosquito population has been a priority. Transiting the Canal you are far enough from shore and the breezes are strong enough that you aren't going to find any mosquitoes. If you are taking a shore excursion into the jungle or on Gatun Lake you might want to take along bug spray to use if needed but do so carefully without spraying everyone else or bathing in DEET.

Where can we find good coffee to take home?

Panama is known the world over for superb coffee, yet the good stuff is incredibly hard to find if you are on a cruise. Sometimes ships will sell "Coffee of The Type Used in The Panama Canal." That tells you nothing! The packages I've seen don't even tell you if it is Panamanian coffee! At the grocery stores, like Super 99 in Colon, you will find the good local brands that people drink in Panama, like Cafe Ruiz, Palo Alto, Sitton and Duran. On the Panama Canal Railway they sell coffee from Boquete, where I live.

People always ask about my coffee. Much of our coffee is sold to Cafe Ruiz and Sitton and is mixed in with everyone else's coffee to make good Panamanian coffee. But the really good, premium stuff we hold out for ourselves and process naturally by hand.

How can I get from the airport to the pier in Colon?

The best, easiest, and possibly cheapest way is using the cruise line transfer. There are cabs at the airport who will take you but it is very expensive! It takes over an hour and the cab driver isn't going to have a return fare so is probably going to charge you close to double. A lot of Panama City cabs are using propane with a tank that may take up much of the trunk space.

If you are staying overnight at a hotel in Panama City you can ask the front desk to arrange something. You'll end up with someone's brother-in-law giving you a ride.

It is easiest and best to use the cruise line transfers. A car or van will run about $70 to $150 depending on the number of people, size of the vehicle, and where you are staying in Panama City.

I'm confused. Which Canal itinerary is best?

This is a frequent question, and, as I've said, there is no one "best" itinerary. It all depends on you, your time frame, your budget, your interests and the cruises you've taken before. Do you want to focus on the Panama Canal, or do you want it to be just another experience of many?

The nice thing is that with the 100th Anniversary of the Canal and the completion of the new locks, there is a lot of interest in the Canal so cruise lines have developed a lot of great itineraries. I particularly like the ones that give you time to get off the ship and experience a full day exploring Panama before or after the Canal transit.

Repositioning cruises are generally offered in spring and fall and are longer and generally attractively priced. However, most repositioning cruises simple transit the Canal without allowing you opportunity to see Panama.

You just need to choose what you want to do and what works out best for you.

There appear to be so many excellent tour choices in Panama. How do I decide?

Most cruise lines, when they list available tours, will list the most general, most popular tours that give you the best "overview" of a place first. As you move down the listing you'll find tours that concentrate on a particular aspect of a port, and near the end you generally find tours that are designed to appeal to more "active" people, or people who have visited that port previously. Which tour is best for you depends on your interests and your physical abilities. Unfortunately most people only have a single day, so you've got to choose a single tour that is most in line with your interests. There is no one tour that is "best" for everyone.

You'll discover that Panama has so much to offer that you'll want to come back and visit again!

Our itinerary says we will do a daylight transit but also that we enter the Canal at 5 am. What time does sun rise? Won't it be dark?

Cruise ships almost always make a daylight transit of the Canal. The pilot comes on board around 5 am. The sun is up by 6:30 am which is when you should be entering the first lock.

Why do we have to get up so early?

You don't! It's your cruise; you can sleep all day if you want. But if you came to experience the Panama Canal you will want to experience the entire transit. Early morning on Canal day as the sun is coming up is absolutely magical! The pilot will generally come on board at 5 am. By 6 am you are generally moving into the locks. It's your choice, but I'd suggest an early wake up call.

Where can I find Indian crafts, Kuna molas and Embera baskets?

You will find some of this craft work in gift shops all over Panama and maybe the shops on board will even bring some on board to sell the day you are in the Canal. The best place to buy Embera crafts is on the Authentic Embera Village tour, since there all of the money is going directly to the Indian family who made the craft. There used to be a big Indian craft market at Pier 6 Cristobal when that was still in existence. The operators of the new piers will only allow the Indians to sell their crafts if they pay exorbitant prices for stores just like the same big stores you see in every cruise port. There is a great selection of craft items behind the YMCA in Balboa, a regular stop on some of the Panama City tours. If you are going independently and visit the Old City (the original city which is different that Casco Viejo) there is also a big Indian craft market right next to the famed Old Panama Tower. There are several stores in Casco Viejo that have a great selection of Indian crafts as well.

Our ship is going to be in the Canal over the Holidays; will that make a difference?

No, the Panama Canal operates 24 hours a day 365 days a year. I was actually in the Canal doing a turn around cruise on Christmas Day. Santa managed to locate the ship and arrived on the fore deck while we were in Gatun Lake! All of the tours operated as scheduled.

Spending the holidays at sea is a fantastic idea . . . all the celebration and fuss . . . without any work! What could be better?

Christmas Day in the Canal

Which cruise line is best?

You think I'm crazy? For fifteen years I ran successful "cruise only" agencies and frequently was asked this question. My answer has always been the same, "It depends." All of the cruise lines work hard to cultivate a particular niche of the market and aim their product at a particular type of guest. You need to find one that is a good fit for you and meets your expectations.

The Canal itself is the same regardless of the cruise line. I'd look at itineraries and I'd look at the type and amount of information and background they give you about the Canal transit. On Caribbean cruises, World Cruises and other itineraries, people book to get away, to escape bad weather or to see "the world." On Canal cruises people book for one very specific reason: The Panama Canal. So you want to find a cruise that focuses on the Canal, and where it isn't just "another cruise" with bingo and line dancing as highlights.

Where is there duty free shopping? I've heard Colon has a huge free port?

There are Duty Free shops at the airport and at or near some of the cruise terminal areas. These are the same Duty Free shops you see at airports around the world.

Panama is not known for "duty free shopping" like in St. Maarten, the Virgin Islands, Aruba, etc. Colon does have the world's second largest Free Zone but that is not "duty free shopping" in the cruise ship sense of the phrase. A free zone allows manufacturers and companies to import huge containers of goods that can be assembled, or labeled, or just broken up and shipped off to other ports without paying any import or export duty. Buyers come from all over the world, and particularly this region, to buy container loads of goods. Major companies stockpile goods and parts to be able to conveniently ship them around the world from Panama, the "crossroads of the world."

If you have your passport and cruise card or are a crew member sometimes you will be allowed into the Colon Free Zone, but you will be disappointed. It is a vast city set up for wholesale, not retail. And while you may find an occasional little store that will sell retain, you have to know where you are going and it can be very time consuming.

What is the difference between an eastbound and a westbound transit? Is one any better than the other?

As you undoubtedly know by now because the Canal runs north-south, going from the Pacific to the Atlantic is Northbound and from the Atlantic to the Pacific is Southbound.

I frankly can't think of any reason why one way is better than another. If you come up with a reason, please let me know.

The only one possible advantage of going Southbound is that on most ships, because of changing time zones, they turn the clock back and you gain an extra hour of sleep so 5 am doesn't seem quite so early.

We're cruising with a disabled family member. How accessible are the tours in Panama?

It really depends on the nature of the disability. Be sure to discuss this with the shore excursion desk on board. They are in touch with the tour operators and know what, if any accommodation can be made. Although Panama is making great strides, we do not have anything to compare with the Americans With Disabilities Act and for the most part "accessibility" is a new concept.

Natural, totally non erotic, and forgotten about in the first ten minutes

We're traveling with our children, grade school through high school. The Authentic Embera Village tour looks very interesting but I am concerned about the nudity.

First, talk with your kids. I suspect they have been exposed to a whole lot more nudity than you've ever imagined, including a whole lot else! Attitudes toward nudity are pretty much cultural, and even within a culture attitudes vary at different times. A little child sees bare breasts and thinks "lunch" and when he's a teenager he is off to his room locking the door. In the context of the Embera Village it is very natural, totally non erotic, and forgotten about in the first ten minutes.

It will be fantastic experience for you kids regardless of their age. I would encourage you to let your younger kids just run off and play with the Indian kids and make new friends. The Indian kids love this and so do the children of guests. Kids tend to cross cultural differences and barriers much more quickly than adults. Let your kids get painted with the black juice or *jagua* fruit tattoo ink. Don't worry, it only lasts for about six weeks and if your kids go back to school with Embera body decoration they will be the envy of all their classmates! And you might try it yourself! Just imagine going back to work with black decorations on your face!

Where can I find Panama Hats?

The real Panamanian "*campesino*" hats run $10 and up, but are rarely found in Panama City, and usually not in gift shops. They don't look like your stereotype of a "Panama Hat." The Panama Hats you are probably thinking of are the ones made in Ecuador. You'll find cheap made-in-China ones for $10 and up in most tourist shops, the good ones for $50 and up, and the really good Montecristi ones for as much as $500!

We are embarking and disembarking our cruise in Colon. Is it feasible to rent a car and see the country safely in two weeks time? I'm very interested in the non city experience, in seeing rural Panama, both coast lines, the mountains etc.

Absolutely. Driving in Panama City is a hassle and not for the faint of heart. But once you are outside of the city, driving is fine. Main roads are generally in good condition. Except for one small section of the Pan American Highway, now being rebuilt, the Pan American Highway is a good road and the seven hour trip from Panama City to Boquete is interesting and gives a good view of the lives of most Panamanians outside the city. All the major rental car companies have offices in Panama City as well as in David should you choose to fly to David and rent a car. Here's my suggestion for two weeks.

Days 1-4 – Panama City area. You can hire a cab for around $25 to $30 an hour. The front desk of your hotel can give you suggestions. See Old Panama, the old French area of Casco Viejo including the Interoceanic Canal Museum, Opera House and Golden Altar. See the Canal itself including the Miraflores Locks visitor center. Your driver can call and check the schedule so you are actually at the visitor center when a ship is in the locks. Or you can try the Hop On Hop Off bus in Panama City. [City-Sightseeing.com] Arrange an all day tour to the Embera Puru maybe through Anne Gordon, a *gringa* who married an Embera guy. [EmberaVillageTours.com] they will pick you up at your hotel and it will be a memorable day.

Days 5-6 – Stay at the beach. Decameron is an all-inclusive beach resort that's about an hour from Panama City. [Decameron.com]

Days 7-10 – Fly to David, rent a car, and visit Boquete. We have hiking expeditions, river rafting, canopy zip line tours, coffee tours and more.

Days 11-12 – Fly to Bocas del Toro, a funky, laid back, somewhat noisy town in the Caribbean islands.

Days 13 – 14 – Fly to the San Blas Islands and visit the Kuna Indians.

Day 15 – Fly home.

That will give you a whirlwind tour of Panama and you'll be anxious to return for more. Of course you can work out a much shorter itinerary as well.

Are there any beaches nearby to the ports in Panama?

Not really. Panama has fantastic beach areas and beach resorts, but they just aren't near to Panama City and Colon.

Why are there no shore excursions to the San Blas Islands?

There just isn't enough time for a shore excursion to visit the San Blas Islands, but it is one of the things that you want to arrange when you return to Panama. It's definitely at least an overnight trip.

Is it possible to just rent a car and do your own thing in Panama?

Anything is possible, but . . . not recommended. You have to be nuts to drive in Panama City or Colon. If you are planning to spend time in Panama outside the cities either before or after your cruise, renting a car may work well. All of the major car rental agencies are at Tocumen International Airport. If you are just spending a day or a few hours in Panama, it will take you that long to get anywhere, and you may well miss the boat and spend the rest of your life driving in circles!

Is it safe to just walk around town without a shore excursion? What could we see and what would we miss?

Short answer: no, and you'd miss everything.

There is nothing really to see in Colon and it is not an area where it is safe to wander around.

At Amador you are out on the end of the Amador Peninsula and except for some shops and restaurants there is nothing there. It's a twenty minute ride into Panama City proper. At night I wouldn't just wander around in the city without knowing which areas are safe and which areas are "iffy". I wouldn't wander around alone Casco Viejo at night without knowing what I was doing. During the day if you take a cab into town you can wander around a mall, but the things you want to see are spread around town and you'd have to keep jumping in and out of cabs.

Our tour leaves at 10 am and doesn't return until 4 pm, but there is only a snack included. My husband needs to eat regularly because of a medical condition.

You didn't hear this from me, because every ship in the world is going to tell you not to take any food off the ship. There are some places in the world (Australia, New Zealand and the US for example) where they are incredibly anal about this; Panama is not. I'm sure there must be signs, somewhere, but I have never seen any actual agricultural inspection, although I suspect this is going to change as Panama moves toward "First World" status.

For most cruise passengers missing a meal is not an ordeal but a needed privilege! But there are people who do need to have something to eat on a regular basis and, I agree, it isn't too smart to take people out over lunch time without giving them something to eat or at least the opportunity to purchase something.

My wife, p-l-e-e-a-s-e don't tell anyone, always sticks a box of Fruit Loops from the buffet in her purse or back pack. If you take a bagel sandwich, an apple, or some nuts and dried fruit from the noontime buffet, I doubt if you will get thrown in the brig. Packaged items, like a little box of cereal, generally aren't problems, except of course in Australia and New Zealand.

Why are so many of the tours in Panama so long? Seven or eight hours are a long time!

Unfortunately the things that you really want to see aren't right next to the pier. The "better" tours in Panama are all the longer ones.

How can I find out if you are going to be lecturing on my cruise?

Heck, I'd like to be on them all! Obviously, that's not possible and there is a whole world out there to explore. You can ask the cruise line; in fact I'd like it if you do! You can check my schedule on my blog at RichardDetrich.com.

We're only going to be in Colon for a few hours. Is there anything to see or do?

Unfortunately the short evening calls are mainly "service calls" to pick up guests returning from shore excursions. There's really nothing to see or do in Colon, nor is it particularly a safe area. You'll spend most of your time in a long line waiting to get back on board. There are some gift shops at Colon 2000 and a Super 99 where you can pick up essentials.

Can you drink the water? What about mixed drinks?

In most parts of Panama water is pretty safe, but I think visitors are always advised to take along bottled water. It is hot, humid and you need to keep hydrated, so take a big bottle from the ship.

Almost all ice in Panama is made commercially and is fine in drinks.

Are there bathrooms on the buses?

Generally no. The buses in Panama may not be what you are used to in other parts of the world. Ease up on the coffee the morning of your tour. Go before you leave the ship. If you need to go en route, tell the driver and he will find a place to stop. Public restrooms, although they have western-style toilets (i.e. not squat toilets), generally aren't the cleanest (as is true everywhere in the world) and usually do not provide toilet paper, so stick a small roll in your backpack or take along a pack of Kleenex.

This is usually easier for men, since it is culturally appropriate, except in cities and built-up areas, to just go beside the road.

I understand there are a lot of North Americans and Europeans moving to Panama - what's the deal?

Oh, bless you for asking! Panama has become a very attractive destination for expats from around the world. The lower cost of living, beautiful beaches and weather is attracting many Baby Boomer retirees. Others, maybe fed up with the direction their home governments are taking or looking for a "safe haven", are relocating to Panama. If you want the whole story pick up my book ESCAPE TO PARADISE: LIVING AND RETIRING IN PANAMA.

The Bill

TOTAL TOLL 3,070 Berths $411,380

Estimated Additional Costs MV JUST CRUISING
Advance Transit Reservation Fee $25,000
Regular pilotage No Charge
Tug services $11.445
Line Handlers $4.745
Wires to Locomotives $3,600
Inspection Fee $118
Security Charge $440
"Orange Box" Rental Charge $161
Sanitary Inspection Fee $173
Medical Disembarkation in Locks $632
Disembarkation & Escort Four Photographers $585
Vessel Internet Information Charge $135
Launch Services $364

TOTAL FEES $47,398

TOTAL COST   **$458,778**

Key Dates in Panama History

- January 9, 1503 – Christopher Columbus built a garrison at Rio Belen

- 1509 - Spanish colonization began in what is today Colombia, Ecuador, Venezuela and Panama

- September 25, 1513 – Balboa claimed the "Southern Ocean" (later renamed the Pacific) for Spain

- 1519 – Panama City was founded

- January 27, 1671 – British privateer Sir Henry Morgan captured Panama City

- December 26, 1848 – First American Invasion as California-bound gold seekers arrived en Panama

- 1850 – Colon founded as the terminus of the Panama Railroad

- 1855 – Panama Railroad opened

- 1880 - Ferdinand de Lesseps began the French effort to build the canal

- May 3, 1881 - *Compagnie Universelle du Canal Interoceanique* incorporated under French law

- February 4, 1889 – The French effort was abandoned and *Compagnie Universelle du Canal Interoceanique* declared bankrupt and dissolved

- 1894 - Philippe Bunau-Varilla became stockholder and spokesman in the New Panama Canal Company, offering to sell the company's assets to the US for $109 million, asking price later reduced to $40 million

- June 19, 1902 - US Senate voted in favor of Panama as the canal site

- June 28, 1902 - The Spooner Bill authorized US to construct canal and purchased concession from France for $40 million

- September 17, 1902 - US troops sent to Panama to keep railroad open as local Panamanians struggled for independence from Colombia

- January 22, 1903 – Hay-Harran Treaty with Colombia giving US right to build a canal was passed by Senate, but not ratified by Colombia

- October 10, 1903 - Philippe Bunau-Varilla met with US President Theodore Roosevelt warning him of imminent rebellion in Panama

- November 3, 1903 – With US NASHVILLE standing by in Panama and Bunau-Varilla standing by in Washington, Panama proclaimed independence from Colombia with the only casualties being a shopkeeper and a donkey

- November 6, 1903 – Panama officially declared independence

- November 7, 1903 – The US officially recognized the Republic of Panama

- November 18, 1903 – Claiming to represent the newly created Republic of Panama, the Frenchman Bunau-Varilla granted the US a strip of land across Panama and the rights to build a canal and in return the US agreed to protect the new country

- February 3, 1904 – US Marines clashed with Colombian troops attempting to re-establish Colombian sovereignty in Panama

- February 23, 1904 – The US paid Panama $10 million for the Canal Zone

- May 4, 1904 – The Second US Invasion began as the US took over construction of the Panama Canal

- 1904 - Panama adopted US dollar as its currency calling it the "Balboa"

- 1904- Dr. William Gorgas took over as chief sanitary officer

- November 8, 1906 – US President Theodore Roosevelt visited Panama becoming the first US president in history to leave the country while in office

- 1907 - George Washington Goethals took control of the Canal Zone and construction

- August 24, 1909 – The first concrete was poured in the locks

- 1912 – The Chagres River was damned

- October 10, 1913 – US President Woodrow Wilson pushed a button in Washington triggering an explosion in Panama, exploding the temporary Gamboa Dike and allowing water to fill Gatun Lake

- August 15, 1914 – With the world occupied by a World War, the Panama Canal quietly opened with the ANCON making the first official crossing Southbound from the Atlantic to the Pacific

- April 20, 1921 -Thomson-Urrutia Treaty signed – US paid Colombia $25 million in return for Colombia's recognition of Panama's independence

- January 9, 1964 - Anti-U.S. rioting broke out and 21 Panamanian civilians and 4 US soldiers were killed including 6 Panamanian teenagers; now celebrated as a national holiday called "The Day of the Martyrs"

- January 10, 1964 - Panama broke off relations with the US and demanded a revision of the original Canal treaty

- October 11, 1968 - Panamanian President Arnulfo Arias was ousted in a coup by General Omar Torrijos

- August 10, 1977 – US and Panama began negotiation for Panama Canal turnover

- September 7, 1977 – US President Jimmy Carter and General Torrijos signed the Torrijos-Carter Treaties abrogating the Hay-Bunau Varilla Treaty and setting 1999 for the turnover of the Canal

- April 18, 1978 - US Senate ratified the Torrijos-Carter Treaties by a vote of 68 to 32

- October 1, 1979 – Under terms of the 1977 Panama Canal Treaties the US returned the Canal Zone to Panama, excluding the Canal itself

- July 31, 1981 – General Torrijos died in a plane crash

- August 12, 1983 - General Manuel Noriega assumed command of the National Guard

- 1985 – Dissident leader Hugo Spadafora was decapitated – Noriega later sentenced in Panama to 20 years in prison for the murder

- February 25, 1988 – Panamanian President Eric Arturo Delvalle removed Noriega as commander and was subsequently ousted as President and Noriega took control

- March 18, 1988 – Noriega declared a "state of urgency"

- April 8, 1988 – US President Ronald Regan issued an Executive Order blocking of all property and interests in property of the Government of Panama

- May 7, 1989 – Voters rejected Noriega but Noriega refused to recognize election results

- May 9, 1989 – US President George Bush in the light of "massive irregularities" in Panamanian elections called for Noriega to step down

- May 10, 1989 - Noriega nullified elections won by his opposition

- May 11, 1989 – US President Bush recalled US ambassador and beefed up US troops stationed in Panama

- October 3, 1989 – Noriega foiled attempted coup and had coup leaders executed

- December 20, 1989 – US invaded Panama with "Operation Just Cause" – the "Third US Invasion"

- December 24, 1989 – Noriega took refuge at residence of Papal Nuncio in Panama City

- January 3, 1990 – Noriega surrendered to US forces, was flown to Miami and arraigned in Federal District Court in Miami on drug-trafficking charges

- January 18, 1991 - US acknowledged that the CIA and US Army paid Noriega $322,226 from 1955-1986 and that Noriega began receiving money from the CIA in 1976 giving credulence to the claim of Noriega's lawyers that he was the "CIA's man in Panama"

- April 9, 1992 – Noriega convicted of drug and racketeering charges, sentenced to serve 40 years as a POW, entitling him to maintain his rank as a General . . . of an army of one since Panama had abolished the military

- 1995 - Noriega was convicted in Panama in absentia for the 1989 murder of officers involved in a failed coup

- October 1, 1996 – Fort Amador was transferred to Panama

- November 1, 1999 – US turned over Howard Air Force Base, Fort Kobbe and other territories to Panama

- December 14, 1999 – Former US President Carter symbolically turned over Panama Canal to Panamanian President Mireya Moscoso

- December 31, 1999 – US officially turned over Panama Canal to Panama

- 2000 – "Fourth US Invasion" began as North American and European retirees relocated to Panama

- September 1, 2004 – Panamanian President Martin Torrijos proposed an $8 billion expansion of the Panama Canal

- October 22, 2006 – Voters approved $5.25 billion Panama Canal Expansion proposal by 78%

- September 3, 2007 - Construction began on the Panama Canal Expansion adding a "third lane" of new locks

- April 26, 2010 - Noriega completed US prison sentence and after lengthy legal fight was extradited to France where he began serving sentence for money laundering, not as POW treated as a General, but as a common criminal

- September 4, 2010 – The one millionth ship transited the Panama Canal, a Chinese vessel named FORTUNE PLUM, carrying steel and crossing from the Pacific to the Atlantic

- December 2011 - US and France agreed to let Noriega be extradited home to Panama where he faces a 67-year prison term. Noriega was incarcerated in El Renacer Prison in Gamboa, next to the Panama Canal

- February 2012 – Panama introduces a one Balboa coin equal in value to $1 US because of the short lifespan and high expense of US paper $1 bills

For Further Reading

Since this book only briefly hits the highlights of the history of the Canal and Panama, hopefully you will be intrigued and stimulated to do further reading.

I've just listed resources here, but if you visit my blog, RichardDetrich.com, I have an annotated list with comments about those books that are really worth buying .

Abbot, Willis J. PANAMA AND THE CANAL: IN PICTURE AND PROSE.

Detrich, Richard. ESCAPE TO PARADISE: LIVING AND RETIRING IN PANAMA.

Dinges, John. OUR MAN IN PANAMA: HOW GENERAL NORIEGA USED THE US AND MADE MILLIONS IN DRUGS AND ARMS.

Doggert, Scott. PANAMA: LONELY PLANET.

DuTemple, Lesley A. THE PANAMA CANAL: GREAT BUILDING FEATS.

Frair, William. ADVENTURES IN NATURE: PANAMA.

Galbraith, Douglas. THE RISING SUN.

Green, Julie. THE CANAL BUILDERS.

Independent Commission of Inquiry on the US Invasion of Panama, THE US INVASION OF PANAMA: THE TRUTH BEHIND OPERATION JUST CAUSE.

Keller, Urlich. THE BUILDING OF THE PANAMA CANAL IN HISTORIC PHOTOGRAPHS.

Kempe, Frederick. DIVORCING THE DICTATOR: AMERICA'S BUNGLE AFFAIR WITH NORIEGA.

Koster, R.M. & Sanchez, Guillermo. IN THE TIME OF TYRANTS: PANAMA 1968-1990.

Lindsay-Poland, John. EMPERORS IN THE JUNGLE: THE HIDDEN HISTORY OF THE US IN PANAMA.

Mc McCullough, David. THE PATH BETWEEN THE SEAS: THE CREATION OF THE PANAMA CANAL 1870-1914.

Noriega, Manuel and Eisner, Peter. THE MEMOIRS OF MANUEL NORIEGA: AMERICA'S PRISONER.

Parker, David. PANAMA FEVER

Perkins, John. CONFESSIONS OF AN ECONOMIC HIT MAN.

Ridgely, Robert S and Gwynne, John A. Jr. A GUIDE TO THE BIRDS OF PANAMA.

Panama Canal by The Numbers

Republic of Panama

- Panama 28,703 square miles (74,340 square kilometers), little smaller than South Carolina
- 1,547 miles (2,490 kilometers) of coastline
- Highest Point: Volcán Baru 11,401 feet (3,475 meters)

Transit

- New York to San Francisco via Canal 6,000 miles (9,656 kilometers) compared to 14,000 miles (22,531 kilometers) around Cape Horn
- From beginning to end the Canal is 50 miles (80.5 kilometers)
- 35-40 ships a day 365 days a year, 24 hours a day since 1963 for a potential maximum of 14,600 per year
- About 225 passenger ships per year - over $46 million in tolls 2011
- Flags & Designation:
    - "Zulu" – Priority Transit
    - "Hotel" – Pilot on Board
    - Southbound - Even numbers
    - Northbound - Odd numbers
    - "Bravo" – Flammable cargo on board
    - "Tango" - Toxic or radioactive material on board
- Average transit time 8 – 12 hours
- Cruise ships get priority transit
- Top five customers US, People's Republic of China, Chile, Japan and South Korea
- 36 tug boats

Atlantic Side

- Bay of Limon 4.5 miles (7 kilometers) long and 2.5 miles (4 kilometers) wide
- Bay of Limon Breakwaters 6 miles (9.6 km) long and 425 ft (130 meters) wide at the base
- From Limon Breakwater to Gatun Locks is 5.4 miles (7.2 kilometers)

Pacific Side

- Bridge of The Americas built 1962 by US at cost of $20 million. Total length 5,425 feet (1,654 meters) in 14 spans. Main span 1,128 feet (344 meters). Center part of main span is 850 feet (259 meters) and at highest point is 384 feet (117 meters) above mean sea level. Clearance under the main span is 210 feet (64 meters) at high tide.

Locks

- Gatun Locks – 3 stages – raises or lowers vessel 85 feet (26 meters)
- Gatun Lock chambers 110 feet (33.5 meters) wide, and 1,000 ft (304.8) meters long
- Lock gates throughout operated by 15 HP motor and hydraulic arms, originally 50 HP motor operated giant gears
- Culverts deep within the walls 18 feet (5.5 meters) in diameter
- 14 lateral culverts
- 70 holes in floor 4 feet (1.2 meters) wide
- Each steel lock leaf is 65 feet (19.8 meters) wide, 7 feet (2.1 meters) thick and from 47 to 82 feet (14.3 to 25 meters) high and weighs from 390 to 730 tons
- Tides on Atlantic 1-2 feet (.5 meter), Pacific tides can be as high as 23 feet (7 meters)
- Pedro Miguel is one chamber – raises or lowers ship 29 feet (8.8 meters) between level of Gatun Lake and Miraflores Lake
- Miraflores Lake is man-made transitional lake about 1.3 miles (2.1 kilometers) and is 54 feet (16.5 meters) above sea level
- Drop from Miraflores Lake to Pacific approach varies due to tidal differences on the Pacific between 43 feet (13.1 meters) at extreme high tide and 64.5 feet (19.7 meters) at extreme low tide

Locomotives

- $1.9 million each, electric powered by third rail, 50 tons, 2 winches
- 100 locomotives each weighing 50 tons
- Powered by 290 HP traction units
- Towing capacity 178 to 311.8 kilo depending on speed
- Maximum return speed 10 miles per hour (16 kilometers per hour

Gatun Lake & Water

- Not unheard of to have rain falling at 3 to 4 inches (76 to 102 millimeters) an hour
- Can get up to 200 inches (5 meters) of rain a year, average 130 inches (3.3 meters)
- Each transit uses 53.4 million US Gallons (202,000 cubic meters) during transit
- Gatun Lake has area of 164 square miles (425 square kilometers) at normal level
- 1,100 miles (1,770 kilometer) shoreline
- About 85 feet (25.9 meters) deep prior to current Canal expansion project

Gatun Dam

- 2100 feet (640 meters) thick at bottom
- 7,500 feet (2,286 meters) long at the top
- 98 feet (30 meters) thick at the top
- At normal level of Gatun Lake top of dam is 30 feet (9 meters) above lake level
- Crest of dam spillway is 16 feet (4.9 meters) below normal lake level
- Spillway dam has 14 electrically operated gates each 46 feet (14 meters) wide by 20 feet (6 meters) high
- Capacity of spillway is 140,000 cubic feet (4,100 cubic meters) of water per second more than the maximum flow of Chagres River
- If necessary lock culverts theoretically can release additional 49,000 cubic feet (1,400 cubic meters) of excess water per second
- Dam contains 22 million cubic yards (17 million cubic meters) of material and weighs some 30 million short tons (27 million long tons)
- Dam covers 290 acres (1.17 square kilometers) of ground
- Earth and rock in Gatun Dam could build a wall 5 feet (1.5 meters) high and 1 foot (.3 meters) thick all around the earth at the Equator
- Lake stores 4,200,000 acre feet of water (5.2 cubic kilometers) which is about as much water as comes down the Chagres River in an average year

Excavations & Gaillard Cut

- Total 232 million cubic yards excavated by US

- French excavated 78 million cubic yards, 30 million cubic yards of which were useful to the US
- Added together about 262 million cubic yards more than four times the volume originally estimated by de Lesseps
- Gold Hill 662 feet (201.8 meters)
- Continental divide taken from 210 feet (64 meters) to 40 feet (12.2 meters) above sea level
- Centennial Bridge opened in 2004, built by Panama at a cost of $120 million. Total span 3,451 feet (1,052 meters), main span 1,051 feet (320 meters) clears canal by 262 feet (80 meters). Supporting towers are 604 feet (184 meters) high. West tower set back 164 feet (50 meters) to allow for future widening of Canal.
- Average depth of Canal channel is 43 feet (13 meters) and the minimum depth is 41 feet (12.5 meters) although changing as Canal is deepened as part of expansion program
- Width varies from 500 to 1,000 feet (152 to 305 meters) and is increasing as Canal is enlarged as part of expansion program

Cost of Construction

- Panama Canal cost Americans around $375 million including the $10 million paid to Panama and the $40 million paid to the French company
- Completed with final figure some $23 million below the 1907 estimate
- Lives lost:
    - 20,000-25,000 estimated lives lost during French era
    - 5,609 lives lost during US construction
    - Approximately 500 people died for every mile of the Canal

Revenue

- Preferential fee $25,000
- No show forfeit
- Late 50-100%
- Passenger ships pay $134 per berth
- In 86 years US operated Canal paid Panama the original $10 million, plus $250,000 per year after the first nine years, or a total of $29,250,000
- In the first year of Panama's operation the Canal made a direct transfer to the government of $252 million

- During first four years of Panama's operation Canal made direct transfers to the government of $1.1 billion
- Annually has been contributing around $400 million per year
- When expansion completed direct transfer to government estimated to be $1.2 billion per year
- Canal generates over $2 billion per year
- $5.25 billion is cost of expansion program

Coming from Richard Detrich . . .

The Little Railroad That Could
The Story of The Panama Railroad

The fascinating story of the world's first "trans-oceanic" railroad . . . the railroad that made the Panama Canal possible . . . and is still rolling along over 155 years later!

Have you ever thought of escaping?

Ever thought of moving somewhere less expensive, with less hassle . . . more romantic . . . maybe even living in Panama?

ESCAPE TO PARADISE is jam-packed with what we've learned and helpful hints of what to consider if you've ever even thought of escaping to Panama or anywhere else.

We lived in Ventura County, California for eighteen years. For most of that time we rarely knew our neighbors. Yes, we waved, and said "Good morning!" and knew their names, but we didn't really know them. Most Southern Californians set themselves off from their neighbors with high stucco walls designed for back-yard privacy.

When we moved to the Hillside in Ventura we finally had neighbors who were neighbors, people we knew. We could commiserate over garden problems, borrow an egg, a tile saw or go for assistance in an emergency.

My next door neighbor, Shaun, was a techie and do-it-yourselfer who, fortunately for me, had every power tool ever invented. Shaun was also a wine aficionado and along the way discovered, and introduced me to Trader Joe's "Two Buck Chuck" Syrah. Then, at only $2 a bottle for a surprisingly good wine, we could afford a lot of neighborly conviviality.

When we were in the depths of trying to buy our property in Panama, sell our house in Ventura, and make it work and pull this all together, we were sipping "Two Buck Chuck", sitting on Shaun's patio and watching the sun set into the Pacific. In all seriousness, Shaun said, "Richard, you know you've got to make this work, because if you can do it, then we'll know that anyone can escape."

If we could do it, so can you!

Escape To Paradise

Richard Detrich

"Moving to another country is a big decision, but Richard's book helps you think through all the benefits of moving to Panama. Get ESCAPE TO PARADISE! It's a GREAT book and the best information I have found anywhere about relocating to Panama." *Jackie Lang*

"Your book . . . is entertaining, informative, and a quick read. Once I started reading it, I found it difficult to put down." *Harry Kooiman*

"My husband and I both enjoyed this book immensely! We made the move ourselves to Boquete six years ago If ONLY we had had this book to help prepare ourselves when we were first considering the move! . . . If you have any thoughts about finding your own paradise, and particularly finding your paradise in Panama, you MUST buy this book!" *Sharron "Squirt" James*

Made in the USA
San Bernardino, CA
27 January 2013